Public Policy and Administration : Series 1

PUBLIC POLICY AND ADMINISTRATION: Normative Concerns

Books by the Same Author

1. Development Policies and Administration in India, (*ed.*) 2000
2. Human Rights and Criminal Justice Administration in India, (*ed.*) 2000
3. Non-Governmental Organizations in Development, (*ed.*) 1997
4. Development and the Social Science Method, 1993
5. The Social Science Perspective and Method of Public Administration, 1992
6. People's Participation in Development Administration in India, 1984
7. Tamil Translation of F.L. Schuman, International Politics, 2 Vols, 1965, 1967

Public Policy and Administration : Series 1

PUBLIC POLICY AND ADMINISTRATION: Normative Concerns

Edited By

PROF. (DR.) MRS. NOORJAHAN BAVA
Department of Political Science
University of Delhi, Delhi

UPPAL PUBLISHING HOUSE
NEW DELHI-110 002 (INDIA)

UPPAL PUBLISHING HOUSE
3, Ansari Road, Daryaganj, New Delhi - 110 002
Phone : Off. 3273756 Fax : 3286571, Res. 2242884

First Published 2000
ISBN 81-7658-003-1

THIS IS A PUBLICATION UNDER UGC'S DSA PROGRAMME OF THE DEPARTMENT OF POLITICAL SCIENCE, UNIVERSITY OF DELHI

Printed in India

Published by B. S. Uppal for Uppal Publishing House 3, Ansari Road, Daryaganj, New Delhi, Laser typesetting by DV Graphic Prints (P) Ltd., Karol Bagh, N. D. and Printed by Arora Offset Press, Guru Ram Das Nagar, Delhi - 31

PREFACE

The Thrust Area of Research on Public Administration and Development of the Department of Political Science, University of Delhi, under the DSA Programme decided to bring out a book on Public Policy in its meeting held in March 1995. The present book entitled *Public Policy and Administration: Normative concerns* is the fulfilment of that decision.

Design and Format of the Book

A vast and clean canvas was made available to the chapter contributors of this work as they were free to choose and brush the theme or focus of their papers **as they thought fit to do**. In her circular letter to the chapter writers dated 4 March 1999, the Editor Prof. Noorjahan Bava, Department of Political Science, University of Delhi had indicated the broad theme of public policy and administration, within the framework of which one could make his/her choice of the specific topic or issue or focus. The response for the **invitation** of papers was so overwhelming and so good that the Editor had to take the spot decision to publish them in three series with titles that reflect the broad theme/area each highlights. Accordingly Series I carries the title: PUBLIC POLICY AND ADMINISTRATION: NORMATIVE CONCERNS; Series II: DEVELOPMENT POLICIES AND ADMINISTRATION IN INDIA; and Series III: HUMAN RIGHTS AND CRIMINAL JUSTICE ADMINISTRATION.

The layout of Series I is based on the following design:

Based on the criterion of thematic unity the book contains four parts including the Editor's Introduction Part. What is common to all the parts is that the subject matter of each part has a judicious mix of both theoretical and empirical aspects of the main issue or theme it deals with.

What is unique to each part is that it focuses on a particular sub-theme of the main theme of public policy like public policy, political science and public administration or public policy process and analysis or, ethics in public life.

Part I entitled ***PUBLIC POLICY SCIENCES: ANCIENT AND MODERN*** comprises as many as seven chapters. In the Editor's INTRODUCTION: *Public Policy Process, Analysis & Research: Political Science and Public Administration as Meta Policy Sciences* **Prof.Noorjahan Bava** after examining the dynamics of the policy process posits the thesis that the study of political science and public administration is the true, original, oldest, integrated meta policy science - the policy science of policy sciences in terms of its fulfillment of Lass well's three-fold criterion: interdisciplinarity, contextual and problematic and normative orientations.

Prof. M.M. Sankhdher in his chapter on *Indian Approach to Political Management* and **Dr.Ruchi Tyagi** in her paper on *Administration in Ancient India: A Study of its Administrative and Financial Structures* highlight the more than 5000 year old ancient Indian Policy Texts – the *Vedas, Sukraniti*, Kautilya's *Arthsastra* and the *Mahabharata* respectively and their contribution to evolution of thought on management science and public administration. M.M.Sankhdher believes that "there is no area of management, whether political, economic, social, educational or industrial, where **classical wisdom of the ages** is not applicable". He optimistically advocates that with suitable modification and reinterpretation, traditional Indian concepts such as **Aham Brahma Asmi, Karma yoga, dharma, bhavantu sukinah**, can be applied to current situations and an useful management system based on Indian ethos can be developed. Not only such a spiritual-ethical model of management behaviour can be developed and used at home, it can also be exported to the rest of the world. *Vedanta* provides this system of human engineering which can reform current political management and administrative structures. Dr.Ruchi Tyagi concludes that the ancient Indian polity was typically a monarchy and it was a Welfare State at that. Promotion of the moral, material, aesthetic and spiritual life of the people - the praja was the supreme goal of the government which was sought to be achieved through decentralised governance. Her study throws up a wealth of information on central, provincial, divisional, district and town and village administration as well as financial administration in ancient India. Far from being a modern institution bureaucracy existed as the mainstay of ancient kingdoms and empires. Belonging to the same genre but 1600 years old, *is Thiruvalluvar's Thirukkural*", another invaluable treasure house of politics and ethics of Southern India. In this chapter **Prof.Noorjahan Bava** makes an attempt to bring another unit of ancient Indian heritage on good conduct, good society and good governance to the reach of the readers. Written in the form of couplets in Tamil language and translated into many European languages, the *Kural* is a master-piece of ancient Tamil literature and statecraft.

In **the modern policy texts section** we have included the chapters related to the theme: **Win-Win Public Policy**. In Chapters Five, Six and Seven dealing with "Win-Win Policy", 'Universal Values and Win-Win Policy' and 'Win-Win Public Administration, **Prof.Stuart S.Nagel**, Professor Emeritus of Political Science, University of Illinois, USA and a doyen of policy analysis has made an important contribution to the glossary/vocabulary of policy studies by coining the concept "Win-Win" policy and applying it to empirical studies. He defines a win-win policy as a "public policy that is capable of achieving both conservative and liberal goals simultaneously. It is not a compromise policy and it is feasible both in theory and practice." A win-win policy solution becomes a "Super-Optimum Solution" (SOS) when the gain from the policy goes beyond the initial best expectations of all the sides or players and does not include unsubstantive gains.

Part II entitled ***NATION-STATE, SOVEREIGNTY AND GLOBALIZATION*** contains **Dr.Wolfgang Reinicke's** superb analytical framework to study the impact of globalisation policy on the nation states. In his chapter *Globalization and Public Policy: An Analytical Framework*, Dr.Reinicke, a German economist by education and training applies the political economy approach to the issue of globalization and examines its adverse consequences on the internal and 'defacto' sovereignty of the nation-states. He argues from the perspective of neoclassical and neorealist schools of international economic thought and emphasizes that while **globalization** is a threat to **internal sovereignty** of modern nation states and it weakens the ability of the governments to provide public goods and act in public interest, the growing **interdependence** amongst and between the nations of to-day jeopardises their **external sovereignty**. The information and computer revolutions along with electronic commerce have contributed to the further dilution of the sovereignty and melting down of the borders of the nation-states.

Part-III is dedicated to an all time important theme of ***ETHICS AND PUBLIC ADMINISTRATION.*** Mr.T.N.Chaturvedi, former CAG of India, **Dr. Rosamund Thomas,** a distinguished academic and veteran administator **Mr.U.C.Agarwal**, former Chief Central Vigilance Commissioner, Government of India analyse the important question of ethics in public life and how to deal with the growing menace of corruption.

In his study entitled *Accountability and Ethical Dimensions of Good Governance,* **Mr. T.N. Chaturvedi** examines the evolution, significance and various aspects of accountability, ethics in public life, parameters of good governance and the need for electoral and legislative reforms in the Indian context. **Dr.Rosamund Thomas**, Director, Centre for Business and Public Sector Ethics, Cambridge, United Kingdom, has in her detailed study on *Ethics in Public Life and Corporate Governance in the United Kingdom Today*, focuses on several important issues of ethical conduct in public life: origin of modern ethics in public life in UK, the Codes of Conduct and prevention of corruption in that country, the Law Commissioner's proposal for "a new offence of corruption covering both the public and private sectors and proposals for the new offence of "misuse of public office", the institutional reforms leading to the establishment of the new Office of the Parliamentary Commissioner for Standards, change of nomenclature of the House Common's Committee of Privileges into `Committee on Standards and Privileges', etc. Dr.Rosamund Thomas draws attention to Seven Principles of Public Life recommended by the Nolan Committee viz. Selflessness, Integrity,

Objectivity, Accountability, Openness, Honesty and Leadership. She also highlights in her chapter the recommendations of the Cadbury Committee (1990), Greenbury Committee, and now the Hampbell Committee on the need for ethics in corporate governance.

In his paper, *Administrative Corruption: Causes and Cure*, Mr.U.C.Agarwal, brings his rare insights of an insider/experienced administrator to bear on the analysis of the problem of growing administrative corruption in India. He says that although corruption was there in British Indian administration, it has grown over the decades following India's independence. Today it has assumed alarming proportions. One of the many suggestions that Mr.Agarwal has put forward to tackle the menace of corruption is the *political will* to uproot this evil. He says that in ancient monarchies, the king used to be the roll model for his subjects in life. In to-day's democracies the political masters who are also the public servants must set high standard of probity in public life so that the civil servants and administrative staff can emulate him.

Part IV focuses on ***PARADIGMS OF DEVELOPMENT***. In her chapter entitled *Approaches to Development Policy* **Prof. Noorjahan Bava** discussees the various dimensions and approaches to the value-laden, umbrella concept of development — its social, political, economic, personality, cultural, environmental, spatial-temporal, material-spiritual aspects and third world perspectives on development.

1 May 1999
New Delhi

PROF.NOORJAHAN BAVA
Project Director and Editor

ACKNOWLEDGEMENTS

The University Grants Commission's Department of Special Assistance Programme has been in operation for the last 10 years in the Department of Political Science, University of Delhi. It is a faculty research programme under which several thrust areas are carrying on research in Political Science. One of the thrust areas - Public Administration and Development of the Department of Political Science has been quite active during the last five years 1995-99 and conducted many seminars and conferences. It has also published several books, chapters in books and research articles in prestigious journals like for instances, Noorjahan Bava, 'The Welfare State and the Liberalization Policy in India' in *Indian Journal of Public Administration*, Vol.XLII, No.3, 1996, pp.334-346 and Noorjahan Bava, "India and Win-Win Policy" in *Developmental Policy Studies Journal*, Vol.4, Issue 4, Winter 1998, pp.14-30.

During the last-five years, two important books were brought out by the Public Administration and Development Group. They are: 1. Noorjahan Bava ed., *Non-Governmental Organizations in Development*, New Delhi, Kanishka Publishers, 1996 and 2. R.B.Jain, ed., *Environmental Stewardness and Sustainable Development*, New Delhi, Friedrich Ebert Stiftung, 1997.

Third in the series of books published by the Thrust Area on Public Administration of the Department of Political Science, University of Delhi is the present book edited by **Professor Noorjahan Bava** entitled *Public Policy and Administration*, New Delhi, Uppal Publishing House, 1999. It has Three Series. Series I : *Normative Concerns; Series II : Development Policies and Administration In India; and Series III : Human Rights and Criminal Justice Administration.*

I am deeply indebted to the three international chapter writers. My sincere and grateful thanks to (1) **PROF.STUART S.NAGEL**, Professor Emeritus, Department of Political Science, University of Illinois, USA for his generous contribution of three papers: *Win-Win Policy, Universal Values and Win-Win Policy and Win-Win Public Administration; and* (2) **DR. WOLFGANG REINICKE** of the **BROOKINGS INSTITUTE,** for his excellent paper on *Gobalization and Public Policy: An Analytical Framework.* My grateful and profound thanks also go to The Brookings Institute Press 1775 Massachusetts Avenue, N.W. Washington D.C. 20036 - 2188 who are the **publisher** of the book as well as to Dr.Wolfgang Reincke, the author for permission granted gratis to include the Second Chapter of the book entitled *Globalization and Public Policy* into the First Series. (3) My profound thanks are also due to **DR. ROSAMUND THOMAS**, Director. Centre for Business and Public Sector Ethics, Cambridge, U.K. for her permission to incorporate into our book her important and useful empirical study - *Ethics in Public Life and Corporate Governance in the UK Today*, the copyright of which vests in her. Together they provide an international, global and comparative perspective to the study.

This anthology of essays would have been impossible but for the Publication and Contingency grants given by the **University Grants Commission.** My grateful thanks to the UGC for the financial assistance.

I also thank Prof.V.R.Mehta, Vice-Chancellor, University of Delhi who is the Chairman of the Advisory Committee of the DSA Programme, Prof.Abad Ahmad, Pro-Vice-Chancellor and Shri P.C.Gupta, Joint Finance Officer of the University for their help and cooperation.

My profound thanks are also due to Prof.Subrata Mukherjee, Head of the Department of Political Science, University of Delhi for all the interest, encouragement and help extended to me as the Project Director and Editor of the book. I also thank the administrative and DSA staff of the Department for their help and cooperation in this connection.

My profound thanks are also due to each one of the chapters writers from different disciplines and institutions. Without their enthusiastic and timely response to my invitation for papers, this work would not have fructified. In fact their response was so tremendous and incredible that I was virtually inundated by a large number of papers which have been organized according to their thematic unity into the above three series.

I also thank the computer operator Mrs.Neena Dua for the good work done in this connection.

Thanks are also due to the Librarian and staff of the Indian Institute of Public Administration and University of Delhi Central Reference Library and South Campus Library for their help.

Last but not least, this study could not have been accomplished without the time, moral and material support and assistance of every sort extended to me by the members of my family. A profound thanks to each one of them for their sacrifice. A very special thanks to my husband Colonel Mohamed Mathar Bava, A.S.C. (Retd) for his help and cooperation without which this work would have been a sheer impossibility.

1 May 1999
New Delhi

PROF.NOORJAHAN BAVA
Project Director and Editor

CONTENTS

MODERN POLICY TEXTS

PART - II

THE NATION-STATE, SOVEREIGNTY AND GLOBALIZATION

PART - III

ETHICS, POLITICS, AND PUBLIC ADMINISTRATION

PART - IV

PARADIGMS OF DEVELOPMENT

CONTRIBUTORS

1. Mr.U.C.AGARWAL, IAS (Retd.), Former Central Vigilance Commissioner, Government of India

2. Dr.NOORJAHAN BAVA: Professor, Department of Political Science, University of Delhi, Delhi

3. Mr. T. N. Chaturvedi, M.P., Vice-President of Indian Institute of Public Administration, and former Comptroller and Auditor-General of India.

4. Dr.STUART S. NAGEL: Professor Emeritus, and Coordinator, Policy Science Organization, Department of Political Science, University of Illinois, USA

5. Dr.WOLFGANG REINICKE, Senior Fellow, Brookings Foreign Policy Studies Program and Senior Economist in the World Bank's Corporate Strategy Group

6. Dr.M.M.SANKHDHER, Former Professor, Department of Political Science, University of Delhi, Delhi

7. Dr.ROSAMUND THOMAS, Director, Centre for Business and Public Sector Ethics, Cambridge, U.K.

8. Dr.RUCHI TYAGI, Reader, Department of Political Science, Kalindi College for Women, University of Delhi

PART - I

PUBLIC POLICY SCIENCES : ANCIENT AND MODERN

Chapter 1

Editor's Introduction

Public Policy Process, Analysis and Research : Political Science and Public Administration as Meta Policy Science

Noorjahan Bava

The Nature of Policy Decision Making

Policy making is a **multidimensional, multifaceted and complex process.** Research is but one (and often minor at that) among the number of frequently contradictory and competing sources that seek to influence what **is an ongoing and constantly evolving process. The public policy process evolves through policy cycles,** with each cycle more or less bounded, constrained by time,funds, political support, and other events and circles back on itself, iterates the same decision issue time and again, and often does not come to closure. Choosing not to decide can also be an outcome. This perspective calls for a modification of the **traditional** understanding of policy making (Rist).[1]

In the traditional approach decision making in the policy arena is viewed as a 'discrete event' undertaken by "defined set of actors" working in "real time" and moving to their decision on the basis of an analysis of their alternatives. It gives the impression that a group of decision makers assemble at particular time and places, review a problem (or opportunity), consider a number of alternative courses of action with more or less explicit calculation of the advantages and disadvantages of each option, weigh the alternatives against their goals or preferences, and then select an alternative that seems well suited for achieving their purposes. The result is a decision (Weiss, 23).[2]

Weiss proceeds to demolish the traditional view when she writes:[3]

> "Given the fragmentation of authority across multiple bureaus, departments, and legislative committees, and the disjointed stages by which actions coalesce into decisions, the traditional model of decision making is a highly stylized rendition of reality. Identification of any clear-cut group of decision makers can be difficult... Which opinions are considered, and what set of advantages or disadvantages are assessedmay be impossible to tell in the **interactive, multiparticipant, diffuse process of formulating policy. The complexity of governmental decision making often defies neat compartmentalization."** (Emphasis added)

In the Indian context of a federal polity, a parliamentary democracy, the Union Cabinet is the architect of the policies of the Union Government, into the making of which policy inputs and demands are generated by line and staff agencies and by bureaucrats in the various ministries, departments, public sector enterprises, boards, Planning Commission, National Development Council besides interest groups like trade unions, Confederation of Indian Industry, Indian Chamber of Commerce and Industry, Farmers Organisations, Government Employees association, unions and confederations, teachers unions, citizen/voluntary/NGOs etc., etc. The members of Parliament, its various committees, the Supreme Court and High Courts also make policy decisions, and lay down guidelines apart from the direction from Ministers.

Role of Policy Research in Policy Process

In the traditional view what is the relation between policy research and policy decision making? The traditionalist thinks that good research will, because it is good, influence the policy process – there is a kind of "linear relation" of research to action. However, it is not a 'viable' way, writes Rist, to think about how knowledge can inform decision making.

According to **qualitative** research school, research can be the basis for more informed decision making, and research has more of an "enlightenment function" whereas traditionalists think that research has "an engineering function" (Janowitz[4], 1971; Patton[5], 1988; Weiss[6], 1988).

Critiquing the traditional view, it is argued by the qualitative researchers that increased personnel, greater allocation of resources and growing sophistication of quantitative methods have not had the anticipated or demonstrated effect of greater "clarity and understanding of the policy issues" before the country. The quantitative methods include Operation Research, Pricing Theory, Cost-Benefit and Discount Cash Flow Analyses, Critical Path Method, Programme Evaluation Review Technique, Programme Planning Budgeting System, Management Accounting and Management Information Systems, and project management methods. Further the tendency to greater "complexity" has left both the policy makers and the citizens less able to understand the issues and understand how their actions might affect the present conditions (Rist).[7] Further, it is pointed out that what policy researchers tend to consider as improvements in their craft - the state-of-art method have not significantly enhanced the role of research in policy making. The proliferation of persons, institutes and centres conducting policy related work has led to more variation in the manner by which problems are defined, more divergence in the ways in which data are analysed and findings reported. The policy maker now confronts a "veritable glut of information".[8]

Viewing policy research as serving an enlightenment function suggests that policy researchers work with policy makers and their staff over time to create a **contextual understanding** about an issue, build linkages that will exist over time, and strive constantly to educate about new developments and research findings in the area. This is in contrast to the engineering perspective, where it is presumed that sufficient data can be brought to bear to determine the direction and intensity of the intended policy initiative, much as one can develop the specifications for the building of a bridge. If the policy direction is sufficiently clear and explicit, then the necessary information relevant to the development of the policy can be collected as this view would contend, and **the policy actions can be deliberate, directed, and successful**. But the reality is that policy environment is too complex with too many competing and contradictory factors and actors competing to influence the policy process and decisions with the result the potential policy direction is not clear or predictable.

This not to decry the importance or relevance of policy research to decision making process. In fact systematic knowledge generated by research is an important and necessary input\component in the decision making process and seldom enough research-based information is available to policy makers.

Redefinition of Policy Decision Making

It is important to remember that the relevance and usefulness of policy research will not become apparent unless there is a reconsideration and redefinition of what is understood by decision making in the policy process. A redefinition is needed of the context in which to look for a linkage between knowledge and action. The use of the concept of 'policy cycle' can bring about this redefinition of policy decision making.

The Policy Cycle and Qualitative Research

There are two levels of decision making in the policy arena. The first involves the determination of the broad parameters of government action, such as national agricultural policy, industrial policy, health and educational policies. At this level policy research input is likely to be small. The setting up of national priorities, **the national agenda is a political act** which is preceded by interaction and deliberation amongst a host of people, institutions, organizations, structures and processes. Politicians, party leaders, members, bureaucrats, legislators, citizen groups, media persons, professional associations, universities, academics, and researchers are involved in the national agenda setting.

At this level, any research study or funding may be quoted in support of the contention that the issue deserves national attention, but it is incidental to the more basic task of first working to place the issue in the national agenda. During this phase if any one wants to influence the policy process, it can be done through personal or organizational contacts between key actors. The role played by the media will be also crucial to the political parties-ruling as well as the opposition interest groups and citizen bodies.

Once the issue is on the agenda of key players or organisations within the policy establishment, there are possibilities and scope for utilization of policy research. This is the second level of the policy decision-making-**the level where there are concerns about transplanting policy intentions into policy and programmatic realities.**

A **policy cycle** consists of three phases: **policy formulation, policy implementation** and **policy accountability.**[9] Each of these phases has its own order and logic, its own information requirements and its own policy actors. At each one of these phases of policy cycle, qualitative research can be useful in making available relevant, and timely information to the bureaucrats, political masters and legislators - the key actors in the policy process.

I

DYNAMICS OF THE POLICY PROCESS

Policy may be defined as a set of instructions from policy makers to policy implementors that spell out both **goals, values, objectives and the means or strategies** for their achievement. Policy is a declaration of the government of what it intends to do during its tenure in office – the decisions and actions that it proposes to take as spelled out in the election manifesto of the party in power to meet the election promises. An election manifesto of a political party is a potential policy statement of the party which, if voted to power will work towards the fulfilment of the mandate.

The policy process consists of the various **interfaces** of (i) policy planning (ii) policy formulation (iii) policy enactment into public laws (iv) policy implementation (v) policy monitoring and evaluation and (vi) policy accountability. **Decision-making on policy matters is undoubtedly the legitimate core function of the Government**. It is the legal and constitutional prerogative of the political party in power in all modern states.

Policy Context (Environment)

The policy process always operates in a particular **context** - political, economic, social, cultural, ecological, and ethical **environment**. This requires the adoption and application of an **integrated, holistic, interdisciplinary, all-encompassing, systemic approach and methodology and perspective** to public policy problems, their analysis, and policy decisions. Indeed **the** truly **integrated social science perspective of politics and public administration** is called forth for coping with problems of the policy process.[10]

The Political Context

A modern democratic polity-developed or developing governs itself according to its **Constitution**, which is the embodiment of the **collective political will** of its people and the **basic or fundamental law** of the land. The State is founded and governed according to its philosophy and principles. The constitution lays down the principles governing the nature, structures, institutions and processes of the government, relation between its executive, legislative, judicial branches, the government - citizen interface, the fundamental rights and duties of the citizen; it lays the foundation for the type of economy - liberal, capitalist, market driven/laissez-faire economy or state-led socialist economy or mixed economy, and shows the direction for the future development of the polity, economy and society. A constitution thus embodies the cherished values, goals and aspirations of its people and functions as the guiding post and lighthouse of the people governed by it. It contains the **superordinate goals** towards the realization of which every government - its leader the prime minister or the president and other ministers pledge themselves and are accountable for their performance.

In the Indian context, for instance, the superordinate or fundamental goals consist of the establishment and maintenance of a **Sovereign, Democratic, Socialist, Secular Republic** wherein there shall be for every citizen **justice, equality, freedom, fraternity, dignity of the individual** and **national unity**.

Based on the constitutional goals the government of a democracy spells out its various policy goals in policy statements (Science and Technology Policy), resolutions, (Industrial Policy Resolutions), planning documents (Five Year Plans) and Cabinet decisions. Parliamentary/legislative enactments, statutes and laws, judicial decisions, interpretations and directions also establish, determine, and amplify the regime goals and values. In a parliamentary democracy such as Britain and India the constitutional and legal power to take decisions on all policy matters - the power to set the national agenda and to prioritise the goals, determine the strategies, provide for the necessary resources and means to achieve the goals vests with the Chief Executive i.e. the Cabinet headed by the Prime Minister which is collectively responsible to the Lower House - House of People of the Parliament for all its policy decisions and actions of commission and omission and each Minister is accountable for the policy and good administration of the department(s) under his charge. In a Presidential democracy like the United States the president is, the chief executive, chief administrator, chief legislator, chief policy maker and chief of the government and head of the state.

Political Environmental Factors

Many factors originating from the constitutional and political context and environment impinge the policy process and influence and shape public policies. A political system includes all of the institutions, structures, processes, and behaviour which function and transform the demands (inputs) into governmental decisions (outputs) on policy matters. This includes a large number of factors such as the constitution and its philosophy, the political party system and its functioning, including the election manifesto, the electorate and its voting behaviour, structure and behaviour of the executive and legislative bodies, the socio-economic background, profile, behaviour, attitude, belief and values of the bureaucracy, role of administrators as catalyst of socio-economic development and nation-building, as guardians of public interest and national interest, interest (pressure) group activity, lobbying, organizational strength and activities of citizen bodies, voluntary agencies and non-governmental organisations, the formal constitutional and legal political and administrative arrangements, political attitudes of both elites and the masses, political customs, traditions, conventions and cultures, the resource allocation system, the judicial system and its functioning, public and informal channels of power etc., etc.. The list of political system characteristics which might conceivably affect public policy is boundless.[11]

In the context of the American government and politics it is usually the most highly educated, prestigiously employed and wealthy people who are found to be highly supportive of government policies.[12] Public policy is more likely to conform to elite opinion than mass opinion. But elites themselves must be responsive to environmental forces: these forces generate demands for governmental, administrative activities and provide the necessary resources to support public policies. Decision makers everywhere appear to be constrained by lack of material and financial resources to support public policies. They cannot long ignore pressing environmental problems such as increasing poverty, environmental pollution, growing inequalities, violence, unemployment, crimes against women and the downtrodden. Virtually the government in all developing nations are faced with resource crunch.

Public Policy Process : Citizen Participation Through NGOs, Interest Groups and Political Parties

Interest group activity provides a linkage between environmental forces and public policy. The interest group structure of a society clearly reflects its social-economic composition. Modern urban institutional societies spawn a multitude of interest groups, the multiplicity and diversity of which reduces the likelihood of any single interest group influencing the policy process to further its own interests in all fields at the cost of others. However, in less developed nations such as India few interest groups and lobbies such as the Confederation of Indian Industries (CII), Federation of Indian Chambers and Commerce (FICCI), Sugar Industry Lobby, Farmers Organizations, Trade Unions, Teachers Unions, Students Unions – all try and sometimes succeed in influencing government's decisions on policy matters.

Group activity is linked to party competition which in turn is related to economic growth and development. **Studies show that interest-groups are more directly influential in policy-making in societies where the party system is weak and underdeveloped.**[13] In the absence of strong cohesive parties, interest groups play a direct role in legislative affairs, with little moderation of their influence by intervening party influence. In contrast, where political parties are strong and cohesive, interest groups, inspite of their numerical strength and activity, their (interest groups') influence on the policy process is filtered through and moderated by party organs.[14]

It has been found that in industrially developed societies like the US, **party** and **constituency** influence are most important on broad social and economic issues whereas on the narrower issues, political parties are less likely to take a stand, and constituents are less likely to have either an interest or opinion. Under such circumstances, the **legislator** is freer to respond to the pleas of organized groups on highly specialized topics than he is on major issues of public interest. The absence of both party and constituency influence on certain types of issues contributes to the effectiveness of organized interest groups. Economic interests seeking to use the law to improve their competitive position are a major source of group pressure on these specialized topics.[15]

However, the actual policy impact of interest groups is **difficult** to measure. Businesses subject to excessive Governmental regulations are very active in lobbying. Organized pressure also comes from associations of state governments upon the federal government and pressure of government employees through their associations and trade unions upon the government on matters of pay revision, super annuation benefits, administrative reforms, etc.

Public Policy Process : The Bureaucractic, Executive and Legislative Interface

The public policy process is directly under the influence of the executive and legislative organs of the government separately and combinedly. The bureaucracy which is the instrument of the political executive has both direct and indirect influence on the policy process. True, policy making is the legitimate power vested in the political executive and legislature but these bodies can do very little without the crucial role played by the top echelon of the bureaucracy (the higher civil service) in every government department or bureau. **The higher civil service shapes and moulds public policies.** Not only does it offer policy advice to the Minister on matters of important public issues, but also furnishes and supplies the necessary policy data, inputs, information and statistics to the Minister thereby facilitating him to take sound or informed decisions in the public and national interest.[15a]

The legislatures of modern states often pass laws in skeletal form, leaving the details - rules and regulations to be framed by the civil servants of the respective administrative departments. This practice of **delegated legislation** has led to **administrative policy-making** by the higher civil services on the one hand and exercise of enormous **discretionary powers** on the other. Discretionary power can be misused and abused by the bureaucrats and thereby endanger democracy, freedom and rights of citizens.

Before the actual implementation or execution of policy decisions, the middle level bureaucracy working in the field formulates its **operational policy** within the framework of the administrative and general policy imperatives and only thereafter the policy is actually implemented under the guidelines of their departmental bosses. The policy goals of the government can be frustrated by the decisions, actions/inaction of the administrators as well as by unnccessary political interference at the implementation stage.

Public Policy and the Judiciary

The judiciary also hands down policy decisions during the course of their interpretation and enforcement of various laws and statutes to specific cases. Since the seventies of this century the public interest litigation has expanded the jurisdiction of courts in India, USA and England for example and it has enhanced the power of the courts to give directives and orders to the defaulting public servants in the concerned administrative departments and government to take necessary steps to redress public grievances or improve the quality and standard of public life or pay damages to the aggrieved citizens. Judicial activism is a result of administrative failures and mismanagement in this country.

Environmental Context–Socio–Cultural–Economic–Ecological–Ethical

As stated earlier the imperative need to adopt a truly interdisciplinary systemic and holistic approach to the process of taking decisions and actions related to policy formulation, implementation and evaluation as well as policy analysis and policy research renders it inevitable for all concerned with various policy-related work to keep the **political, social, cultural, economic, ecological and ethical environmental factors at the centrestage** of their work, study and analysis.

The political environmental factors include amongst others all the activities going on in terms of the **internal** environment and dynamics of the political system (including the politics – administration relationship, government – people interface, citizen participation through NGOs in the policy process, and government interest groups – legislators dynamics. It also involves the linkages between **external** environmental conditions, political – administrative activities and public policy.[16] In systemic terms 'environment' means anything that lies **outside** the boundaries of the political system, yet within the same society, economy, culture, ethical and ecological (natural-physical-chemical) systems. For the political and its administrative system **interacts** not only with each one of its substems but also with other systems of the outer environment and the international/world/global system as a whole.

The non-political environmental factors include technological development, population growth rate, extent of urbanization, literacy rate, level of adult-education, characteristics of the economy, its level of economic development, rate of economic growth, extent of modernization of society, presence or absence of gender equality, citizen participation and involvement in the process of development, the occupational structure, the class\caste system, racial composition, ethnic diversity, mobility patterns, prevalent myths, beliefs and codes, role of the press, the media, ecological factors such as land-man ratio, availability of resources, natural endowments, ecological balance or degradation, environmental pollution and so on. The policy process and its various interfaces are prone to be affected and influenced by any of these environmental factors in varying proportions and combinations in every policy decision of the Government .

Economists have contributed a great deal to the systematic analysis of public policy. Governmental activity is closely related to the level of economic development in a society. Economic development signifies improvement in the standard of the quality of life of a people, it includes social well-being. It is not the same as economic growth which is quantitative. The Gross National Product – per capita is not an accurate measure of the economic development of a society. However economic theory links all economic environmental factors such as employment opportunities, level of income, industrilialization, urbanization, adult education, longevity of life, child mortality rate, availability of number of doctors and beds per 1000 population, etc. The **political economy** approach – the western and Marxist versions links the political and economic variables involved in the policy process.

Dye's study - **Politics, Economics and the Public** shows that four of the most commonly described characteristics of a political system – (1) ruling party (2) degree of interparty competition, (3) level of voter turnout and (4) extent of malapportionment were found to have less affect on public policy than environmental variables reflecting level of economic development – urbanization, industrialization, wealth and education. The study revealed that "economic development variables were more influential than political system characteristics in shaping public policy in the states" of the United States.[17]

II

THE POLICY PROCESS AND QUALITATIVE POLICY RESEARCH

In this section we deal with the question: how best policy research as a tool can serve policy makers, policy implementors and policy evaluators ? It is argued that **qualitative** policy research leading to policy advice to various actors involved in the public policy process will greatly enhance the standard and relevance of the information offered for advice on which informed decisions will be based; and that there is place for qualitative research on policy issues in **each** phase of the policy cycle i.e. formulation, implementation and accountability.[18]

Policy Information

In general the principal actors involved in policy formulation are the "legitimate" or formal policy makers" people who occupy positions in government that entitle them to authoritatively allocate values, assign priorities and also provide for resources. These people include legislators, (elected representatives of people), elected officials and appointed high level civil servants (of the rank of deputy secretary, joint secretary and Secretary in the case of India) representing different constituencies – electoral, administrative and bureaucratic. The policy making process also offers points of access to various interest groups , citizen bodies and NGOs to exercise influence. Thus policy making usually involves a diverse set of authoritative or formal policy makers, who operate within the governmental arena plus a diverse set of special interest and other constituency groups from outside arenas, who press their demands on these formal leaders.[19]

At the policy formulation stage there exists a definite need for the three types of information: the first set of information need revolves round an **understanding** of the policy issue at hand. In the words of Charles Lindblom, "Policy makers are not faced with a given problem. Instead, they have to identify and formulate their problem."[20]

The second set of questions that call for information have to do with past policy initiatives, decisions and actions on policy matters – what programmes and projects were previously been initiated? How long did they last? What levels of funding was required? What are the achievements?

The third cluster of questions relevant to the policy formulation stage focuses on what is known of the previous policy efforts and their impacts that would help the policy makers to choose among available present day policy options.

It is argued that qualitative research is "highly relevant" to the third type information needs in the policy cycle.[21] There is an additional contribution that qualitative research can make at this stage of the policy process, and it is that of studying the intended and unintended consequence of the various policy instruments cr tools that might be selected (1989).[22] Key among the activities in the policy formulation stage is the selection of the most appropriate policy strategy to achieve the desired objective. Central to the design of this strategy is the selection of one or more tools available to the government as the means to carry out its intentions. Qualitative studies of how different tools are understood and responded to by target populations is of immense importance at this stage of the policy process (Rist).[23]

Although the demand for this type is great, the supply is extremely limited. The research community can profitably explore this area of policy tools further by qualitative research However, it must be pointed out that even though qualitative research at this stage is relevant, its applications can be problematic because there is not enough time between commissioning of a research study and the availability of its findings to the policy makers in time. Thus applications may have to rely on existing research – that may or may not exist. This underlies the need for good quality research on topical social issues and such studies can find their way into the policy arena.

Policy Implementation

The second phase of the policy cycle is that of policy implementation. It is the stage at which policy initiatives and goals established during policy formulation are to be transformed into programmes, procedures and regulations. At this point the concern becomes one of how to use the available resources in the most efficient and effective manner in order to have the best impact of the programme.

At the policy implementation stage the information needs cluster into several areas. First, there is a pressing information need on the implementation process per se. Qualitative researchers, through case studies, and programme monitoring and evaluation, can inform programme managers in charge of policy implementation.

The second type of information required at this stage is to find out whether the initial condition that existed at the time of launching of the programmes has improved or worsened or remained static; and what is the extent of involvement or participation of the target group? Qualitative research can identify the 'problem' areas and bring to the notice of the project management in time to take mid course correction steps that are essential to carry the programme to its successful end or to decide to jettison the programme.

Policy Accountability

At this phase of the policy cycle the type of information that is required from research is about the performance of the programme- what is the impact or outcome of the programme? At this stage the researcher has to evaluate the impact of the programme on the extent of achievements of the goals that it had set about to achieve initially. Qualitative research allows for the study of both anticipated and unanticipated outcomes, changes in understanding and perceptions as a result of the programme or policy, the direction and intensity of the social change that results from the programme, the strength and weaknesses of the administrative/organizational structures charged with its implementation etc. The findings of evaluative studies undertaken by independent qualitative researchers will carry great reliability and validity which is good for the government to fortify itself from future pitfalls.

Conclusion

Qualitative research can also be useful in the deeper understanding of the policy tools available to government and how each can be more or less effectively used to achieve policy objectives. Such information can clearly inform the policy makers in all the three stages of the policy process. The emphasis on qualitative research is not to be construed as a negative judgement on **quantitative** research. It is always possible to adopt the right mix of both these types of research. A basic factor that need to be kept in mind before choosing the type of research - qualitative, quantitative, a mixture of both for policy studies is to pay due attention and weightage to the preponderant, dynamic fast changing political process scenario; the freedom of operation (decision-making) open to the authoritative-formal political masters and policy makers; and above all the political compulsions such as the impact that policy decisions shall have on the electoral fortunes of the policy makers and their political party.

III

POLITICAL SCIENCE AND PUBLIC ADMNISTRATION: THE META POLICY SEIENCE

At the end of fifty years after 'policy sciences' made their appearance in the academic firmament in 1950s, the policy scientists are deeply divided. The movement is faced with theoretical, methodological and practical problems. This paper posits the thesis that political science and public administration emerge as the *true original* science of government and will ever remain the true, credible, integrated social science of social sciences. T*he study of Politics and Administration constitutes the genuine, all encompassing Meta policy science.*

After a survey of the chequered history of the discipline of Public Administration from its genesis in 1887 with the publication by Woodrow Wilson of the seminal essay on *The Study of Administration* till the 1960s, Golembiewski (1977) identified three comprehensive paradigms in the intellectual field, viz. *Traditional, Social-Psychological* and *Humanistic/Systemic*. He examined their relative strengths and weaknesses on a nine-point scale: guiding political philosophy, focal unit of analysis, central emphasis, central concepts, implied metaphor of organisation, guiding principle, central focus, model for motivation and control of behaviour and dominant role for officials.[24] As a 'developing discipline', public administration witnessed the emergence of a new paradigm - *the Public Policy Paradigm*, the fourth in the series since the fifties.

IV

PUBLIC POLICY PARADIGM

With the political scientist Harold Lasswell's essay on "The Policy Orientation" in *The Policy Sciences*, authored with Daniel Lerner (1951), the study of public policies came to be newly christened as Policy

Sciences. It also hearalded the birth of the public policy paradigm in public administration. However, the fact remains that Political Science is the oldest policy science everknown to mankind by definition, substance, scope, content and the process. *The process of government and administration together constitutes the heart of the policy process,* i.e. public policy is the traditional concern and legitimate core area of political science. If Politics is policy and policy is politics, political science stands out as the tallest and unique policy science amongst all social sciences. Political science is the *mother* of all policy sciences. Together with its intellectual baby – *public administration* which is directly and indirectly concerned with all the interfaces of the public policy process – policy planning, policy formulation, implementation, monitoring and evaluation, political science and public administration the mother and child rightly deserve the claim of being the *Meta policy science – the policy science of policy sciences a la* Aristotle[25] who christened the study of politics as *the Master Science* and *a la* Yehezkel[26] Dror who coined the concept of *metapolicy* – policy on policies.

Historically speaking political science originally meant what we now call *policy science* – the application of knowledge to the concerns of the prince, of those who seek to foster the *good society*. The first chair in political science was established in Columbia University in 1857. One of the earliest appearances of the term was in the 1890s when the Columbia University's graduate social science faculty was founded as the *Faculty of Political Science*! This faculty came to include departments such as *economics, sociology, history, anthropology, statistics, public law* and *government*. The Department of Government was thus considered as one of the political or policy sciences (Bava, 1993).[27]

Political Science has been the intellectual home of the study of public administration. At first political scientists taught and guided students of public administration. As the executive machinery of the government - as government in action, the art of public administration has come to be treated as a *profession* with its own professional ethics and standards for its members. With the clarion call given in 1887 by

Woodrow Wilson, Professor of Political Science for a separate study of public administration, many universities in the United States, England, France, Germany and India established independent departments or schools of public administration. Being rooted in public law and in political science, and directly concerned with the public policy process, public administration has over the decades developed into an *interdisciplinary* and *applied social science* and the "*meta social science*" - the social science of social sciences - the integrating and synthesising social science with emphasis on public interest (public good), public service, public law, public policy, public finance, public debt, public personnel, public accountability etc. (Bava, 1993).[28]

As a policy science, a role which filled the traditional *normative* concerns of the classical writings about politics (later came to be known as political theory) the field of *government drew on other social sciences. Its interests were normative, historical or analytic in a policy sense. That is, it did not involve efforts at systematic generalisation along the lines of other social sciences.* But while political science as the study of state, government and politics was emerging as a separate field, other disciplines continued to exhibit considerable interest in politics. This was particularly true of early sociologists in the United States and Europe. In their effort to *generalise* about institutions and social behaviour, they could not ignore as important a set of institutions as the *political* or the formation of attitudes and group norms in *politics*. Thus thinkers like Max Weber, Robert Michels, Vilfredo Pareto, and Emile Durkheim involved themselves in political analysis as part of their sociological concerns (Bava, 1993).[29]

Development: The Mother of the Social Science

The integration of social sciences was bedevilled by three factors - (i) crises in the explanandum of social sciences, (ii) pluralism in methods of social explanations and (iii) non-utilization of social science knowledge for policy-making process. The emergence of developing nations since the Second World War and the issue of development which became the centre of politics, administration, economics, international trade and diplomacy in the developing and developed nations facilitated the integration and synthesis of all social sciences into *the social science*. As Martin Seymour Lipset succinctly put it:[30]

> "The concern for development has forced the social sciences to think in terms of conceptual approaches which includes the polity, economy, society and personality. As a result, for the first time, there has been a real movement towards *the social science rather than social sciences*."

Iriving Harowitz echoes the same view when he observes that the *integrated social science* is precisely the contribution of the historical phenomenon of *development*.[31]

The Integrated Social Science is Interdisciplinary

The multidimensional, multi-faceted, multi-level umbrella concept of *development*[32] (including sustainable development) calls for the *interdisciplinary, integrated, holistic, global, systems perspective on* the part of students, scholars, development planners, policy makers and public administrators who are concerned with forecasting, planning formulating, implementing, monitoring and evaluating various developmental policies, plans, programmes and projects in different sectors of the economy and at different levels in order to achieve such development goals as growth with social justice, increased production/ productivity, removal of poverty, unemployment, illiteracy, illhealth, inequality and ignorance in both rural and urban areas.

The imperatives of development has led to the *linking* rather than the breaking of the boundaries of the social sciences. *The social science* perspective on the part of all concerned with public policy process in all governments and nations alike becomes inevitable since development involves normative, empirical, environmental, economic, political, social, cultural, scientific, material, spiritual, temporal, spatial, individual, personality and group oriented dimensions and aspects at grassroots, sub-national, national and international levels. Further, the interdisciplinary and integrated social science approach is essential to solve all development problems as the latter involve issues of international trade and aid, cooperation, peace and understanding, technology transfer, exchange and sharing of information for development; and democracy, decentralisation and devolution of political, administrative and financial powers to people and governments at lower levels.

Politics (Public Policy) and Public Administration As the Integrated Social Science and Applied Field[33]

Political Science and Public Administration - the traditional, classical fields of public policy making and administration together qualify the status of the *integrated social science*. The study and practice of public administration is truly *interdisciplinary* (multidisciplinary) as well as *applied* in nature.

The role, functions, powers and position of public administrators in the policy process establishes and highlights the unique position of the *art* and *practice* of public administration as the integrating, synthesising, all encompassing, comprehensive process of government. Public policy making on development matters and administration of diverse policies - political, economic, social, cultural, scientific and technological - plans, programmes and projects are the *core* areas of the study of *Development Administration*, a sub-field of the mother discipline Public Administration : Planning, formulation, implementation, monitoring and evaluation of public development policies, plans, programmes and schemes are *multidisciplinary exercises* i.e. calling for pooling of knowledge, skills, conceptual tools and techniques of all the sciences - social and natural (physical) taught at universities and centres of higher learning within and between nations. All social and natural sciences (experts in these fields) meet at the altar of public policy planning and formulation processes. *Truly development policy and administration call for the integrated social science perspective of Public Administration.* It is at various interfaces of the public policy processes that planners, politicians, administrators and experts are required to use their integrated socially relevant knowledge and take rational and sound policy decisions on matters of public affairs subject to "bounded rationality" (Simon, 1945).

Sound public policies thus call for the integrated social science perspective. Since the profession and practice of public administration is concerned with all the phases of the public policy process in order to protect public interest, provide public services, to facilitate development of the individual citizens and of the nation, and to safeguard the unity, territorial integrity and sovereignty of the country in which it operates, its approach and perspective to all problems of governance has got to be a truly integrated and holistic one. Such a perspective is equally applicable to the people positioned at both the ends of the spectrum of government - the politicians and administrators - members of the political and permanent executives.

V

POLICY SCIENCES

Early Stirrings

The present day "Policy Sciences" may be a 20th century invention started by Harold Lasswell and Daniel Lerner in 1951 but the act of seeking and tendering advice to the ruler(s) is a *political* exercise and it is certainly not a 20th century innovation but an ancient practice.

History is replete with examples to support the view that policy examinations, discussions and policy advice have been practised in one form or other eversince people have been making political decisions or exercising power and authority over others. The practices of seeking policy advice on public affairs or matters, policy writings and treatises on governance have a hoary past and a great history. In fact the institution of policy advice can be traced to the beginning of both civilization and government itself. It is universally true that the establishment of formal authority - government over a group of people occupying and living in a definite territory and submitting to the orders and commands of the ruler(s) - be he a tribal or clan chief, a war hero, a charismatic person, religious or social leader or a king, monarch or emperor or a few benevolent persons (aristocrats) or malevolent persons exercising power (oligarchs) or a tyrant or dictator or just the people (the *demos*) led to the practice of rulers seeking advice of the wisemen or the learned or the experienced or the saint or sage on matters of statecraft and even on their private life. This has been found to be true in all forms of government - *monarchy, aristocracy, oligarchy, tyranny, dictatorship,* and *democracy.*

To take a few historical instances, the more than 5000 years old Indian *Vedas* (scriptures) contain many words of wisdom or valuable teachings and advice for both the rulers and the ruled (Bava, 1992)[34] One of the earliest recorded examples of policy analysis is The Code of Hammurabi, (18th century B.C.) consisting of 282 laws believed to have been given to King Hammurabi by a Babylonian god which aimed at establishing an unified and just order over many aspects of public life, from family and marital relations to public office (Dunn, 1981).[35] To take a western illustration, the famous Greek Trojan Horse episode during the war between the city-states of Troy and Corinth is an example of how the rulers acted upon policy advice tendered by a Greek god or the oracle. From Plato's Academy and the courts of Chinese emperors to the modern centres of policy studies and research, people have been trying to better personal and institutional relationship by applying knowledge to government (de Leon and Overman, 1998)[36]

The art of systematic policy counselling probably developed with the onset of increasing relations between the state and church, between states and between state and subjects or citizens. The first recorded Indian treatise on governance - Kautilay's *Arthsastra* dates back to the 4th century B.C. In Western Civilization, it was not until the Italian Renaissance that policy advice assumed a more institutionalized basis, the writings of Machiavelli being the most celebrated illustration, (de Leon and Overman, 1998).[37] It is very interesting to note that despite many centuries separating the lifetime of Kautilya and Machiavelli and despite one being a product of eastern civilization and other of the western civilization, there are some remarkable similarities in the policy advices that both are credited with. For instance, on the political issue of the relationship between politics and morality both Kautilya and Machiavelli shared the common view that morality must be kept out of politics; that politics is the art of capturing, maintaining, increasing the power of the ruler (state); on the means and ends question, both held the same view that ends being the most important sought after goals, the use of any means that can lead to the realization of the goal(s) in question should be adopted by the ruler.

After *The Prince* on matters of statecraft, and Thomas More's *Utopia* (1516) on social life, *Bacon's New Atlantis* applied scientific knowledge to issues of government. The worldly philosophers such as Eramsus and English philosophers - Hobbes's *The Leviathan* and Locke's *Two Treaties on Civil Government* set the intellectual tones for the subsequent study of politics and administration as the precursor of the policy sciences.[38] The writings of the 18th century English political philosophers such as Burk, Bentham, Hume and J.S.Mill go to establish the influence of the ideas of these thinkers on the English rulers and the "growing political acceptance of knowledge" based professional advice in the development of the art of governance and administration. The increased involvement and interaction of political philosophy with political events was apparent with the French philosophers – Montesquieu's *The Spirit of Laws* (1748) and Rousseau's *Social Contract* (1762) during the French Revolution. The American *Federal Papers* (1787-1788) elaborated the profound influence of political doctrines such as the doctrine of *popular sovereignty* (from Rousseau), of *limited government* (from Locke) and of *separation of powers* (of Monstequieu) on the framers of the Constitution while structuring The American Government. However, despite the influences that the ideas of political philosophers had upon establishment of government or exercise of power, there was nothing of the sort of "conception of policy process or what composed of good policy; certainly there was no explicit research or literature on these issues."[39] Dickens and Shaw were probably more influential in affecting British social welfare legislation than Booth and Webbs just as the Tarbells and Sinclairs were the key movers in the American Progressive Movement.

In the academic world, *Economics* was beginning to mature as a set of possible insights into policy issues with Adam Smiths' *The Wealth of Nations* (1776) and influence of the writings of David Ricardo on English agriculture and freetrade policies of the government. *History* was in the vanguard in *contextual* studies but the historians' works were largely descriptive and retrospective and never prescriptive or of contemporary perspective. The influence of Darwin's evolutionary laws was writ large on political and social philosophers - Herbert Spencer and T.H. Huxley who believed in social Darwinism - in the social evolution and organic theory of the state. Finally, the study of politics was starting to define itself in matters pertaining to issues of governance. In 1887 the study of public administration was originally propounded by Woodvow Wilson who felt that it was "getting to be harder to run a constitution than to frame one."

In short, the academic disciplines were beginning to apply their skills and insights to social problems such as *suicide* by the famous sociologist Durkheim. Socially relevant knowledge was beginning to be slowly and gradually used for problem solving in society. Although there was no "systematic and routinized examination of public policy issues" prior to the start of the 20th century - and "certainly not from an organised institutional basis", the disciplines which would emerge as constituents of policy sciences were starting to fall into place as differential and separate disciplines and became more keen to protect their boundaries and respective distinctive identities rather than adopting integrated, coordinated, interdisciplinary approach to social problems. This trend of differentiation continued and affected the policy sciences well into the 20th century.[40]

Conclusion

To-day policy sciences are in a quandary. In the present scenario, the credibility and claim of *political science and public administration as the meta policy science*-the policy science of policy sciences remains unchallenged for *three* reasons. Firstly, in terms of the three-fold criterion of Lasswell's policy orientation, viz., interdiciplinarity, contextual and problem-orientation, and explicitly normative perspective, political science and public administration most eminently fulfil the criterion. Secondly, *the science of politics and public administration is the original, genuine, oldest policy science, the integrated social science* and the use of policy advice and suggestions from the adherents, analysts and followers of other academic disciplines depends, in the ultimate analysis, on the beliefs, values, compulsions and decisions of *the policy makers (political leaders) and administrators in the government of the day* and the problems that the latter faces. Thirdly, public policy process is the traditional and legitimate concern and cornerstone of the *process of governance* - of politics and administration, as such, constitutes the cornerstone of the disciplines of political science and public administration. This only goes to prove the *primacy* of political and public administrative disciplines as the public policy science *vis-a-vis* other social and natural sciences, the relevant knowledge of which can be used at the altar of the various interfaces of the public policy process only *after* it's (knowledge) internalisation, acceptanc and assimilation by the political executive and the higher echelon of the bureaucracy-the higher civil services.

NOTES & REFERENCES

1. Ray C-Rist, 'Influencing the Policy Process with Qualitative Research, 'in Norman K. Denzin and Yvonna S. Lincoln, eds. *Handbook of Qualitative Research*, Thousand Oaks, London, Sage, 1995
2. Weiss, C.H. 'Evaluations for Decisions: Is Anybody There ? Does Anybody Care ?' *Evaluation Practice* 9, (1), 23
3. *Ibid*, p 26
4. Janowitz, M. *Sociological Methods and Social Policy*, New York, General Learning Press 1971
5. Patton, M.Q. *Qualitative Evaluation and Research Methods*, (2nd ed.) Newbury Park, CA : Sage, 1988
6. Weiss, C.H. 'Evaluation for Decisions'.
7. Rist C.R. 'Influencing the Policy Process', op. cit. p545.
8. *Ibid*, op. cit. pp 545-46
9. *Ibid*,
10. Noorjahan Bava, *The Social Science Perpective and Method of Public Administration : Public Policy and Development Administration Approach*, New Delhi, Uppal, 1992
11. Thomas R. Dye, *Understanding Public policy*, New Jersey, Prentice-Hall, Englewood Cliffs, 1972, pp 231-232

12. *Ibid,* p 231
13. *Ibid,* p 245
14. *Ibid,* p 248
15. *Ibid,* p 273

15a. For details on the role of the bureaucracy in policy planning, policy implementation and evaluation see Noorjahan Bava, *The Social Science Perspective and Method of Public Administration : Public Policy and Development Administration* Approach, New Delhi, Uppal, 1992, pp52-58

16. Thomas R. Dye Understanding *Public Policy,* p 281
17. *Ibid,* p 282
18. Ray C Rist, 'Influencing the Policy Process', in K. Denzin and Yvonna S. Lincoln, eds. *Handbook of Qualitative Research,* p 548
19. Nakamura, R.T.& Smallwood, F. *The Politics of Policy Implementation,* New York, St. Martins, 1980, as quoted by Ray C. Rist in *Handbook of Qualitative Research,* p 548
20. Lindblom, C.E., *The Policy Making Process,* Englewood Cliffs, NJ : Prentice-Hall, 1968, p 13
21. Ray C. Rist, op. cit. p 548
22. Salmon, L.M., *Beyond Privatization : the Tools of Government Action,* Washington D.C. : Urban Institute Press, 1989
23. Ray C. Rist, op. cit., p 549
24. Golembiewski, "Public Administration as a Field : Three Comprehensive Paradigms" in Golembiewski, *Public Administration as a Developing Discipline: Perspective on Past and Present,* New York, Marcel Dekker, Inc., 1977, Vol.I Chap2, pp.35-73.
25. Aristotle, *Politics.*
26. Yehezkel Dror, *Public Policymaking Reexamined,* Scranton, Pennsylvania, Chandler Publishing Company, 1968; - *Design for Policy Sciences,* New York, American Elsevier Publishing Company, Inc., 1971 and - *Ventures in Policy in Policy Sciences: Concepts and Applications,* New York, Elsevier, Inc., 1971.
27. Noorjahan Bava, *Development and The Social Science Method: An Interdisciplinary and Global Approach,* New Delhi, Uppal Publishing House, 1993, p.4.
28. Ibid, p.178.
29. Ibid, pp.4-5.
30. Martin Seymour Lipset, *Politics and the Social Sciences,* New Delhi, Anand R.Kundalji for Wiley Eastern Pvt. Ltd. 1972, pp.xiii-xiv.

31. Iriving Horowitz, *Three Worlds of Development*, New Delhi, Oxford University Press, 1966.

32. Noorjahan Bava, *Development and the Social Science Method*, Chapter 2, Development and the Birth of the Social Science, pp.152-178.

33. Noorjahan Bava, *The Social Science Perspective and Method of Public Administration*, New Delhi, Uppal Publishing House, 1992.

34. *Ibid.*

35. Dunn, W.N. *Public policy Analysis*, Englewood Cliffs, NJ. Prentice Hall, 1981.

36. Peter de Leon and E.Sam Overman, "A History of Policy Sciences" in Jack Rabin ed. *Handbook of Public Administration*, New York, Marcel-Dekker, Inc. 1998, pp.467-507.

37. *Ibid*, p.468.

38. *Ibid*, p.468.

39. *Ibid*, p.469.

40. *Ibid*, p.470.

Chapter 2

An Indian Approach to Political Management

M.M.Sankdher

There is no area of management, whether political, economic, social, educational or industrial, where *classical wisdom of the ages* is not applicable. With suitable modification and reinterpretation, traditional Indian concepts can be applied to current situations and a useful management system based on Indian ethos can be developed. Apart from using it indigenously, a spiritual-ethical model of management behaviour can be profitably exported to the rest of the world. Vedanta provides this system of human engineering which reforms current political management and administration structures.

Adding the spiritual dimension to current management techniques implies an improvement of individual character, which, in turn, improves one's motivation towards organizational and professional life. Instead of being a competitive entity clamouring for more and more power, pelf and profits, soulless efficiency and materialistic goals, an insightful statesman can strive to develop a holistic, integrated framework of governance that includes righteous conduct and an awareness of the inter-connectivity between citizens, organization and oneself.

The traditional Indian approach to governance is infused with values including family integrity and work ethics (*karma yoga*). Vedantic tenets postulate ethics and morality as practical expedients for public administration, management policies, and results. Politics and ethical behaviour are complementary since ethics can be a successful political strategy and observation of scruples a better guarantee for social relations than fraud or deception. The enduring success of statesmanship depends more upon the quality of human conduct than temporary gains by unscrupulous means.

The soul-killing consequences of stark materialism can be mitigated only by a spiritual approach of trusteeship to reward, wealth and resources both individually and organizationally. If the concept of service rather than acquisition of political power is adopted, the whole scenario becomes transformed.

Recognizing and incorporating sincerity in the exercise of power is the first step towards improving human relationship systems. One learns to adjust to political crises and face them with greater self-confidence. The concept of *A'ham Brahma Asmi* (I am Brahman), indicates that each one of us has the capacity for omniscience, omnicompetence and omnipotence, which provides a tremendous boost to sagging morale. State leadership can usefully invoke this *mantra* of self-empowerment. It is a great aid to success as it provides impetus to positive energy from within and is an inner mechanism, which dissolves negativities in citizen -relations and the environment.

The core of successful political management lies in one's clarity of vision, plan of action and implementation. A successful agenda depends on the mobilizing ability to mobilize resources – natural and manpower – for maximizing policy implementation. While it is generally believed that a materialistic approach is more effective in managing national resources, it would be interesting to experiment how administering one's spiritual life contributes to positive gains. Take, for instance, the goal of *sarve bhava:.tu sukhinah*, (may all be happy), where achieving maximum happiness without exploitation and injustice demands a higher state of consciousness on the part of political actors. Would such a goal aid function in the long run, develop deeper and strong citizen-state relationships and strengthen moral commitment? If sacrifice and service are higher values than self-gratification, does sublimating desires not lead to more lasting solutions?

The spiritual perspective comes from a level of consciousness where we rise above our physical needs and cravings, and *dharma* holistically integrates body, mind and soul. Consciousness of duty, rather than fighting for one's rights, is the essence of *dharma* as one's function is performed in harmony with others and conflicts resolved through selfless conduct. If *dharma* governed *artha* and *kama*, there will be no discord or hostilities, and even if there are any, mutual understanding can help in their resolution. If our sights are clear and transparent, management of human relationships such as those between rulers and ruled become smooth on account of the awareness of the inherent unity of souls.

Mismanagement is caused by short-sightedness in our affairs. In order to understand our problems better, we must completely cleanse any false ego or prejudices from our minds. Our ancient scriptures prescribe maturity of thought and conduct, abiding values of life, sound character and integrated personality as qualifications for political leadership. Traditional knowledge stresses the need for transformation for spiritual self-realization as it helps not only in conceptualization but also in policy execution. The examples of rulers, such as, Janak, Ram, Ashok, Harshvardhan and Chandragupt Maurya are for any one to see.

Indian philosophers, rulers, saints and sages have always practised concentration - it raises our level of consciousness to enable insights and wisdom. It is a method for elevating the lower self or ego to a higher Self where the "I" ceases to exist and one is equipped to take impartial, judicious and objective decisions. One learns to see the whole rather than the parts, which makes a tremendous difference in attitudes. Modern decision-making techniques are scientific but they cannot be effective without the art of reflection which, in turn, is enhanced by contemplation and meditation. By including these practices in our daily life, we discover a profound feeling of detachment or transcendence, which is the *talisman* for successful ventures in business, politics, commerce and industry management. Maharishi Mahesh Yogi has taught these subtle techniques to management cadres through his Transcendental Meditation programs. They can equally be applied to politics by transforming our vision of power as a moral service to people in the Gandhian framework.

The negative approach to politics as if it is a dirty game, the last refuge of a scoundrel and that it leads inevitably to corrupt practices, needs to be replaced by a positive one, of selfless service, sacrifice and helping the people.

Besides proficiency and talent, a politician should be inherently good or cultivate goodness. Traditional methods create leadership that subordinates. Family patterns can be introduced to encourage familial feelings with colleagues and in the groups and parties replacing conflict of interests by harmony. Secondly, in the place of competitive struggle, the Indian experience suggests *sahanau bhunaktu* (let us all share) the fruits of enterprise.

To conclude, the conventional approach to management differs radically from its Western counterpart. Unless there is a higher level of consciousness in the political class, there can be no change in the political process or behaviours. The basic differences are:

1. *Aham Brahma Asmi* (I am Brahman) is the principle of maximum potential in every individual for competence, productivity, creativity and fulfillment. This is also reflected in the *mantra, tat tavamasi* (you are that), indicating a unity between the self and the universal Self. Here, governance is defined as that which infuses self-confidence and the capacity for excellent administration, organizational skills, work-ethics and functional efficiency and competence.

2. A holistic disposition implies the end of dualism between rulers and ruled, co-operation rather than confrontation and a reconciliation of contrary interests. In a system inspired by this principle, a person works for his evolution and for others' in the same measure. It is a mechanism for transformation by which a government concentrates on solving society's problems by resolving private and public interests for greater benefits without dependence on external agencies. This promotes functional autonomy, which is conducive to overall growth and corruption free politics.

3. Spirituality invokes subtle and tangible forces in management, such as, norms and scruples, courage and vision, which override narrow materialistic consideration and power interest. Deeper human awareness and drives are better incentives than money, machines and goods. The vision that the source of enterprise and excellence is within us and the feeling of working for higher goals help enormously.

India has a natural soil for such traditional theories and practices. Although the above concepts are traditional and Indian in the sense that they have their genesis in India, they are universal and modern in their application and effectiveness.

Aham-Brahmasmi Model

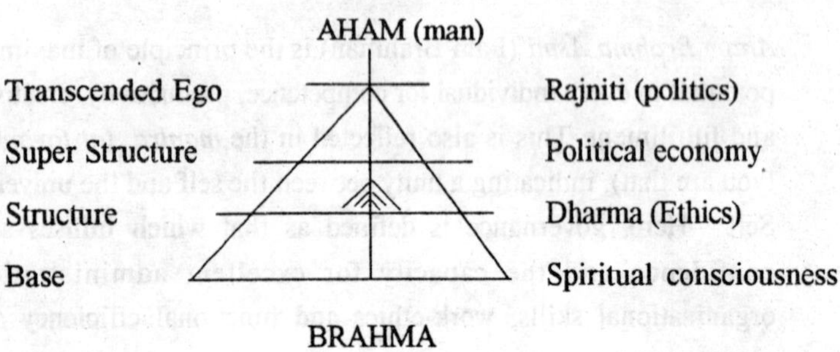

Chapter 3

Administration in Ancient India : A Study of its Administrative and Financial Structures

Ruchi Tyagi

Promoting the moral, spiritual and material well being of the people by properly administering the law of the state was repeatedly emphasized as the objective of the polity by Ancient Indian political thinkers.[1] They tried to protect the interests of the people by recommending and bringing about a decentralized administrative machinery. Several types of states like republics, oligarchies, diarchies and monarchies were prevailing in India in ancient times, but eventually monarchy became the order of the day owing to various factors and causes. The classical theory of Indian kingship, however, illustrated the role of the king as an administrator and the promulgator of law. Since the king was not able to discharge the functions of the state single handedly, he, for the development and welfare of the state had to depend and rely on his competent ministers, the departmental heads, and also on decentralized machinery of the administration including the provincial, divisional and district administration alongwith town and village administration.

Ministry

Ministry or a council of advisers has been regarded by ancient Indian political thinkers as a very vital organ of the body politic. In the *Rigveda* and the *Atharvaveda* we find no mention of king's ministers. The *Samihitas* of the *Yajurveda* and the Brahmana literature, however, mention in several places some high functionaries, known as *ratnins* (jewels), who probably formed the king's council. The *ratnins* consisted of royal relatives, departmental heads and courtiers. To the first of these categories belong the Crowned Queen and the Favourite Queen, who are invariably mentioned by all authorities[2] and perhaps the crown Prince. This would suggest that queens in the Vedic age were not merely consorts of kings, but played some part in the adminnistration. Purohita, the royal chaplain, also figures in all the lists of *ratnins*. Amongh the departmental heads included in the list of *ratnins* figure *Senani* (the commander-in-chief), *Suta* (the commander of the chariot corps of the royal army, *Gramani* (the most prominent among the village headmen), *Sangrahita* (the treasurer) and *Bhagadhuk* (the tax collector).

After the disappearance of vedic *ratnins* a more effective body of council of ministers came into existence. This was variously described as *mantrins, sachivas* and *amatyas.* The *Jatakas* frequently refer to ministers. The Mauryas and the Sungas had a regular council of ministers known as *Mantri-parishad,* which figures both in inscriptions and literature. The Saka rulers of Western India ruled with the assistance of a council of *mati-sachivas* (councillors) and *karma-sachivas* (administrative heads of departments). *Mantrins* (ministers) *figure frequently in the Gupta inscription.*[3]

So far as the strength of the ministry is concerned, *Manu* holds that the ministry should consist of 7 or 8 members; the latter number is prescribed by the *Mahabharata.* The *Sukraniti* recommends a ministry of ten. Manu and Kautilya agree with each other in stating that the actual number of ministers should depend upon the needs of the situation in the state concerned.[4] To ensure despatch and secrecy, there often used to be smaller cabinet of important ministers consisting of three or four members only.

In the selection of servants, Sukra lays more on work, character and merit rather than on caste or family. Only in marriages and dinner parties, considerations of family need be compulsorily observed. But when the question is of appointement to political offices, neither the superiority of caste nor of family is to be asserted. Only work, character and merit are to be respected and given due consideration.

Kautilya describes an elaborate system of recruitment of the Amatyas and other officials who were to be *Dharmopashuddha* (morally and ethically pur), *Arthopashuddha* (honest in financial matters) and *Charitropasuddha* (of good or pure character). Sukra enumerates the characteristics of good administrators, as truthfulness, good family, good habits, contentment with salary, sweet tongue, efficiency, parity, firmmess, skilfulness and aversion to evil ways etc. He warns that cheats, miserable, greedy, passionate, vicious, gamblers, atheists, vain, envious, ferocious, irreligious persons cannot be good servants.

The scope of the work of the ministry inlcuded the whole administration. It was to enunciate new policies, to ensure their success ful working, to remove any difficulties that may crop up, to supervise and direct the state policy regarding taxation and expenditure, to take steps for the proper education and training of the princess, to participate in their coronation and to direct the foreign policy, both with reference to internal feudatroy kings and external independent status.[5] In order to divide the work among the ministers, Sukra gives us same idea of their portfolios. According to him, the ministry, whose strength was to be ten was to consist of (1) *Purohita* (the Royal Chaplain or the Priest), (2) *Pratinidhi* (the Viceroy), (3) *Pradhana* (the Premier), (4) *Sachiva* (the War Minister or the Commander), (5) *Mantrin* (the Foreign Minister or the Councillor), (6) *Pradvivaka* (the Judge), (7) *Pandita* (the Scholar), (8) *Sumantra* (the treasurer or the Collector), (9) *Amatya* (the Revenue Minister) & (10) *Duta* (the Spy). The status and pay of each succeeding minister were lower than those of the preceding one.[6]

Ministerial appointments were made by the king. Personal factors counted for a good deal in determining the position and powers of ministers. When kings were strong and powerful, they were the centres of power and the administration was known as 'King-centred) *(rajayatta-tantra);* when they were weak and incapable, ministers were the virtual rulers and then the administration was known as ministry – controlled *(Sachivayattatantra).* In normal times, howerver, power was shared by both and the administration was dependent equally both on the king and the ministry.

SECRETARIAT AND DEPARTMENTS

King and his council of ministers, however, together constituted the brain centre of the govenment organism. But just as the brain can function through the instrumentality and cooperation of a number of senses and organs, so also the king-in council requires the assistance of a central secretariat and the heads of a number of departments.

The secretariat might have gradually evolved in the post-Vedic period, when the art of writing was coming into more extensive use; kingdoms were developing into empires; functions of government were becoming more numerous; some kind of a Central Secretariat must, therefore, have existed in courts of legendary kings like Yudhishthira and Jarasandha; or historical emperors like Ajatasatru or 'Maha Padma Nanda'.[7]

The *Arthasastra* shows that the secretariat had developed into a full-fledged and well-developed organisation in the Mauryan period. The officers of departments were called *Lekhakas* or writers. These *Lekhakas,* however, were not mere clerks, Kautilya lays down that *Lekhakas* were to be of the status of *amatyas,* whose position and pay were to be inferior only to those of ministers (mantrins).[8]

The efficiency of the administration depended to a great extent upon the ability of the secretariat officers and the accuracy with which they drafted the orders of the Central Government. "Government is writ and writ is government" says Kautilya; 'royalty does not reside in the person of the king, but in his sealed and signed orders' says Sukra. A great care, therefore was taken in the selection of the secretariat officers. They were required to possess almost as high qualifications as that of ministers, so far as education, ability and reliability were concerned. Above all they were to be experts in drafting. It was their duty to listen to the oral orders of the king or ministers and to draft them properly and accurately in as short a time as possible. They were to look into the previous files, assure themselves that there was no contradiction of earlier views or orders and then frame the wording of the new communique, which was to be characterised by relevancy, completeness, sweetness, dignity and lucidity. Redundancy was to be avoided; facts were to be stated either in their chronological sequence or according to their importance; the description was to be impressive and cogent reasons were to be adduced for the action that the government was taking.[9] When the communique was ready, it was to be shown to the minister or head of the department concerned and then submitted to the king for his final approval and signature. After the royal signature, the office used to seal the document and forward it to its destination.

The secretariat altogether had a big record office. Ordinary or routine orders were not naturally preserved for a long time, but those which granted lands or assigned revenues were kept with great care for future reference. In all cases of land grants, the enttry of the transaction was made at the secretariat as soon as possible; the delay in this connection was regarded as irregular and officers responsible for it were censured.

One of the most important duties of the Central Government and secretariat was the supervision and control of the provincial, district and local administration. For this purpose, (i) tours of inspection have been recommended to the king and his officers by several writers.[10] (ii) the Central Government used to have its own reporters and informers to keep it in touch with the developments in the provinces. These appear to have acted independently of the officers of the local government. (iii) Kautilya gives us a very detailed description of the spy system in which spies moved in guise of students, ascetics, merchants, nuns, prostitutes or astrologers etc. These spies were to report on the conduct of both officials and non-officials. It was their duty to see that public funds were not misappropriated, justice was properly administered and sedition promptly punished.

The decision of the central government were communicated to the local authorities by the secretariat through its special messengers. The work being responsible, it was usually entrusted to high officers.

In general different departments were presided over by heads, who were called *adhyakshas* in the Mauryan age and *Karmasachivas* in the Saka administration. Curiously enough, Smritis refer to them in a very general and vague way; it is the *Arthasastra,* which supplies detailed information, which is very largely confirmed by inscriptions.[12] So far as the number of departments is concerned, the epics usually refer to eighteen departments, which are called *tirthas.*[13] The *Asthasastra* also refers to this number of departments, but it does not hesitate to increase their number by five or six. The number of departments contemplated by Sukra seems to be twenty. If we group these departments under the heads of administration well known to the modern time it would include: the (i) The Department of the Royal Household including a royal physician, Poet-Laureates or a learned men, a royal astrologer and also the special officer for the management of the harem; (ii) Military Department, as referred to by Kautilya, included six heads of departments, the *Ayudhagaradhyksha* (in charge of the armoury), the *navadhyaksha* (in charge of the naval forces), the *avsadhyaksha* (in charge of the cavalary), the *hastyadhyaksha* (in charge of the elephants); the *rathadhyaksha* (in charge of the chariots) and the *pattyodhyaksha* (incharge of the infantry); (iii) The Department of Foreign Affairs was divided among several officers and had a large staff of the intelligence department; (iv) Revenue department, which had a large number of superintendents incharge of the Crown-Lands *(Sitadhyaksha),* forests *(Aranyadhyaksha),* state herds *(Godadhyaksha)* waste-lands *(Vivtadhyaksha),* and land-records *(Mahakshapatalika).* The principal tax collected by the Revenue Department was the land tax, which was usually in kind and a large army of officers had to be employed to supervise its collection. The Revenue Department was also known as Treasury Department under the charge of *Koshadhyaksha.* (iv) the Department of Industry and Commerce used to supervise cloth industry, distilleries, prostitutes, slaughter-houses, mines, pearl fishery, the production of gold, etc. A survery of *Arthasastra* shows that Kautilya was in favour of state control of important and lucrative trade and industries. Mines, pearl fishery and the production of gold were under state-control and management; private individuals could come in only as lessees. Cotton industry, forest development and salt and wine production were controlled by state. In the industries in private sector the state was keen to ensure that the labour was not exploited and the public was not cheated. (v) the Department of Commerce having a large number of superintendents, was to put the governemnt products in the market under favourable conditions, to organise the import of goods required inthe locality and to supervise their sales at reasonable rates, to export merchandise, to control the prices and to supervise the tolls and also the weights and measures. (vi the Judicial Department, headed by the king himself as the fountain sources of justice, consisted of village panchayat and town council at grass-root level, government courts, royal courts, *dharmadhyakshas* (presiding judges) and *dandadhayakshas* (judges of criminal courts). (vii) the Police Department was usually responsible for extermination of thieves and dacoits, (viii) the Ecclesiastical Department was headed by the royal chaplain *(purohita)* or the minister *(pandita)* and was to preserve religion and morality; to discourage the obsolete socioreligious customs and to compose necessary and desirable changes. Their duty was to encourage all religions impartially; no distinction was usually made between Hinduism, Buddism and Jainism when distributing state patronage in aid of hospitals, education and poor relief.

At this point, however, this can be submitted that all these departments existed in the administrations of moderate-sized states of the ancient period. The evidence of the *Arthasastra* is strikingly confirmed by the data of inscriptions in several respects.

The *Arthasastra* gives us detailed information about the pay of different dignitaries and officers. The queens, the crown-prince and important ministers like the commander-in-chief received 48,000 Panas a year; the chamberlain, the treasurer and revenue minister received 24,000; ordinary members of the ministry and wardens of the marches,

12,000; superintendents of horses, chariots and elephants, 8,000 Panas; army doctors and horse trainers, 2,000 etc. It is difficult to state whether the Panas were silver or copper coins. THe salaries must have varied with the size and resources of the state also.

About the recruitment of these officers to various departments, it has been acknowledged that many of them especially those who worked in the commere or minig departments, required high technical qualification. Smritis emphasisze that only thsose who were specially qualified for them should be appointed after thorough test. Sukra even suggests that the state should give scholarships for training youngmen for the different technical posts. Birth and high connections must have counted then in the selection to posts where no special training was necessary, the subsequent career must have depended largely on the merit of the new entrant. It, however, appears very probable that the *mahamatyas* of the Mauryan age or the *Kumaramatyas* of the Gupta period formed a class of officers, similar to modern ICS. or IAS. Persons who belonged to this class were usually of high birth, often recruited from the members of ex-royal families, which had been superseded by the empire. Their posts often used to become hereditary, as those of the ministers.. The system of paying these officers by the assignment of lands of government revenues must have made many of these posts hereditary.

Provincial, Divisional, District and Town Administration

As in modern times so in ancient days, the scheme of terriorial division was not uniform in India. Some districts and divisions were small, while others were large. This was partly due to difference in population and fertility and partly to political causes. In case of small kingdoms, like Pallavas or Vakatakas, they had only one territorial division the district variously called *vaishya* or *rashtra.* The administrative divisions of a big empire like the Mauryan were almost similar to those of the Union Government today. It was divided into provinces often as big as in modern India. These provinces were divided into divisions. The divisions were divided into districts or vishayas and the latter into subdivisions variously termed as *pathakas, pethas* or *bhukits.* These latter were divided into smaller groups of villages, each one containing from 10 to 15 villages.

Provincial Government

Provincial administration in the modern sense of the term existed only in big kingdoms. The Mauryan empire was divided into seveal provinces. Five of them are known at present Uttarapatha, Avantirashtra, Dakshinapatha, Kalinga and Prachya with Taxila, Ujjanini, Survarnagiri, Tosali and Patliputra as their respective capitals. Under the Sungas, the administration of Malwa had the status and powers of a provincial government. The status of *Mahakshatrapas* ruling at Banaraas, Mathura and Ujjaini in the empire of Kanishka was also similar to that of provincial governors. In the Gupta empire, Kathiawar, Malwa and Gujarat had provincial administrations.

Heads of the privincial administrations were officers of very high status. Very often princes of the blood royal were appointed to them. Thus under the Mauryas, Bindusara, Asoka and Kunala had all served as viceroys in the different provinces of the empire; under the Sungas the crown prince Agnimitra was serving as viceroy in Malwa. Ofcourse princes of the blood royal were not always available for appointment to the viceregal posts; then they went to the most senior and trusted officers of the empire, who were military generals as well. Military leadership was regarded as an essential qualification not only for ministerial but also viceregal post.

Viceroys also acted as the incharge of supervision and guidance of civil and revenue administration of the province. This was done obviously in the light of the orders received from the capital. Besides maintaining law and order and supervising revenue collection, the viceroys had to take steps for developing the resources of their provinces by constructing and repaining works of public utility like irrigation tanks and canals and to strengthen the foundation of the empire by ensuring good government and promoting public condidence. Almost all the departments that existed at the imperial capital must have their replicas in the provincial headquarters.

The government taxes and revenues must have been first collected at the provincial headquarters. The balance that remained after meeting the charges of the provincial administration must have been sent to the imperial capital.

Divisional Administration

The next administrative unit roughly corresponded to the size of a Commissioner's Division consisting of three or four districts. It was called a *bhukti* under the Guptas and Pratiharas; *rashtra* under the Rashtrakutas and *mandala* under Cholas and Chalukyas and *Rajjukas* under Mauryan administration.

Asoka had followed a policy of decentralization and granted large powers to the *rajjukas.* Subject to the general imperial policy, they had full administrative powers in civil, revenue and criminal affairs. They could confer favours or impose punishments as demanded by the situation.Under the Rashtrakutas, on the other hand, their powers appear to be restricted.

Divisional Commissioner had extensive powers over their subordinate officers. If the latter became disloyal or disaffected, they were arresed by them and sent up for further action. The Divisional Commissioners had sufficiently strong military forces under their command which were used for controlling subordinate officers and local feudatories, When a big campaign was planned by the king, a greater part of these forces were naturally sent to the capital.

Divisional Commissioners were also at the head of the revenue administration. The term *rajjuka* used to denote them or the district officer implies an intimate connection with the measurement and assessament of lands. Revenue settlement of villages or their reassessment necessitated by various causes must have been carried under their supervision.

Asoka's exhortation to his rajjukas to follow a uniform policy in punishments implies that they had judicial powers as well. The same must have been the case with the Commissioners of the Division. Probably they constituted the highest court of appeal of the Division.

The patronage to appoint various district officers which the Divisional Commissioners exercised must have varried with different administrations. So far as the existence of popular councils at the Divisional headquarters is concerned (which definitely existed at village level), it is, however, difficult to say whether there was a regular popular council to guide and advise the Divisional Commissioners. Though they are mentined in context of Rashtramahattaras under the Rashtrakutas and Adhikarins under Kalachuris in Malwa; they, probably, were the notable citizens of the Division, but not the members of a constitutional popular conucil.

District Administration

The *vishaya* of our ancient records usually corresponded with the district of the modern administration, consisting of about a thousand to two thousand villages. The head of the vishaya was naturally called *vishayapatti* or *vishayadhyaksha* in the Mauryan administration. *Sahasradhipa* of *Manusmriti*,[18] who was in charge of a thousand villages, is probably to be idenitified with him. The nadu was smaller division in Tamil country, but the powers of its heads were probably similar to those of a *vishayapati*

The district officers, like the modern collectors, were responsible for maintaining law and order in their districts. They also had to supervise the collection of government taxes and revenues. They were assisted by a large subordinate staff, like the *yuktas,* ayu*ktas, niyutas* and *vyapritas.* They were also known as *gopas* in the Mauryan age and as *dhruvas* in Gujarat in the post-Gupta period.

In order to maintain law and order, the *vishayapati* used to have a small military force under them. The officers of the poice department known as *dandapasikas* or *chorodharanikas* worked under the directions of the district officers. There is no definite information as to whether the different officers of commerce, industry and forest departments were subject to the immediate general supervision of the *vishayapati* (though working under the direct orders of the heads of their respective department at the Capital). Whether the *vishayapati* exercised any judicial powers is also not known at present.

Unfortunately, no information is available as to how the members of the district council were elected or selected. The bankers and merchants were represented by the president of their guilds. The same was the case with the writers class. Regarding the other members of the council, A.S. Altekar is of the view that persons of different classes, who had by their age, experience and character, acquired a pre-eminent status, were coopted to the council by a general consenus of opinion.[19]

The district administration was well organised in the Gupta period. It had its own records office in charge of a *pustapata* (record keeper), who kept accurate records of the dimensions and ownership of not only cultivated but also the waste land, and also of house sites in towns and village. Even when waste lands, the ownership of which was vested in the state, were to be sold, the sanction of the popular council was necesary. Some of the land-grant charts even bear the seals of the district administration. Seals of the district administrations of Rajagriha and Gaya were found at Nalanda, showing that their communication to outsiders bore the impress of their official seals. All business was transacted methodically; even when the *vishayapatti* himself wanted to purchase some wastelands, he had to appear before the council and take its permission.

Sub-Divisional Administration

Between the district and the village there were some administrative divisions, whose nature and dimensions varied from age to age. Manu recommends that ten villages should form one administrative unit, and ten of the latter should consitute a bigger one, consisting of 100 villages, which would roughly correspond to the Modern Tehsil or Taluka. The district which according to Manu was to consist of a thousand villages which includes ten Tehsils. The *Mahabharata* suggests some variation in this decimal system of administrative units and recommends intermediate groups of twenty or thirty villages.[21]

A number of these village groups constituted something like modern Tehsil or Taluka, which was known as *pathaka, peta sthali* or *bhukti* in the different provinces. *Kharvataka* and *dronamukha* consisting of 200 and 400 villages respecitively were also sub-divisions of *vishayas* corresponding to modern Tehsils.[22]

The Tehsildars of the Central Government carried on the administration of their areas with the help of hereditary revenue officers, known as *nadgavundas* in karnatak and *desagramakutas* in Maharashtra.

The sub-divisional officers in charge of the *pathakas, pethas* and *bhuktis* were helped and guided in administration by popular councils which formed a salient feature of the village administration. During Chola rule in the Tamil country, the *Nadu* assembly included the representatives of the village. It took active part in the periodical assessment of the land revenue as well as in the classification of land. It also took suitable steps to secure relief in land tax when there was a case to justify it. They also gave donations of their own and administered charitable endowments given by others. At times, they even decided the cases of accidental homicides not amounting to murder.

Town Administration

The administration of major towns, as in modern times, differed from that of an unimportant town in the moffusil. Very little is known about the town life of Vedic period or of the period of Samhitas and Brahmanas. On the eve of the invasion of Alexander the Great, the Punjab was studded with a large number of towns and cities, most of them autonomous to a great extent, being governed by their own councils. Probably, the very experienced elders were coopted on them by a general consensus of public opinion. The chief officer of the town was called *sarvarthachintaka.* During Gupta period, this presiding officer was called *purapala.* If the town was also a fort, it used to have another imperial officer called Kottapala. Very often the *purapalas* were themselves military captains. Sometimes, they were selected from among scholars, some of whom were interested in promoting the study of six systems of philosophy. It is quite possible that they might have combined the literacy qualifications with military ability as well.

The *purapala* goverror was assisted by non-offical committee, variously called as *goshthi, panchakula* or *chaukadika* in the different parts of the country. All classes and interests were represented on the committee. Sometimes towns were divided into wards and each ward sent its own members to the committee. How the representatives were selected is not known. Probably, elderly persons, who had earned the regard of the residents by their experience, character and ability, must have been sent to the council by a general consensus of public opinion.

The *puanchakula* usually consisted not necessarily of five but often of a larger number of representatives thus sent by the different wards. It used to have *vara* or an executive of it own for the speedy and convenient despatch of business. The number of members of the executive committee must have varied to the needs of each case. It was their duty to look after all the executive work, the collection of taxes, the investment and recovery of public funds, the administration of trust funds etc. The *varikas* were assisted in their work by a permanent office and staff. The former was called *sthana* in Rajputana and used to keep carefully all records of important documents. A permanent secretary *(karnaika)* was in charge of the records and correspondence of the committee. Important documents were carefully drafted by him under the instructions of the committee. He must have had a sufficient clerical staff under him.

An officer called *Kauptika* used to be appointed for collection of market dues, which probably formed the main stay of the local finacne. Sometimes the dues of the Central Government in custom duties and even the pilgrim tax were collected by the town committee on its behalf.

Kautilya's *Arthasastra* and the Megasthenis account give us a brief description of the corporation of Pataliputra during the 4th and 3rd centuries B.C. Being imperial capital, thronged with foreigners, its constitution was somewhat different, but it followed the same general principles which governed ordinary town committee. It consisted of a body of 30 members divided into five sub-commiittees. Out of these sub-committees, the one dealing with foreigners, watching their movements and providing for their needs, must have existed only in big capitals or busy ports. The second commmittee dealt with vital statistics and registered carefully the births and deaths. The third committee, which supervised over the manufacture of articles, must have existed only in industrial towns and cities. The fourth and fifth committees dealt with the fixation of fair wages, the supervision of the market, the supply of pure and unadulterated goods and the collection of the different dues from the merchants.

These duties were discharged by most of the town and village boards throughout Indian histroy. The public works committee, usually known in Tamil country as the tank or the garden committee in later times, does not find any reference here. Probably Pataliputra being the imperial capital, its needs in this connection were met by the officers and departments of the Central Government. None of the sub-committees is seen administering trust funds for the benefits of the community, as was invariably done by the town councils and village committees in later times. Probably this work was done by some purely non-official bodies, as indicated in *Arthasastra.* Pataliputra being the imperial capital of a big empire, it is but natural that many officials must have been appointed on the board like the superintendent of markets, tolls, weights and measures etc. referred to in the *Arthasastra.*

Village Administration

Since earliest times, the village has been the pivot of administration in India. Its importance was significant in an age when communications were slow and industrialisation was unknown. In the vedic age, states were small to further enhance the importance of village. In later times, even when kingdoms became large, there was no change in the situation, for, the village was the natural pivot of administration in a rural society. Even the kings like Bindusara used to convene a meeting of village headmen to discuss the important questions of administrative policy. The villages were, indeed the real centre of social life and important units in the country's economy. They sustained the edifice of national culture, prosperity and administration.

The Village Headman :

The village administration was usually carried under the supervision and direction of the village headman. He is called *Gramani* in the Vedic literature and figures freqently in the *Jatakas.* The *Arthasastra* attests to its importance in the administration and inscriptions of almost all the provinces refer to him during the first millennium of the Christian era. He was called *gramika*k or *grameyaka* in northern India, *mununda* in th eastern Deccan, *gramukuta* or *pattakila* in Maharashtra, *gavunda* in Karanatak and *mahattaka* or *mahantaka* in U.P. Sukraniti observes him as the father and mother to the villagers, who as a man of people tried to protect their interests.[24]

In general, there was only one headman for each village. His post was usually hereditary, government having the right to nominate another scion of the family if the succession of the son was not approved. By caste he was usually a non-Brahmana. Being the leader of village-militia, he often belonged to the Kshatriya caste. Sometimes Vaisyas too aspired for and obtained the office.

The headman was the most important officer of the village administration. His order was represented on the council of *ratnins* in the Vedic period and he appears almost like a village king in the *Jatakas.* Defence of the village was the most important duty of the village headman. Owing to slow communications, the help of the Central Government could not be always expected at the nick of the time. The villagers, therefore, had to be self-reliant in defence.[25]

The collection of the government revenue was the next important duty of the village headman. He was the custodian of the necessary records and used to carry out the work of collection in consultation with the village council, of which he was the ex-officio president and used to guide its deliberations and activities. He was usually remunerated by rent free land and could also get a number of petty dues in kind which the villagers had to pay to the government.

The Village Office :

The village office had to keep records of rights and transfers of the village lands and papers connected with the government dues and their realisation. Correspondence had to be carried on with the district authorities and central government. The decisions and resolutions of the village council had to be duly recorded. All this work was entrusted to another village officer known as village accountant. His post was hereditary in most provinces and was paid rent-free land. In Tamil country, he was appointed by the village assembly.

Apart from the village headman and the accountant, *Sukraniti* refers to four more village officials, *Sahasadhipati* (magistrate), *bhagahara* (revenue collector), *Sulkagrahak* (toll collector) and *pratihara* (gate-keeper)

Village Assembly :

Probably all respectable householders were entitled to become the members of the Primary Assembly of the village. There is numerous evidence to show that the village assembly primarily included all the village householders in Maharastra, Karnataka and Tamil country who were invited by the beat of the drum for the meeting of the Village Assemblies. The different terms were used to denote the Great Men of the village, i.e *mahattamas* in U.P., *mahattaras* in Maharashtra, *mahajanas* in Karnatak and *perumakkal* in Tamil country. These village elders used to organise works of public utility and recreation, settle the disputes between their residents and act as trustees for the property of minors.

The meeting place of the Primary Assemblies varied according to local conditions; sometimes it was the hall of the Assmebly, some times the pavilion of the local temple, sometimes even a tamarind or a banyan tree. All respectable householders were entitled to attend; in actual practice about 200 or 300 persons generally participated in the meetings. The Assemblies used to meet when the Village Council had to be constituted or when matters of unusual importance were to be considered or when donations were to be accepted on behalf of the community. Probably the village headman presided over the meetings and the village accountant kept the record of the proceedings in the village office especially when grants were accepted or tax exemptions granted.

Village Council :

The executive committe or village council or village *Panchayat* appears to have evolved into regular bodies in the Gupta period, at least in some parts of India. They were known as *Panchamandats* in Central

India and *gramajanpadas* in Bihar (Nalanda). In Bihar, the village councils had developed into formal bodies, meeting regularly to transact administrative business and communicating their decisions to outsiders in formal and sealed communications. In Tamil country, the village executive was elected by the Village Assembly after obtaining the consent of all the villagers assembled.

Administration of Village Uttaramerur :

The most detailed picture of the working of the executive committees of the Village Assemblies *(Sabhas)* is to be obtained from the famous inscriptions at Uttaramerur (or Uttaramallur), a village still existent in Chingleput district. The administration of this village was carried on by five sub-committees of the *Sabha.* All the members worked in the honorary capacity and held office for one year. They coud, however be removed earlier, if found guilty of mis-conduct. It was felt that all experienced and qualified residents of the village should get an opportunity to serve in various sub-committees. One of the rules, therefore, provided that a member who had served once on a sub-committee was not to be re-appointed to it during the next three years. Persons with loose character or found guilty of misappropriation of public funds were debarred from membership. Members were to be within the age group of 35 to 70 years. They were required to own a house and at least 1/4 *veli*k (abut two acres) of tax-paying land. It was felt that those who deal with pubic funds should be persons above need. The property qualifications were halved in case of scholars of Vedic literature or Smritis or bhashyas (philosphy). It is worth noting that no government officers were included in these committees.

Each *Sabha* was usually the architect of its own constitution. The earliest known constitution, that of the *mahasabha* of *Mananlainallur* was framed by that body itself at a special meeting of villagers convened by a beat of drums. When amendments became necessary in the constitution, they also were usually considered and passed by the *Sabha* itself.

At Uttaramerur, members of the different sub-committees were selected by drawing of lots. Several nominations were made for each of the thirty wards of the villages; the name of each nominee being put on a separate ticket. All the tickets for each ward were put in a pot and a young child, who was quite innocent of what it was called upon to do, was asked to pick up one ticket. That person was declared elected for each ward whose name was on the ticket so taken out. There was no room for canvassing or party-politics.

It does not seem that election of the modern type giving rise to party jealousies and rivalries was prevailing anywhere. Persons were periodically elevated to the council by the consensus of public opinion as expressed in a general meeting of all the respectable householders of the village. Caste consideration did not sway in the selection of the council members. Many non-Brahmanas worked on it in the Gupta age. On the judgements of many village *Panchayats* in the Maratha period appear the signatures of not only non-Brahmanas, but also of untouchables.

Thirty pesons who were thus selected were later assigned to different sub-committees. The first committee was in charge of village gardens and orchards; the second supervised the village tank and the distribution of its water; the third discharged the important function of settling disputes; the fourth gold-committee was to assay gold for all people impartially; and the fifth committee was known as *panchavara* committee. In addition to these five sub-committees, there was a general committee of supervision known as Annual Committee or *Samvatsara-Varyam.* The number and functions of the sub-committees naturally varied according to the needs and circumstances of each village. Accordingly, a land-survery committee, a temple committee, education committee find references therefor.[28]

Sub-committees of the Chola type did not probably function in northern India as well. Here the village council consisted of five members only; it is expressly called a *panchamnadab* in a Gupta inscription and *panchkuli* in several medieval records.

Functions of the Village-Council

Several records from south India make it clear that the village council was responsible for collection and even remission of the land revenue, to negotiate with government for concessions in case of famine and similar calamities and also to auction the land in case of defaulters. It is doubtful, whether the same powers were enjoyed by village councils in Karanatak, Maharashtra and other parts of northern India. Novertheless, the ownership of the village waste lands was vested in the village councils.

The settlement of the village disputes was one of the most important functions of the village councils. Though serious crimes, or crimes involving capital punishment or cases of accidental homicides not amounting to murder were excluded from the jurisdiction of the village council as far as civil cases were concerned. Disputes involving rights to properties worth several thousands could be settled by them. Evidence of the Smritis, inscriptions and Maratha records observe that the decisions of the village councils, duly arrived at, must be enforced by the state.

Many temples had their own separate management committees. When, however, such was not the case, the village councils or one of its sub-committees would supervise the temple administration with a view to see that worship was duly arranged, funds properly utilised and repairs to the temple elegantly carried out.

In some areas, the village councils used to transact business as bankers as well. They used to receive perpetual deposits and guarantee the utilisation of their interest properly. They used to capitalise the value of the government tax of a particular land and make it tax free on receiving its capitalised value arranging to pay the tax out of the interest annually accruing.

In case of calamities like famines, they used to raise public loan by mortgaging the common lands at least in the Chola period.

The village councils used to organise several works of public utiltiy. Efforts were made to bring forests and wastelands under cultivation in order to increase the wealth of the village. Construction, maintenance and repairs of irrigation tanks and canals engaged the serious attention of the village councils. Repairs of the village roads, widening them by purchasing the adjoining lands; digging up and repairing wells for drinking water; occasionally building rest houses were some of the other functions of village councils. They were also found taking steps to promote cultural and intellectual progress.

So far as the resources of the village councils are concerned, there is enough evidence that the Central Government used to permit the village council to spend a small percentage of the revenues collected in the village for financing its own activities.[29] Fines imposed by the village court upon the offenders were another source of revenue.[30] Village councils had also the right to impose additional taxes and cesses. Religion also considerably helped the village councils by enumerating digging of wells and tanks and founding of poor houses and hospitals among the most approved methods of gaining religious merits. The Central Governement would also occasionally help the village councils by direct grant by giving the requisite material free or at concessional rates.[31]

Relationship Between the Central Government & the Village Council :

Some Smritis occasionally state that the Village Councils derive their power from the king or the Central Government.[32] This statement, however, indicates the greater power of the Central Government. Whereas, the village communities and councils were, on the other hand, of hoary antiquity and derived their powers from very old custom and not from any charter or delegation from the Central Government. When the Central Government became more organised and developed, it often sought to control and curtail powers of the Village Councils. In Uttaramerur usually the village Primary Assemblies themselves determined the constitution of their committees. In northern India as well, the Village Council *(Panchayat)* consisted of only about five members, who were raised to that body by the general approval of the whole community. There was hardly any scope for the Central Government to dictate any constitution.

The Central Government used to have a general power of supervision and control over the village government. This control was exercised by the occasional summoning of the village headman to the district headquarters to explain and clarify matters, as also by the periodical despatch of inspection officers to villages to supervise their account and general administration. If there was a dispute between two Village Assemblies, the case must have been normally referred to the Central Government.

In essence, the Central Government exercised only a general supervision and control over the Village Assemblies and their Councils. It left the initiative to the Village Councils which enjoyed large powers. They made effective arrangements for the defence of the community, collected the taxes of the Central Government and levied their own, settled village disputes, organised works of public utility and recreation, functioned as trustees and bankers, raised public loans to mitigate the miseries of famines, organised schools, colleges and poor houses and arranged for their funds and supervised the manifold religious and cultural activities of the temples. Indeed, they exercised greater power than those that were enjoyed by the bodies in most countries, eastern and western, ancient or modern. They played an important and creditable part in defending the interests of the village and in promoting their material, moral and intellectual progress.

Ancient Indian political thinkers, thus, tried to protect the interest of the people by recommending and bringing about a great decentralization of the functions of the government. Large powers were vested in the district, town and village administrations, which could be effectively supervised and controlled by local non-official councils.

A word of caution, however, must be given. The village councils worked successfully in the past because the people had high regard for truth and character and were instinctively inclined to respect age, experience and ability. Members of the Village Councils were not elected; they were raised to that position by consensue of public opinion. Democracy of the modern type involving voting and party alignments did not exist. It presupposes widespread education, which must be immediately brought about. Fear of God and hell, which has now disappeared, must be replaced by the sense of civic duty, which alone can now induce our elected representatives to place the good of the people they represent above everything else.

Village *Panchayats* (councils) of ancient India exercised wide judicial powers. They decided practically all cases except those of serious crimes. Life in ancient times was simple; judicial disputes were usually confined to local parties and transactions and the law to be administered was known to and understood by all. Modern law is complex and presupposes technical knowledge and assistance; parties to a dispute may often belong to distant places. Village *Panchayats* in modern times, therefore, cannot successfully excercise that wide civil jurisdiction which they did in the past. Continued illiteracy, selfishness, party-factions etc. pose another problems in the context.

Ancient India sought to solve the problem of the finance of the local bodies by localising a part of the land revenue. Most of the villages could get back about 15 to 20% of the proceeds of the land tax from the government of the day. If the state governments, set apart a part of their income from various sources to meet the needs of the Village *Panchayats,* the financial hurdle in their successful working may be removed.

Financial Administration

Contrary to Western presumption that ancient India was predominantly metaphysical; ancient Indian authors like Kautilya and Sukra depicted a balance and harmonious integration amongst the four pursuits of life, i.e. *Dharma* (righteous performance of one's duties), *Arha* (economic activities in pursuance of wealth and power), *Kama* (physical desires) and *Moksha* (final liberation). They were convinced that wealth is significant for the realization of *Dharma* and accepted the notion of maximisation of wealth and territory. They further realized that sound finances are absolutely necessary for a stable and prosperous state. They have included prosperous treasury and ample reserve funds among the essential constituents of the state and have declared that any deterioration in this connection would be one of the most serious national calamity.

Vedic literature supplies meager information about the revenues of the state in their contemporary times. In the earliest period, the king's power was not well established and the taxation seems to have been occasional and voluntary. Later Vedic literature suggested the regular payment of taxes by the people to the king which enabled him and his officers to live in dignity and pomp. During this period, *Brahmanas* were engaged in priesthood, the *kshatriyas* were mostly occupied in territorial annexations and the *Sudras*k held no property. The incidence of taxation, therefore, fell heavily on the *Vaisyas*, who were engaged in the production profession of agriculture, trade and cattle-rearing, Despite of this classification, king is often described as taxing all all his subjects. The state, however, derived its revenues from agriculturists and cattle breeders and also received tributes from conquered chieftains.

Very little is known about the system of taxation during the post-vedic and pre-Mauryan period. The *Arthasastra,* the *Dharmasutras* and *Smritis* provide considerable data, which was altogether supported to a great extent by Greek writers and contemporary stone inscriptions and copper plates, which, however, considered taxation as king's wages and also deliberated upon the divine theory of taxation, in which king was depicted as the servant of the people, getting his wages (sustenance) in taxes for the purpose of continuous protection and growth.[34]

It would be pertinent to discuss the general principles of taxation propounded by the Smritis, epics and *Arthasastra* :

(i) The taxation was to be reasonable and equitable. It was argued that, "Just as fruits are gathered from a garden as often they become ripe, so revenue shall be collected as often as it becomes ripe. Collection of revenue or of fruits, when unripe, shall never be carried on, rest their sources may be injured, causing immense trouble."[35]

"If the calf is permitted to suck it grows strong, O Bharata, and can bear (heavy weight) and pain". The king, therefore, should milch taxes keeping the above principle in view. Overmilching is to weaken the calf and consequently harms the milcher himself.[36]

"The ruler should act like a bee which collects honey without causing pain to the plant."[37]

The king, therefore, was advised to collect his taxes, but with out causing any sufferings to his subjects. The tax, thus, was to be certain, and not arbitrary and the time of payment, manner of payment, and the quality to be paid was fixed.

(ii) The critierion of equitable taxation was that the state on the one side and the agriculturist or the trader on the other should both feel that they have got a fair and reasonable return for their labour.[38]

(iii) In the case of trade and industry, the taxation was to be on net profits and not on gross earnings. It was recommended that "taxes should not be levied without determining the outturn and the amount of labour necessary for its production." It was to be borne in mind that without proper incentive no body would engage in industry. "What profit (result of production) would keep the producer to the production and produce benefit to the king as well" should be the ruling consideration in deciding upon the amount of taxes to be levied on industries."

(iv) In the productions of art-materials used, cost incurred, maintenance of the artist required for producing the article, and the condition of the artist have to be taken into account.[40]

(v) An article was to be taxed once and not twice.[41]

(vi) If increase in taxation becomes inevitable, it should be gradual and not sudden and steep. They should never be realised by a painful mode - "milch the cow but do not bore the udders.[42]

In taxing imports :

(vii) "Sales (price realised), purchases (capital employed) distance travelled, cost of importing, and the total cost, also the risks incurred by the merchant should be fully considered."[43]

(viii) "Imports harmful to the State" and "luxurious (fruitless) are to be discouraged by taxation.[44]

(ix) Beneficial imports should be made free of import duties.[45]

(x) Those articles which are rare in the country, and those which would be needed for future production should be allowed free.[46]

(xi) Certain commodities should not be exported, while their imports are to be encouraged by not being taxed at all. They included weapons and armours, metals, military vehicles, rare things, grains and cattle.[47]

(xii) Principle of countervailing duty was resorted to in certain cases. Foreign favourites and private manufactures in wine and liquors were taxed onthe principle of 'compensation' with reference to the state manufactures.[48]

Economic considerations, therefore, were very prominent. Productive power was not to be hampered; profit and not capital was to be taxed; articles which lead to new industries were to be encouraged; exports which cause 'artificial' prosperity by driving up prices were to be discouraged; no special protection was granted to ordinary industries; taxes were to be gradual, and with reference to capacity and not in an obnoxious form.

Extra taxation was to be imposed only in times of national calamity after taking comprehensive steps to explain the situation to the people with a view to ensure a willing response. This was to be adopted only as the exceptional remedy and last altenative. It was only, to meet the emergencies, that the people could expect to pay extra and higher taxes. Authors of *Mahabharata* and *Arthasastra* alongwith others enlist a number of methods by which the king could obtain extra funds and were not, however, disturbed about the king's having recourse to trickery and assassination. They recommended that the king should explain the necessity to the people; but if this does not bring in the required revenue, he may sell honours or position; or "if the danger is very great take away wealth of corporations or heretics and temples." He may even extort funds from all sinful people. Otherwise proper legitimate collection was to be in accordance with the proportionate tax paying capacity of citizens, which is also the criterion of modern welfare government.

Ancient scholars, thus, propounded sound, applicable and universally recognised principles. Equally sound principles were enunciated about partial or total remission in the normal taxation :

(i) Both the *Arthasastra* and *Sukraniti* recommend that if enterprising persons bring fresh land under cultivation or seek to make it more fertile and productive by irrigating it with water from tanks built by themselves, the state should charge only a nominal tax in the beginning and gradually raise it to the normal rate during a period of four or five years.[50]

(ii) Military villages were exempted from taxation in consideration of the regular supply of recruits, which they ensured for the army.

(iii) Exemption from taxation on the ground of incapacity in case of dumb, deaf and blind persons; students studying in *grurkulas*; hermits practising penance in forests; women (in early times had a negligible amount of property) or poor widows and destitute women (when right of inheritance for women was recognised by society).

(iv) Learned Brahmanas *(srotriyas)* were recommended exemption[51] by *Smritis*, as they vowed to poverty and imparted higher Vedic and Sanskrit education free to all students. In many cases, however, revenues of whole villages were assigned to learned Brahamanas for their maintenance. But, for those holding lucrative appointments or following money-making professions like trade, agriculture and cattle-rearing they were charged normal taxes and cesses at full rates. In general, all Brahmanas had to pay taxes excepting those who were learned and poor and had received no state patronage.

(v) Temples with only a small income were charged with quit rent.

Sources of Revenue Collection :

Various legitimate source of revenue collection acknowledged by ancient authors included (i) various forms of land tax; (ii) duty levied on the sale of commodities in market; (iii) tax on imports and exports; (iv) road cess, canal cess, ferry dues, conveyance cess, tax on roads; tax on markets and fee from passport; (v) taxes received from artisans, fishermen etc.; (vi) taxes levied on prostitutes, gambling houses and wine houses and slaughter houses; (vii) income from properties and monopolies belonging to the king; (viii) forced labour; (ix) fines from law courts; (x) accidental income; (xi) interest on loans advances to the people; and (xii) miscellaneous taxes.

The mainstay, however, of the government revenue was land tax. *Smritis* lay down no uniform rate of taxation. The percentage they recommend varies from eight to thirty three.[53] This variation must be due to the quality of land or the varying practices of the different states or to the different rates charged by one and the same government at different times to meet its varying needs. The normal procedure was to charge one sixth of the produce as the land tax, which the expansionist states, however, found it insufficient. It is diffcult to state whether this percentage refers to gross or net produce. An automatic relief was also obtained to a certain extent in case of adverse change in natural circumstances. The dues were usually collected in kind; that too in two instalments at the time of autumn and spring crops. In case of any failure in payment of land tax, either the land was sold, or interest was charged, but the state is not allowed to confiscate the lands of the defaulting owners.

Trade and industry had to bear their own burden like agriculture. Traders had first to pay **Octroi duties** that were levied on most of the articles imported in town or village at varying rates. The state justified these duties on the ground that it had to spend considerable amount for the up-keep and protection of roads on which the merchantise was carried.[54] The duties were usually collected at the gate of the town or village by custom house officers. They had to be paid sometimes in cash and sometime in kind according to the local usage. These custom duties varied according to the commodities as in modern times. *Manu Smriti* recommendes a 16 percent duty on fuel, meat, honey, ghee, scents, medicines, flowers, vegetables, earthen pots and leather goods. The *Arthasastra*, however, recommends a higher tariff of 4 to 5 percent on medicines, fuel, leather goods, earthen pots and cotton stuffs. Whereas wines and silken pieces were charged a higher duty varying from 6.5 to 10 percent.[56] The tariff, thus, differed from province to province and age to age according to the needs and policy of different government.

Ferry tax, fees for testing and stamping of weights and measures and **shop tax or sales tax** were also referred to by the *Arthasastra* or Megasthenese. Petty artisans like smiths and carpenters were required to work one or two days a month for the state. The central government usually transferred the right to receive the **labour tax** to the local bodies to carry out their schemes of works of public utility. **Weavers** had to pay **tax** of 1.5 panam (a silver coin equal to six anna) per loom. Wine manufactured in private distilleries had to pay an **excise duty** of 5 percent. Though all mines were regarded as state property, but leased out mines were imposed heavy excise duty. Accoding to *Sukranti,* it was to be 50 percent in case of gold and diamonds, 33.5 percent in case of silver and copper and 16 to 25 percent in case of other metals. [59] Excise duty was levied on salt.

Cattle breeding also had to bear its own share of taxation while Manu requires a cattle breeder to pay 2 percent of the herd, Sukra imposes a duty of 6 to 12 percent.[60]

Vishti or **forced unpaid labour** was common in ancient times, those who afford to pay a tax neither in cash nor in kind. They were expected to serve the state in return for the protection they got from it. They were required to work for the state free for one or two days in the month to carry out the public works programmes. The state was to feed them during this period.

Apart from the usual taxation, the state was empowered to levy **extra cesses to meet unforeseen calamities,** or to finance costly works of public utility, or to carry out its plans of ambitious expansion. The *Mahabharata* is reluctant to sanction extra taxation even on such occasions, but it admits that there is often no alternative to it. It, however, urges the state to send special messengers to the people to explain the gravity of the situation and to win their willing assent to the new taxation proposals.[61] *Arthasastra* describes these extra contributions as *pranayas* or benevolences and lays down that the farmers may be called upon to pay about 25 percent and merchants from 5 to 50 percents according to their circumstances.[62]

One can analyse the royal panegyrists, ancient literature and inscriptions to show the fairness, reasonability and practicability of the taxations. These records show how people often tried to declare and protect their rights against undue enchroachments. They might not have been successful in their efforts, when kings were tyrannical and self-willed; but there can be no doubt that they had strength enough to press their claims successfully when kings and their officers were of the normal type. The absence of a popular body like the Vedic Samiti at the centre during the first millennium of the Christian era no doubt tended to increase the number of oppressive demands from the centre; but the village assemblies and their executives were usually strong enough to resist enchroachments on their legitimate rights and interest.

The items of state revenue, other than taxation included the income from state properties, the profits of the state industries and other undertakings, proceeds of fines and the tributes from feudatories.

State property consisted of crown lands, waste lands, forests, mines, treasure-troves, natural tanks and reservoirs and it yielded considerable income.

The ownership in arable lands was vested in private owners in historic times, but their lands would often lapse to the state on account of the absence of heirs of the nonpayment of state taxes or the commission of heinous crimes involving forfeiture of property. To supervise over the administrative arrangements of the state lands was the work of a special officer called *Sitadhayaksha* in the *Arthasastra.*

Waste lands, being under nobody's occupation, were naturally regarded as state property. Though private enterprising in such lands was alwasy encouraged, the administration, in general, of waste land was often left to the local bodies.

The ancient Indian state often claimed ownership in mines and their products. They were an important source of income, if they happened to be of precious metals.

The state claimed ownership in treasure troves also, either because it claimed to be the heir to heirless property or because it regarded them as similar in nature to the mineral yields, both being recovered from the bowels of the earth.

Forests were an important item of state property. A portion of them was reserved for breeding elephants, another portion was reserved for king's game. The remaining area was utilised for fuel and tinber.

The state in ancient India used to organise several industrial concerns. It used to have a weaving department to produce cloth; distilleries for manufacturing wines; slaughter houses; and herds of sheeps, buffaloes, goats, cows and elephants. Small fee was charged by the state from private individuals. Goldsmiths were engaged or licensed to manufacture silver and golden wares and ornaments for the public. Boats were hired for transporting the merchandise. The state would also license and control gambling and prostitution. All these activities brought considerable income to the state treasury.

Tributes, altogether, formed a considerable source of income in the budget of imperial states. Fines were also one of the items of state's income. Petty fines imposed for small offiences tried by village courts were usually assigned to the headman or the village community. In case of crimes tried inthe state courts, the fines may have gone to the central treasury.

Items of Expenditure

Mahabharata, early Smritis, inscriptions and copperplates provide little information about the items of expenditure in the state budget. The *Arthasastra* in nutshell, and *Sukraniti* in detail provide us information about the state expenditure.

The *Arthasastra* give us different items of stae expenditure. It refers to the royal establishment and throws very little light on the money spent on the different state departments. It does not also tell us what percentage of the state income was spent on each item of expenditure included in the royal household. Though Kautilya refers to the salaries of ministers and some other officers of his ideal state, we do not know its income, and so can form no idea about the reasonableness of the emoluments received by different officers. It is, further, almost certain that state in ancient India usually paid their officers either by the grants of land or by the assignnment of land taxes. Cash payment was rather an exception.

Sukra gives us some definite idea of the percentage of the state income devoted to the different items. According to his analysis, the state income was to be spent as follows.[63]

1.	Fighting forces *(balam)*	50%
2.	Charity and donations *(danam)*	$8^1/_3$%
3.	People *(Prakritayah)*	$8^1/_3$%
4.	Civil Administration *(adhikarinah)*	$8^1/_3$%
5.	Privy Purse *(atmabhoga)*	$8^1/_3$%
6.	Reserve Funds *(Kosha)*	$16^2/_3$%

Elsewhere, Sukra[64] give us the budget of a feudatory having an income of 1,00,000 a year as follows :

Privy Purse	18,000 or 18%
Prakritis	3,600 or 3.6%
Lekhaska	1,200 or 1.2%
Queens & Princes	3,600 or 3.6%
Scholars	2,400 or 2.4.%
Army	48,000 or 48%
Elephants, horses and guns	4,800 or 4.8%
Reserve fund	18,000 or 18%

A comparison of the two budgets show that the smaller a kingdom, the greater was the percentage of the state revenues spent on the king and his court and retenue. The percentage of the revenue spent on the works of public utility was small. It is possible to argue that the item *Prakriti* in the first budget may refer to the people in general, and might have thus covered the expenditure onthe works of public welfare like the building of roads, digging of wells and tanks, maintenance of rest houses etc. But the word has also the meaning of ministers and officers and 16% revenue spent on *Prakritis* would then be the expenditure on the civil administration. At several places in his book, *Sukra* has used *prakritis* in the sense of ministers and officers and praja in the sense of people or subjects. Only the item charity *(danam)* of the budget which included grants for *sattras* (poor houses), hospitals, monasteries and temples also catered for the works of public utility. The last two mentioned institutions used to run schools and hospitals in many cases.[65] The Brahmana donees of *agrahara* village also used to promote the cause of education and culture by imparting free education to deserving students.

The budget of the normal state provided an allotment of 8% for the social, cultural and nation building activities of the state. But the actual amount spent was somewhat larger, for the amounts spent by the local bodies out of the revenues assigned to them by the Central Governemnt were not included in the above budget.

The privy purse at 81/3 percent cannot be regarded as too high. 10% was the ideal that was placed before the rulers of the Indian states by the British Government and the Union Government after independence in 1947 had generally accepted it in its policy of inergers and unions.

The military expenditure at 50% of the central revenues is undoubtedly very high. From about 500 A.D. militarism was rampant and warfare common. If a state wanted to live and maintain its independence, it had to spend heavily on its fighting forces. It may, howerver,be noted that every pie of this huge expenditure was spent within the country and that the heavy military budget went a long way not only in fostering material spirit but also in indirectly encouraging trade and industry.

Reserve fund or treasury claimed 162/3% of the revenues. It has been observed by a number of Muslim authors how it was customary for Hindu rulers to have large treasures handed down by their predecessors, which they would touch only on very grave occasions. Public and state loans were unknown, and the state could tide over crisis only if it had a rich treasury and full over flowing granaries.

Treasuries in ancient Indian states were of two types, public and secret. The locality of the latter was known only to a select few and it could not be normally touched. The other type of the treasury may by coveniently called the public treasury, the contents of which were entered into usual state documents and could be utilised at any time of normal current expenditure.

Review of Financial Administration :

One can definitely submit that ancient India sought to solve the problem of the finance of the local bodies by localising a part of land revenue. Most of the villages could get back about 15 to 20% of the proceeds of the land tax from the government of the day. Ancient Indian thinkers, indeed, had evolved excellent principles for taxation. The grounds on which remissions were sanctioned and exemptions granted were, also, as a rule, sound.

The state was to gather the taxes like the bee, which sucks the honey without damaging the flower. The trade and industry were to be taxed not on gross earnings, but on net profits. An article was not to be taxed twice and the rise in taxation, when inevitable was to be gradual. The principles of exemption were also sound. The dumb, the deaf, the blind and the widows were exempted from taxation as they were usually poor. Students studying at the *Gurukulas* (educational institutions) were also given the same concession, as also teachers, if they were poor and imparting education free.[66]

The taxation was usually determined by the local customs and traditions. In the later times, however, when the *samiti* disappeared from the scene, government would often impose high and arbitrary taxes. We often find tug of war between the central governments, which wanted to levy new and oppressive taxes and the village *panchayats,* which would refuse to collect them. Very often, however, power prevailed and justice went to the wall; we find villagers migrating *en masse* to escape unbearbale taxation.[67] There can be no doubt that in later times, the interest of the average man in the sphere of taxation was not adequately protected when a greedy tyrant was on the throne. This, however, happened primarily because there was no *samiti* or popular assemble in later times.

The ancient Indian state was not merely a tax-gathering corporation, intersted only in preserving law and order. It is surprising to find that the state in ancient India should have interested itself in a number of ministrant activities of the nation-building type, which are being undertaken by the modern government only in relatively recent times. Private agencies, trade guilds and state department worked side by side to promote national welfare without mutual jealousies. Mines were worked both by the state and private enterprise; guilds banks and organisations often inspired greater confidence than the state treasuries. Private and guilds concerns received subsidies, if they promoted national welfare. The state regarded itself as a protector for the population as a whole and usually contended itself by harmonising the conflicting interests of differnet classes. It tried to keep the scale between the capital and labour, the employer and employee, the producer and the consumer and the merchant and the purchaser by laying down suitable and stringent regulations for curbing the greed of former and protecting the interest of the latter.

The ideals of the ancient Indian state, thus, were all comprehensive. It sought to promote the moral, material, aesthetic and spiritual progress of the whole community. Human ideas about the progress in these different spheres go on changing from age to age and it is no wonder that we may not be able to agree with all that the state in ancient India did or countenanced in order to achieve progress in this fourfold field.

Nevertheless, in their description of finance, financial administration, town planning and the organisation of a vast bureaucracy to control the entire social, economic, educational and religious activities of the people, ancient Indian scholars were very ahead of their Greek and Roman contemporaries to a great extent.[68]

NOTES & REFERENCES

1. *Mahabharata,* Poona : Bhandarkar Oriental Research Institute, 1929-33 XII .5.37-38; *Kautilya Arthasastra,* Tr. by Udaya Vir Shastri, Delhi : Mehar Chand Lakshman Das, 1970 (Hindi), I.3; *Manusmriti,* Tr. By Har Govind Shashtri, Varanasi : Chaukhamba Sanskrit Series Office, 1970 (Hindi), VII.53 ; *Sukra Niti,* Tr. By Brahma Shankar Mishra, Varanasi : Chaukhamba Sanskrit Series Office, 1968 (Hindi), Ch.II.
2. A.S. Altekar, *State and Government in Ancient India,* Delhi : Motilal Banarsidas, 1958, p.161.
3. Ibid., p. 164.

4. *Manusmriti,* Supra no. 1, VII.54; Mahabharata, Supra no. 1, XII.85 ; Sukra Niti, Supra no. 1, II.70 ; Arthasastra, Supra no. 1, I.15.
5. *Arthasastra, Supra no. 1,* VII.1 & I.6.
6. *Sukraiti, Supra no. 1,* II. 70-72 ; Vandana Nagar, Kingship in SÆukraNiti, Delhi : n.a., 1985, p.72-80.
7. A.S. Altekar, *Supra no. 2,* p. 187. Points out that Rome developed the Central Secretariat only in the days of Hadrian (2nd Century A.D.). In India it was developed at least by the 3rd Century B.C.
8. *Arthasastra, Supra no. 1,* II.10.
9. Ibid, *Sukraniti, Supra no. 1.,* II.172 also prescribes similar qualifications.
10. *Manusmriti, Supra no. 1,* VII.122-44; Arthasastra, Supra no. 1, II.9 ; SÆukra Niti, Supra no. 1, I.374-5.
11. *Ibid.,* I.11-12.
12. A.S. Altekar, *Supra no. 2,* p.192.
13. *Ramayana.* II.100.36. *Mahabharata, Supra no. 1,* IV.5.38.
14. *Arthasastra Supra no. 1,* I.8.
15. *Sukra Niti, Supra no. 1,* II.17.
16. A.S. Altekar, *Supra no. 2,* p.210.
17. *Ibid.,* p. 213-14.
18. *Manusmriti, Supra no. 1,* VII.115.
19. A.S. Altekar, *Supra no. 2,* p.216-17.
20. *Manusmriti, Supra no. 1,* VII.115.
21. *Mahabharata ; Supra no. 1,* XII.87.3.
22. *Arthasastra, Supra no. 1,* II.
23. *Manusmriti, Supra no. 1,* VII.121.
24. *SA. Eukra Niti, Supra no. 1,* II.343.
25. *Arthasastra, Supra no. 1,* II.1.
26. *Ibid.,* III.10.
27. K.A. Nilkantha Sastri, *Studies in Chola History and Administration,* Madras, 1932. P.131-145.
28. A.S.Alketar, *Supra no. 2,* p.234.
29. *Ibid.,* p.240.
30. *Arthasastra, Supra no. 1,* III.10.
31. *Ibid.,* II.1.
32. *Yajnavalkya Smriti,* Tr. By Umesh Chandra Pandey, Varanasi : Chaukhamba Sanskrit Series Office, (Hindi), II.30.

33. V.P. Varma, *Studies in Hindu Political Thought and its Metaphysical Foundations,* Delhi : Motilal Banarsidas, 1974, p.69-70.
34. K.P. Jayaswal, Hindu Polity ; A Constitutional History of India in Hindu Times, Bangalore : The Bangalore Printing and Publishing Co., 1967, p. 320-1.
35. *Arthasastra, Supra no. 1,* II.21.
36. *Mahabharata, Supra no. 1,* XII.87. 20-21.
37. *Ibid.,* XII. 88-7-8.
38. *Manusmriti, Supra no. 1,* VII.127 ; *Sukra Niti, Supra no. 1,* IV. 2.19.
39. *Manusmriti, Ibid.,* VII, 129 ; Mahabharata, Supra no. 1, XII. 87.16.
40. *Mahabharata, Ibid.,* XII, 87.14.
41. *Sukraniti, Supra no. 1,* IV. 2.111.
42. *Mahabharata, Supra no. 1,* XII. 88. 4, 7-8.
43. *Ibid.,* XII. 87.13 ; Manusmriti, Supra no. 1, VII.127.
44. *Arthasastra, Supra no. 1,* II.21.
45. *Ibid.*
46. *Ibid.*
47. *Ibid.,* II.21 ; 39.
48. *Ibid,* II.25.
49. *Mahabharata, Supra no. 1* Ibid., XII.87.26-39 ; SÆukra Niti, Supra no. 1, IV.2.10.
50. *Arhtasastra, Supra no. 1,* VI.9 ; SÆukraniti, Supra no. 1, IV.2.122.
51. *Manusmriti, Supra no. 1,* VII. 133.
52. *Mahabharata, Supra no. 1,* XII. 76. 4-7.
53. A.S. Altekar, *Supra no. 2,* p.270.
54. *Sukraniti, Supra no. 1,* IV.2.25.
55. *Manusmriti, Supra no. 1,* VII.131-2.
56. *Arthasastra, Supra no. 1,* II.22.
57. *Ibid.,* II.19.
58. Manu (VII.138) prescribed the monthly liability of one day ; while Sukra recommended for double the number of days.
59. *Sukraniti, Supra no. 1,* IV.2.118-9.
60. *Manusmriti, Supra no. 1,* VII.130.
61. *Mahabharata, Supra no. 1,* XII. 87.26-39.
62. *Arthasastra, Supra no. 1,* V.2.
63. *Sukraniti, Supra no. 1,* I., 316-7.
64. *Ibid.,* IV.7.24.

65. A.S. Altekar, *Supra no. 2,* 289.

66. Somnath Dhar, Kautilya and the Arthasastra, New Delhi : Marwah Publications, 1981, p. 119-20.

67. Jataka records this en masse migration. Even under king SÆankaravarman of Kashmir ; also some village in Tanjore district and also under Kulottunga III reference to fiscal oppression can be found which, though as an exception, resulted the same. In A.S. Altekar, Supra no. 1, p.283, also referred to by *Arthasastra, Supra no. 1,* XIII.1; Mahabharata, *Supra no. 1,* XII.57 and Manusmriti, Supra no. 1, VII.130-32.

68. M.V. Krishna Rao, *Studies in Kautilya,* Delhi : Munshi Ram Manohar Lal, 1958.

Chapter 4

Thiruvalluvar's Thirukkural : A Treatise on Good Humans, Good Society and Good Governance

Noorjahan Bava

THIRUKKURAL is a treatise on Ethics and Politics – on good conduct and (good) wise governance. It is the poetic creation and masterpiece of the greatest Tamil poet *Thiruvalluvar* who belongs to the Sangam Age Tamil literature and history of Southern India, approximately the 4-5th centuries A.D. During this period there were three great kingdoms ruling over the southern peninsula, the *Cheras* on the west, *Cholas* on the east and *Pandiyans* in the south with Thanjavur and Madurai as the great flourishing capital cities of the Chola and Pandiyan kingdoms respectively and Tamil as the language of the people and the court (administration).[1]

Thirukkural belongs to the great classics of the world. It is regarded as the greatest Tamil contribution to the wisdom literature of the world. The Tamil word *Thiru* connotes that which is *great, beautiful, elegant, true, respected,* or *revered.* When used as a prefix to the name of a person it denotes great or respected, so and so. Thus the name of Thiruvulluvar literally means Respected or Revered Valluvar. When the term 'thiru' is used as a prefix to any work like *Thirukkural*, it connotes a great work - a beautiful, elegant (poetic) work, a masterpiece or a classic. Generally the term "thiru" is used as a mark of respect or greatness in Tamil culture. Tamil is the oldest non-Sanskrit Dravidian language of the world with rich literature dating back to the ancient period of world history. The great poet Thiruvalluvar appears to have belonged to a class of ministers, advisors, or seers, for, his name signifies a great counsellor (advisor), an 'elegant seer' or 'sacred diviner'. Another view is that he was born in a family of weavers and led a simple, virtuous married life as per his own great teachings. The title of his book Thirukkural literaly means a "great book of teaching" - "elegant or sacred couplets". Thirukkural is not a "religious" text. It is more appropriate to describe it as a *secular* treatise on good conduct, good human behaviour, good society and good governance written in the form of couplets – a great book of "lofty maxims". It is a great work on ethics, morals and good conduct for individuals - men and women, as well as rulers, ministers, warriors, and subjects and citizens. Thus it can be described as a treatise on ethics and politics.

Thirukkural occupies a niche for itself in the world's masterpiece variety of literature comparable to Confucius' *Analects*, Plato's *Dialogues*, Aristotle's *Ethics* and Seneacca's writings. It has been translated in many languages of the world - English, French, German etc. After reading the German translation of the Kural, Albert Schwitzer is credited with the statement: "There hardly exists in the literature of the world, a book of such lofty maxims".[2]

CONTENTS OF THIRUKKURAL[3]

Thirukkural consists of 1330 couplets divided into three books/ chapters or parts - *Virtue, Wealth and Love*. They deal with all aspects of human life - most relevant to the problems of to-day's world.[4]

Part - I of the Kural dealing with *Virtue* is divided into three sections - (1) the *Preface* on God, rain, saint and righteousness (*aram*) (2) Domestic Virtue and (3) Acetic Virtue. The section on *Domestic* virtue includes couplets on subjects like man, woman, children, affection, hospitality, affability, gratitude, impartiality, self control, discipline, purity, patience, envy, covetousness, slander, gossip, conscience, charity and fame. The section on *Ascetic* virtues includes subjects on compassion, vegetarianism, penance, hypocrisy, fraud, truthfulness anger, murder, violence, instability, renunication, realization, desire and fate.

Thus the first part of the Kural is primarily a book of teachings on good conduct and good humans.

Part - II entitled *Wealth* is classified into six sections dealing with (1) Royalty, (2) State Cabinet, (3) Law, (4) Politics, (5) Alliance and (6) Miscellaneous.

The section on *Royalty* consists of subjects such as leader, study, ignorance, listening, knowledge, faults, greatmen, meanness, consideration, forethought, time, tactics, selection, employment, kith, vigilance, just rule, oppression, penalties, benignity, detectives, zeal, sloth, perseverance and fortitude.

The next section dealing with *State Cabinet* deals with issues like ministers, eloquence, law, firmness, offensiveness, ambassador, service, divining, audience, and assembly.

The section on *Politics* includes five subjects - nation, fortification, wealth, army and valour.

The section on *Alliance* is devoted to topics on friendship, testing friendship, intimacy, bad company, false friendship, folly, stupidity, hatred, enemies, enmity, traitors, offending, warning, prostitutes, liquor, gambling and eating.

The last section deals with miscellaneous matters such as nobility, honour, greatness, perfection, courtesy, niggardliness, modesty, family, agriculture, poverty, labour, mendicancy and meanness.

Thus Part - II of the Kural dealing as above with matters and issues of politics, good governance and administration entitles the work to the claim of a treatise on politics or good governance.

The third and last part of the Kural deals with the them of *Love* which is dealt with in two sections. First section deals with secret marriage under which issues like disturbance, signs, intercourse, beauty, love, abandonment and rumour are dealt with. The second section is concerned with the main theme of chaste wedded life with sub-themes on separation, complaining, grief, solitude, memories, dreams, lament, waste, soliloquy, reservation, longings, thoughts, reunion, heart, pouting, feigning and charming.

Part - III of the Kural can thus be described as the book on good society. Part I lays down certain "Dos" and "Donts" for the individual members of society and subjects or citizens of a state.

Kural as a Treatise of Ethics, Politics & Administration

From the perspective of public policy, governance and administration, we have grouped the substance of the Kural under three broad heads - namely - *Good Human Beings* (Good conduct), *Good Society* and (3) *Good Governance*.

Good Human beings & Good Society

Faith in God

In Thiruvalluvar's scheme of things a good human being is one who has faith and belief in God, worships, meditates and prays to Him and reaps His blessings - heavenly life, protection from evil, eternal bliss, and freedom from anxiety. The first ten verses of the Kural starts with the theme God. The opening verse says: "As all alphabets have the letter A for their first, so has the world the eternal God for its beginning. The Kural preaches: "Of what avail is a man's learning if he does not pray to God". Or, "the head that does not bow before God ... is as worthless as organs which do not perform their proper functions."

Righteousness (Aram)[5]

Aram or righteousness should be the centre-stage of one's life and conduct since there is no greater good than virtue or greater evil than the neglect of it. What is best for every one is to lead a virtuous life and avoid vices. One must always do good deeds as far as practicable by thought, word and deed, free himself/herself from envy, greed, anger and bitter words, and do charitable acts which alone can give life its true pleasure and fame. The married state is truly called a life of virtue though the other state is also good provided it is above reproach. A true householder gives succour to the forsaken, poor and the deprived. A virtuous wife is a blessing and good children are its adornment. If a wife does not possess the virtues for house-hold life, that home will have no happiness. Sweet is the music of flute and lute and sweeter still is the little one's (their babies') prattle. It is the duty of the father to ensure that his children hold the foremost place among the learned. A mother's joy will be greater when she hears other praise of her son's virtue and refinement than at the time she gave birth to him. The son's duty towards the father lies in getting the appellation of "a worthy son" from others. The greatest blessing in life is to have sensible children.

Impartiality, Self-Control, Discipline, Fidelity and Patience[6]

The hallmarks of a good human being and a good citizen are: to be impartial in his relations with friends, foes and neighbours alike; not to deviate from the path of equity in adversity or prosperity; to show consideration to others; to practise self-control which will place a man among Gods; there is no boon greater than self-control for man; to guard oneself from the use of foul utterances, for, a burn caused by fire may heal but not a scar caused by a fiery tongue. The greatness of a man who exercises self-control and lives righteously is loftier than the mountains.

Right conduct makes one great. It is deemed greater than life. Right conduct brings nobleness and happiness to life while improper conduct causes unprecedented infamy, misery and ruin. It is good conduct that constitutes high birth, conversly, lapse of conduct will lower one's rank of birth. Fidelity is the mark of perfection in one's character.

Patience is a trait of a good human being just as the earth supports the men who dig at it, bear with those who scorn you, forgive and greater still forget the wrongs done to you. Those who forebear the harsh words uttered by others are greater than the hermit who performs penance by fasting.

Refraining from envy should be the rule of one's conduct. There can be no greater boon than freedom from envy. He who does not care for ethics, virtue or wealth is the one who envies another's prosperity. Envy destroys one's wealth and leads to evil deeds and ruin. Never did envy make one great nor freedom from envy cause loss of one's affluence. The prosperity of the envious and the adversity of the righteous are matters for deep thought.

Avoidance of Avarice, Slander, Gossip, Fraud, Hypocrisy, Anger and Evil[7]

Avoidance of avarice and covetousness is a trait of a righteous person. Those who seek lasting happiness will refrain from the shortlived pleasure derived from misappropriating other's belongings, wealth or property. A good person should always avoid slander, gossip, hypocrisy and fraud. Wealth begotten by fraudulent means may seem to increase for a time, but will eventually disappear altogether. Theft will ruin a person. Just as one's shadow follows one wherever one goes, destruction follows the path of the evil doer. Since evil begets only evil deeds, it should be feared more than fire. If a man cares for the well-being of his own self, he should do no harm whatever to others.

Practising Benevolence, Charity, Compassion, Penance, Truthfulness[8]

The good human being is one who knows that doing good to others is the best virtue of all; the wealth acquired by the worthy through their industry is intended for charity; the wealth in the hands of a liberal person is like an useful tree bearing fruits in the midst of a town square or a medicinal tree with access to all; giving to the poor is charity and enjoying alone the hoarded wealth without giving others is worse than begging; there is no greater boon to man than the renown, popularity and recognition gained by giving the poor.

Truthfulness[9]

Valluvar defines truth thus:

"Speech which causes no harm whatsoever to anyone is what is called truth" (291).

"If a man should utter a lie consciously, his own mind would torture him for the lie uttered (293).

"One who is true in thought and word is greater even than those who perform `thapas' (penance) and do charity (295).

"There is no reputation equal to that of truthfulness. It is capable of bringing all the other virtues and at the same time avert suffering thereafter" (296).

"If one could safeguard oneself against flinching from truth, one need practise no other virtue" (297).

"Outward purity may be secured by the use of water. Inward purity of the heart comes only from truthfulness" (298).

"All lamps are of no avail. The light of truth is the only lamp which the wise cherish (299).

"In all true scriptures we have known, nothing is praised so highly as truthfulness" (300).

Control of Anger[10]

The person who controls his anger towards the weak who is helpless is the one who controls it truly. Anger towards those stronger than oneself is harmful, but there is no harm greater than losing one's temper towards the weak. As anger causes greater harm one should restrain anger towards anybody. Anger is bound to ruin oneself and therefore one should safeguard himself/herself against it. The angry are like the dead and those who control anger are like the sages who have overcome death.

Life free from Crimes and Violence[11]

The good-hearted will refrain from doing harm to others, even one may gain rare attainments by doing harm to others.

The noble-hearted refrain from doing harm in retaliation of harm done to him. The harm done to a person who harbours enmity without provocation will bring irretrievable distress. The best way to punish those who harm you is to make them feel ashamed by doing them good and thinking no more of it. Refraining from the intention of doing harm to anyone anytime is the best policy. Harm will beget harm. The harm we do unto others will bring in quick succession, harm unto ourselves.

Avoidance of the killing instinct, intent and act is the trait of the good and virtuous. According to the teachings of sages and saints, sharing one's food, with others and sustaining other lives is the highest virtue. Avoidance of the act of killing is a matchless virtue against which truthfulness ranks as the second in merit. One should not take the life of another, even though one may come to lose one's own life. Those who destroy life are despised as the lowest of humanity by the great who realize the degradation of killing.

GOOD GOVERNANCE

Leader and his Qualities[12]

The art of governance calls for the qualities of leadership. A ruler is a leader and vice versa. Thiruvalluvar defines the leader thus:

"He is a *lion* among leaders who has these six: an army, subjects, wealth, ministers, allies and fortifications". (382)

"He is a *ruler* who possesses courage, liberality, wisdom and zeal". (383)

"A *noble* leader must be brave, virtuous, adventurous and free from vices and injustice". (384)

"An *able* leader makes and earns wealth; guards and apportions it for people's good." (385)

"The whole world will exalt the country whose leader is easily accessible and is free from use of harsh language". (386)

The leader who speaks sweetly and gives [his wealth] with graceful clemency commands the praise and obedience of the world. He is esteemed as Lord of men who protects his subjects by his upright justice. The world thrives under the shelter of the leader who bears the bold bitter remarks of counsellors. And "He is the light (leader) of leaders who has four things: benevolence, compassion, justice and care for his people". (390)

Learning, Knowledge, Wisdom[13]

The virtue of seeking wisdom, knowledge and information is highlighted by Valluvar as an essential virtue for the good ruler and the ruled - the leader and the masses. On the importance of learning he writes: "Study well those books which are worth studying and then follow the right path according to what you have studied." Letters and numbers are the two eyes of man. The learned alone have eyes on their face, to the ignorant their eyes are their sores. The learned delight in companionship and regret the separation. The student has to be as humble before his teacher as the poor before the rich. Just as the underground spring flows with water as one digs deeper, knowledge flows with deeper study. (396) The learned find their home and town everywhere. Then, why not learn till death? The joy of the learned is to see others enjoy their lore as they expound it. Learning is the lasting wealth, all other material wealth are lost in time.

Ignorance is the mark of the unlettered man. The unlettered should abstain from speaking before the assembly of the learned; and his vanity will suffer if he does. Although the innate knowledge of an unlearned person may be very good it will not be accepted by the wise. Men without learning are like the barren lands. The pomp of a person without deep and subtle knowledge is like the fine painting on a clay doll. The wealth of an unlearned man will give him more sorrow than poverty upon the learned. It is learning that makes one truly high or low in life and not the status of birth.

Hence listening and learning from the wise is the treasure of treasures - the best wealth. "Listen to whatever is good, however little, it will bring you much greatness, it will support him like a staff in moments of depression or on slippery ground. Those who listen, understand and reflect over wise words will not err or do wrong things. One who listens to the wise and the learned in one ear but passes it off through the other is indeed deaf.

Wisdom is a weapon that protects from one's fall. It is the inner fortress that baffles the enemy's entry. Wisdom is that power present in a human being which controls his mind from roaming, from evil thoughts and actions and directs it towards which is good. Wisdom lies in discerning the truth in everything that comes from whatever source. The wise have foresight and the ignorant lack in it; wisdom lies in living in conformity with the world. The wise are universal friends, equal-minded; they fear what ought to be feared; they use foresight to guard themselves against any dreaded evil. In short, those who possess wisdom, possess everything and those who have not wisdom, whatever else they possess, have nothing.

Choice of Ministers and Friends: The Power of Discrimination & Discernment[14]

The successful ruler is one who has the ability to distinguish between good and evil, nobility and meanness, the wheat and the chafe. Valluvar warns the ruler to be careful in choosing his friends and allies and lays down the guideline to weigh the worth and then choose for friendship "men of ripe wisdom who knows the law"; to make *friends* with those who remove the present ills and guard the ruler from future ones and who reprove him when he goes wrong; to choose as his *ministers* only those who are men of wisdom as they are his eyes. The leader who has worthy friends and acts in an able manner need nothing to fear from terrible enemies. There is no stability for a leader without strong supporters. The leader should know that to lose good ministers and friends is ten times worse than facing countless enemies (450).

The leader must have the capacity to discriminate between the great and noble men and the mean and the vulgar and choose good company.

Planning & Choosing the Action Plan[15]

Valluvar lays emphasis on proper planning before the ruler launches his action campaign. He must thoroughly deliberate over the costs and benefits of his action plan - over the output, possible loss and final gain. He must rely on advice of tried and tested friends in the choice of his action plan. He should avoid such types of actions as involve either doubtful gains or the pain of disgrace. The leader will invite only ruin and failure if he launches action without proper reflection and planning as regards necessary means - in terms of men, material and money. The ruler must know that failure is possible despite the adoption of a good plan if the dispositions of men have not been taken into account or to due inconsistent medley.

Among other guidelines for the leader, Valluvar lays stress on forethought, time, tactics, selection and employment of officers and men, the importance of kinsmen, vigilance, just rule, and qualities of benevolent ruler.

- the ruler must weigh the magnitude of his action, his strength and of his allies before resorting to action (attack)
- nothing is impossible to that leader who knows his ability, facts, and limits of his bravery
- He will court defeat and failure who jumps into action without assessing the extent of his strength
- wealth will dwindle due to extravagance, waste and failure to practise economy and thrift.
- the ruler must launch action against the enemy at the right time and with proper means and tact. Choosing the proper time is of utmost importance for success.
- when a rare opportunity offers itself, execute the most difficult plan.
- In adversity feign peace and wait like a heron and strike like its peck when the time is opportune.
- Valluvar advises the rulers to follow certain important *tactics* to win a war.
- Do not strike before supervising the right field for action.
- A strong fortress is of great advantage even to leaders of mighty power and prowess.

- Even the weak can withstand a mighty enemy and conquer in a suitable field strong in defence.
- In deep waters the crocodile overpowers all, out of water others overpower it. Once the right field of action is chosen, only a daring attack is needed to win a victory.

Recruitment and Employment of Officers and Men[16]

The recruitment of officers and men should be based on four tests - virtue, wealth, pleasure and fear of death. Only that person who hails from a good family, is free from faults and dreads dishonour should be selected. The choice of the successful candidate should be made after weighing the merits and demerits of candidates and the one with greater merit should be chosen. A warning at the time of selection is that men without kinsmen and good tradition should not be chosen since they will have no affinity nor shame of sin. If the leader chooses a fool as an advisor, he will have to pay a heavy price. The ruler and his dynasty stand to suffer endless troubles if he trusts a stranger without test. Likewise, to suspect a man after he has satisfied the test will cause endless misery.

Valluvar has laid down a number of qualifications for the state employees. Only that person should be employed who can make the right choice after weighing both good and evil. Only such persons as are capable of increasing the resources and wealth of the kingdom, and preventing evil should be employed. The affairs and duties of the kingdom should be entrusted only to men who possess four virtues – loyalty, love, intelligence, clear vision and ungreediness. Though the staff has to be duly tested and chosen, the nature of their work can change many persons. Wise men of capacity and character should be vested with power and responsibility by the ruler. The leader should exercise vigil over his officers every day. For, if the workers are straightforward the kingdom will prosper.

Rule of Law and Justice

In order that government is carried on with justice, the ruler must consult the wisemen, consider the matters of his kingdom well, and examine them impartially before taking crucial decisions. The subjects look up to their ruler for their welfare and well-being as the world looks up to the sky (rain) for its life. The scepter of the ruler is the symbol of justice, righteousness, prosperity and welfare of the people. The wrong doer and the culprit will be punished including capital punishment to the wicked killers and the life and property of people will thus be protected by the ruler.

He who holds the scepter, the symbol of justice and good governance cannot govern in a tyrannical manner. The ruler who throws away the principles of justice stands to lose both his wealth and his subjects. While justice and peoples' welfare-oriented (good) administration and governance will crown the king with glory, his unjust rule will ruin the kingdom since the rains will fail, cows will yield less, and the sages will stop their blessings. The tyrant will perish swiftly and surely.

Rule of justice is rule of law and law must prevail throughout the kingdom. He is a leader who conducts just enquiries and punishes the law-breaker appropriately to prevent recurrence of the crime.

It is necessary for good governance to employ spies to gather information in a secret manner about the happenings and events in the lives of subjects, administrators, royal household and allies and enemies of the state. It is the duty of the sovereign to keep himself informed about the goings on in his kingdom. The members of the espionage (intelligence) corps must watch keenly the officers, kinsmen enemies and others to gather information. They must go in disguise even as asceties to gather secrets; be fearless and capable of keeping the secret under all circumstances. The reports of one spy should be tested and verified by that of another. The spies must be sent one by one and if three of them agree, the information should be confirmed. The spies should not be rewarded in public lest that would reveal the secret organisation.

The Diplomatic Corps

Ambassadors and diplomats who are essential to carry on relations with allies (other kingdoms) must possess qualities such as devotion, noble birth, courteousness that pleases the ruler, love for the leader, political genius and learned eloquence to present facts. He must be a well versed scholar of Political Science to negotiate successfully with military powers. Mature wisdom, imposing personality and good learning mark the diplomat who acts as the bold ambassador. The ideal envoy brings good to his state by conscise statements, avoiding harshness and by winsome humour. He is an envoy who is well-versed, speaks with persuasion and without fear, knows what is fit for the occasion, knows his duty, his place and proper time to present his facts boldly. The faithful ambassador will negotiate for helpful alliance and assure the well-being, safety and joy of his leader.

Minister

Thiruvalluvar has laid down many qualifications for ministers. The right minister is one who judges the proper means, time and plan of action for attack. The ideal minister is learned, manly, firm, resolute, and zealous in guarding people's welfare. The able minister cherishes friends, disunites the foes and reunites those who had parted. The minister must be capable of comprehending a plan, and selecting the best method. The virtuous, wise, the learned and the brave should become ministers and advisors to the ruler. The minister should have the courage to tell the truth to the king even if it is distasteful to him. The minister who indulges in treason against the Prime Minister or the king is worse than millions of open enemies

Nation

A country inhabited by people with robust health, wealth, rich yields from fields, happiness and defence forces constitute a nation. It is a peaceful land where there are no sectarian divisions among people, no destructive internal enemies and no traitors. That is a real nation which is free from starvation, incurable diseases and free from enemies that are dangerous - a land which yields rich food and needs no foreign aid and a land with rains, springs, rivers, hills and forts.

SOME TRIBUTES TO THE KURAL

Paying tribute to the Kural, Mahatma Gandhi observed, "It is a textbook of indisputable authority. The maxims of Valluvar has touched my soul".

Rev. G.V.Pope commented that "Kural has entered into the very soul of a whole people. It proclaims in sweetest mystic concepts virtue, truth, wealth and joy. Valluvar is a seer of spotless souls."

"The Kural is the masterpiece of Tamil literature - one of the highest and purest expressions of human thought." (M.Ariel)

"The Kural sentences are as binding as the Ten Commandants on the Jews. Kural is as important and as influential as Dante's work on the language and thought of Italy. (Charles E.Grover)

"Men like Thiruvalluvar and Siva Vakyar used their tongues and pens in favour of "Deism and against the ceremonial Polytheism of the Brahmans." (Charles E. Grover)

"Thirukkural alone is enough to edify the world. It contains all things and there is nothing which it does not contain." (Tiru Naganar)

"There is no treatise equal to Kural in any Indian language". (J.Murdoch)

NOTES & REFERENCES

1. See *Books on the History of The Period and Date of The Kural.*
2. Albert Schwitzer, *Indian Thought and Development*, 1951.
3. The threefold classifications of the Kural into books of (i) Virtue, (ii) Wealth and (iii) Love is based on *The Commentary of Kural* by Parimel Alager, one of earliest commentators of the Kural. Parimel Alagar, a native of Kanchi near Madras (now Chennai) lived and taught about 600 years ago. All students of the Kural are greatly indebted to him for his clear and accurate exposition of the couplets. His criticism of the various readings current in his time are both "incisive and dignified".

   According to one view, there were 10 commentaries on the Kural during the medieval period. Out of these only four works have been brought to light - those by Parimel Alagar, Manakkudavar, Kalingar, and Periperumal. Since works of the last three commentators have been discovered only in the early decades of this century, Parimel Alagar's commentary is considered to be the oldest and the most authentic and authoritative one on the Kural.

   The Commentary of Manakkudavar was published in 1925 through the research of K.Ponnuswami Nadar of Madras. Differences in the rendering of the same text have come to light between the works of Manakkudavar and Parimel Alagar.

Commentaries of the Kural by Kalingar and Periperumal were published by Vidvan T.P.Palaniappa Pillai only in 1948. These two commentaries were discovered by the Sri Venakteswara Oriental Institute, Tirupathi (Andhra Pradesh). These Commentaries do not adopt the same numbering of the chapters, their meanings as those of Parimel Alagar.

4. This organization and treatment of the content of Thirukkural is based on the ordering of the theme of the Kural as dealt with in the book *The Sayings of Thiruvalluvar*, Singapore, EVS Enterprises, 4th edition, 1986.
5. *Ibid*, op.cit. pp.4-10.
6. *Ibid*, op.cit. pp.12-17.
7. *Ibid*, op.cit. pp.18-29.
8. *Ibid*, op.cit. pp.22-30.
9. *Ibid*, op.cit. p.410.
10. *Ibid*, op.cit. p.31.
11. *Ibid*, op.cit. pp.32-33.
12. *Ibid*, op.cit. p.39.
13. *Ibid*, op.cit. pp.42-43.
14. *Ibid*, op.cit. p.45.
15. *Ibid*, op.cit. pp.48-63.
16. *Ibid*, op.cit. p.51.

Note: We reproduce *ad verbatim* from the book, *Sayings of Thiruvalluvar*, EVS Enterprises, 4th edition, 1986 the following bibliographical details:

- Book on the History of the Period and Date of the 'Kural'
- Some Tamil Editions of the Kural
- Some Tamil Books on the Tirukkural
- Translation of the Kural and English Books on it.

Books on the History of the Period and Date of the 'Kural'

1. J. Kennedy, 'The Commerce of India with Babylon'. *Journal of the Royal Asiatic Society*. 1898. pp.241 ff.
2. V. Kanakasabhapathi Pillay,*The Tamils Eighteen Hundred Years Ago*. Madras, 1904. An account of the life and culture of the Tamil lands, called from the literature of that age.
3. Seshagir Sastri,*Tamil Literature*. Madras, 1904. Account of the history of Tamil literature to the twelfth century.
4. Tamilian Archaeological Society, *Tamilian Antiquity*. Trichinopoly, 1911-14. Article on the early history of the Tamils, by various authors.
5. Dr. S. Krishnaswamy, *Ancient India*. London, 1911. Essays on the early history of Southern India.

6. M. Sriniavasa Iayangar,*Tamil Studies*. Madras, 1914. Essays on the history of the Tamil people, and their language, religion and literature.

7. G.S. Duraiswamy Pillay,*Tamil Illakkiyam*. Calcutta, 1915. A history (in Tamil) of the literature of the Sangham period.

8. Vincent A. Smith,*Oxford History of India*. Oxford 1924.

9. T.R. Sesha Iyengar,*Dravidian India*. Madras, 1925. An account of the Tamils of the early ages drawn from literature and epigraphy.

10. T.G. Aravamundan,*The Kaveri, the Mankharis, and the Sangham Age*. Madras, 1925.

11. *Cambridge History of India*, Vol. I Cambridge, 1928.

12. E.H. Warmington,*The Commerce between the Roman Empire and India*. Cambridge, 1928.

13. M.S. Purnalingam Pillay, *Printer of Tamil Literature*. Revised, Tirunelveli, 1928.

14. K.A. Nilakanta Sastri,*The Pandyan Kingdom*. London, 1929. History from the earliest times till the sixteenth century.

15. P.T. Srinivas Iyengar,*History of the Tamils*. Madras, 1929, From the earliest times to A.D. 600.

N.B. - The list of Tamil editions and books on the *Kural* is not claimed to be complete, but simply contains those which the writer has come across.

Some Tamil Editions of the "Kural"

1. Arumugam Navalar, Kural : With Parimelalgar's Commentary. Nine Editions to 1919.

2. Dr.Lazarus, Kural : With Parimelalgar's Commentary and English Renderings. Madras 1885 and 1903.

3. V. Sundara Muthaliar, Kural : Text with short paraphrase of each couplet. Madras, 1893.

4. Vadivelu Chettiar, Kural : With Parimelalgar's Commentary. With English rendering and Tamil notes on each couplet. 2 Vols. Third Edition. Madras 1919.

5. Manakkudavar, Kural : Commentary Edited by K.Ponnuswami Nattar, Madras. 1925.

6. Tirukkural, Saiva Siddhanta Publishing Co, Kural : Pocket Edition. Text only. Madras 1924.

7. Jagavirapandyan, Tirukkural Kumaresa Venba, Kural : To each couplet is attached an illustration in the Venba metre. Tuticorin. 1931.

8. K.S.V. Kutchmiammant, Kural : Tirukkural Tipalangaram, A Prose Commentary on the whole book. Marungapuri. 1928.

9. M.R. Arunachala Kavirayar, Kural : Tiurkkural Mulamum Teliporul Vachanamum, Madurai Tamil Sangam. Complete edition with prose versions of each couplet. Tirupparankundram. 1930.

10. Gurusaranalayam, Kural : Tirukkural Vachanam, A prose version of the whole book in simple and elegant Tamil. Madras. 1922.

11. A. Mathavaiyar, Kural : Kural Nanuru, Selected stanzas with Tamil meanings and English translations. Madras. 1925.

12. C. Kanaya Chettiar, Kural : Tirukkural, Madras. 1884.

13. K. Viraraghavan, Kural : Tirrukkural Mulamum and Pozhipppuraiyum, Kanchipuram. 1929. 2nd Ed. 1935.

14. A. Ranganatha Mudaliar, Kural : Tirukkural, With English translation. Triplicane.

15. N.C. Thandapan Pillai, Kural : Tirukkural Aratthupal, South India Saiva Siddhanta. Madras.

16. Selections From The Kural, 100 stanzas only. With Tamil Urai. C.L.S. Madras.

17. S. Subramaniya Aiyar, Kural : Tirukkural Vilakkam, Mylapore, Madras.

18. V.R. Sithambaram Pillai, Kural : Tirukkural Viruttiruai, Arappal only. Tuticorin. 1925.

19. T. Sambantha Muthaliyar, Kural : Tirukkuralasaram, Triplicane.

20. K. Subramania Pillai, Kural : Tirukkural Telipporul Vilakkam, Saiva Siddhanta Publishing Co. Madras. 1928.

21. Swami Suddhananda Bharati, Kural : Tirukkural Inbam, Singapore. 1937.

22. Dr. Subramaniya Sastri, Kural : Thirukkural Kurippu Pt, Triuvaduthurai. 1937.

23. S. Ramanujachariar, Kural : Tirukkural Aratthuppal, Madras. 1938.

24. Dr. P.S. Subramanya Asrai, Kural : Thirukkural Aratthuppal, With Urai. Trichirappalli.

25. Vidwan T.P. Palaniyappa Pillai, Kural : Tirukkural Porutpal, With Commentaries of Kalingar and Paripperumal. Tirupathi. 1948.

26. Vidwan Sundara Sammuganar, Kural : Tirukkural Telivurai, Selection of 50 stanzas.

27. M.E. Virabahu Pillai, Kural : Tirukkural, Yeliya Urai, Simple Tamil translation of the whole work. Thayagarayanagar, Madras, 1954.

28. Dr. M. Varatharasanar, Kural : Tirukkural, Simple Tamil renderings of the whole book. Saiva Siddhanta Publishing Co. Tirunelveli. 1949.

29. G. Devaneya Pavanar, Kural : Thirukkural Thamil Maraburai, Modern Interpretaion by a great Tamil Scholar. 1969.

30. Pulavar Kulanthai, Kural : Thirukkural, Commentary & Modern Interpretation. 1967. Pari Publishers, Tamil Nadu.

Some Tamil Books on the Thirukkural

1. T.Chelvakeswaraya Mudaliar, Kural : Essay on Tiruvalluvar, Madras. 1904.

2. J.M.Nallaswami Phillai, Kural : Tirukkural Vittinpal, Madras. 1923.

3. M.S. Subramaniya Aiyar, Kural : Tirukkural Vilakkam, Madras.

4. M.S. Govindarasanar, Kural : Tirukkural Vilakkam, Tirukk Mylapore. 1923.

5. N. Kapalamurthi Pillai, Kural : Tiruvaluva Nayanar, 1926.

6. R.P. Sethu Pillai, Kural : Tiruvalluvar Nulnayam, South India Saiva Siddhanta Co. Tirunelveli. 1927.

7. T.P. Minakshi-sundaram, Kural : Valluvarum Magalirum, Describes Valluvar's idea of womanhood. Madras. 1930.

Translation of the Kural and English Books on it

1 FR. Constantius Josephus Beschius, Kural : Latin Translation of Books I and II in India Office Library. First published by Dr.G.U.Pope as an Appendix to his edition. About 1730.

2. Rev. G.U. Pope, Kural : The Sacred Kural of Tiruvalluva Nayanar, With introduction, grammar, translation, notes, in which are reprinted Fr.C.J.Beschi's and F.W.Ellis' versions. Lexicon and Concordance. By Rev. G.U.Pope. pp.VI,XXVIII, 328, 80. London 1886.

3. Edited by F.W. Ellis, Kural : Arappal, On the Virtue in Kural. Three series of verses on ethical and erotic themes. Edited by F.W.Ellis. With translation and commentary in English. pp.304. Madras 1816.

4. Rev. W.H. Drew, Kural : The Kural of Tiruvalluvar, With the Commentary of Parimelagar, an amplification by Ramanuja Kavi Rayar and English translation. Parts I and II. Madras 1840 and 1952.

5. T.M. Scott, Kural : Kural Mulamum pozhipuraiyum, Madura. pp.375. Madras 1889.

6. N.E. Kindersely, Kural : Extracts From Tiruvalluvar's Kural, In Specimens of Hindu Literature. pp.51-82. With explanatory notes and introduction. London 1794.

7. French translation of Kural : In the Bibiotheque Nataionale, Paris. Referred to by M.Ariel. 1767.

8. E.J. Robinson, Kural : Tamil Wisdom, Translsations of 24 chapters of the Kural. London. 1873.

9. E.J. Robinson, Kural : Tamil and Poems of South India, An enlarged edition of Tamil Wisdom, London. 1885.

10. E.J. Robinson, Kural : The Divine Paraih,Traditions about Tiruvalluvar.

11. P.G. de Dumant, Kural : French Translation, Portions only. Nacny. 1854.

12. Dr. Graul, Kural : German and Latin Translations of Kural. Portion only Probably used Beschi. Leipzig. 1856.

13. M. Lamairesse, Kural : French Version of Kural, Complete. Pondicherry. 1867.

14. C.E. Grover, Kural : Folk Songs of Southern India, Translations of a few chapters. Madras. 1871.

15. Rev. P. Percival, Kural : Extracts From the Kural.

16. Dr. Ja. Lazarus, Kural : The Kural, Tamil edition with English translation. Madras. 1885.

17. G. de Barrigue de Fontanieu, Kural : Lelire Del' Amour De Tiruvaluvar, French translation of Part III. Paris. 1889.

18. J.M. Nallaswamy Pillai, Kural : A Chapter From the Kural, Translation and Notes on Ch.36 in Tamil Antiquary, Vol.II. No.1. pp. 73-82. Trichinopoly. 1913.

19. Dr. J. Lazarus, Kural : The Kural, A short article in Tamil Antiquary, Vol. II. No.1 pp.52-72. Trichirapalli. 1913.

20. Mr. T. Tirunavukkarasu, Kural : Tirukkural, A gem for each day Selected stanzas, with English renderings for each day of the year. Madras. 1915.

21. V.V.S. Aiyar, Kural : The Maxims of Tiruvalluvar, Introduction and complete translation. Madras. 1916.

22. Rev. J.S.M. Hooper, Kural : Thirukkural, Article in Christian College Magazine. April 1915.

23. K.Vadivelu Chettiar, Kural : Chettiar Thirukkural Mulamum Uraiyum Tamil edition with English translation. Madras. 1919.

24. A. Mathavaiyar, Kural : Kural Nanuru, Four hundred selected stanzas with English renderings. Madras. 1925.

25. V.R. Ramchandra Dikshitar, Kural : Thirukkural of Tiruvalluvar, The whole book in Roman translation with English renderings. Adyar. 1949.

26. Somasundara Bharati, Kural : Thiruvalluvar, A pamphlet on the legends about the poet. Madurai. 1928.

27. Prof. M.S. Puranilingam Pillai, Kural : Critical Studies in the Kural, Biblioteca. Munnirpallam. 1929.

28. C. Rajagopalchariar, Kural : The Second Book of Kura, A selection of Stanzas from Kural, Part II. With English translations and Notes in English. Madras. 1937.

29. Teachers' Publishing House, Kural : Tirukkural Madras. Complete edition with English renderings. Convenient pocket edition. Madras 1949.

30. I.D. Thangaswami, Kural : Tirukkural, Adapatation in English verse or 27 selected chapters. Madras. 1954.

31. J.G. Whittier, Kural : Giving and Taking, Said to be a free rendering of Chapter 9 and 11 of Kural. London. 1889.

32. A. Ranganatha Mudaliar, Kural : Thikurral, Tamil edition with English renderings.

33. Prof. A.Chakravarti, Kural : Thirukkural, With English translation and Commentary and Introduction. A most comprehensive and useful book. pp.LXIX 645. Madras. 1953.

N.B. - The list of English editions and books on the Kural is not claimed to be complete, but simply contains those which the writer has come accross.

Chapter 5

Win-Win Policy

Stuart S.Nagel

Win-win policy refers to public policy that is capable of achieving both conservative and liberal goals simultaneously. Examples could be given from any field of public policy, such as economic, social, environmental, legal, or political policy. Win-win policies should be distinguished from compromises, where both sides retreat partially from achieving their goals in order to obtain an agreement.

As an example, the field of environmental policy involves both conservative and liberal approaches. Conservatives emphasize the role of consumers and the marketplace in restraining business from engaging in socially undesirable activities, like pollution. The liberals emphasize the role of the government in restraining pollution. Conservatives are especially interested in the goal of economic development, which may be interfered with by government restraints. Liberals are especially interested in the goal of a cleaner environment, which may not be achieved so effectively by relying on selective consumer buying.

A neutral compromise approach might involve giving business firms partial subsidies to adopt antipollution devices. Doing so would involve some requirements for receiving the subsidies, but less interference than regulation and fines. Doing so would help promote a cleaner environment, but there still might be evasions by business in view of the extra expense and trouble in complying.

A win-win policy alternative instead might emphasize subsidies to universities and research firms to develop new processes (that relate to manufacturing, transportation, energy, and agriculture) that are both less expensive and cleaner than the old processes. Those new processes then would be adopted by business firms because they are more profitable, not because the firms are being forced or subsidized to do so.

The new processes thus would achieve the conservative goals of profits and economic development, even better than retaining the present marketplace. Such a win-win policy also would promote the liberal goal of a cleaner environment, even better than a system of regulation, and without the expense of a continuing subsidy for adopting and renewing antipollution devices.

A specific example of such an environment win-win policy has been finding a substitute for aerosol propellants and air-conditioning freon that is more profitable to manufacturers and simultaneously less harmful to the ozone layer, which protects against skin cancer. Another specific example is developing an electric car, which saves money on gasoline and maintenance, while at the same time not generating the exhaust pollution of internal-combustion cars. Developing hydrogen fusion or solar energy also may be examples of a less expensive and cleaner fuel for manufacturing processes.

Win-win policies may be capable of achieving both conservative and liberal goals in theory, but not in practice. To be meaningful policies, they may have to satisfy various kinds of feasibility. For example, is the policy of developing solar energy for manufacturing feasible technologically? Is there sufficient funding available to subsidize the needed research if the private sector is not so willing, due to the risks, the large amount of money needed, or the long wait before payoffs occur?

Is there insurmountable political opposition from liberals who do not like government subsidies to make business more profitable? What about the opposition from conservatives who do not like government involvement in developing a research agenda? Is the program feasible administratively in terms of built-in incentives, or does it require a lot of obtrusive monitoring? Does the program violate some constitutional rights? Does the program make provision for workers and firms that might be displaced if the policy is adopted?

Win-win policies may involve creativity, but developing them is becoming easier as a result of experience with the ideas. We now have many different approaches that can serve as a checklist in leading one to a win-win policy. For example, expanding the resources available can enable conservatives to have more money for defense, and liberals to have more money for domestic programs. The government sometimes can be a third-party benefactor in providing vouchers to enable both landlords and tenants, and also merchants and consumers, to come out ahead.

One also can deal with problems like abortion by getting at the causes. These causes consist of unwanted pregnancies that could be lessened through more effective abstinence programs and birth control. Thinking in terms of the goals to be achieved, rather than the alternatives to choose among, can simulate win-win policies. So can thinking in terms of increasing benefits and decreasing costs.

Other approaches deal with early socialization of widely accepted values, technological fixes like the nonpolluting hair spray, and the contracting out of government activities to private firms (which do well as a result of both the profit motive and quality specifications in the contract). Further approaches may involve combining (rather than compromising) alternatives, developing a package with something for each major viewpoint, having international economic communities, adopting a gradual or incremental win-win policy, and arranging for big benefits on one side with small costs on the other.

Win-win policy may be specially relevant as of 1994-1995 because the Democrats control the presidency and thc Republicans control Congress. That division means that neither purely liberal not purely conservative legislation is likely to pass in view of the Republican congressional majority, the availability of the filibuster to the Democrats in Congress, and the availability of the veto to the president. It is possible that some compromise legislation might pass, such as health care without an employer mandate or required forms of health insurance. Even better would be win-win policies such as promoting real economic growth through greater productivity related to increasing labor skills, new technologies, competition, and tariff reductions.

NOTES & REFERENCES

For further details of win-win policy, see Lawrence Susskind and Jefrey Cruikshank, *Breaking the Impasse: Consensual Approaches to Resolving Public Disputes* (Basic Books, 1987) and such Nagel books as *Policy-Analysis Methods and Super-Optimum Solutions* (Nova Science, 1994), *The Policy Process and Super-Optimum Solutions* (Nova Science, 1994), and *Developing Nations and Super-Optimum Policy Analysis* (Nelson-Hall, 1993).

Stuart S.Nagel is professor of political science at the University of Illinois, Urbana. He is secretary-treasurer and publications coordinator of the Policy Studies Organization.

Chapter 6

Universal Values and Win-Win Policy

Stuart S.Nagel

This is a follow-up to the previous note in the spring 1995 issue of the *Policy Studies Journal* entitled "Win-Win Policy". Its purpose is to provide further examples regarding the question, "What policy issues are worth providing examples for?"[1]

The General Set of Values

In anthropology and sociology courses, human beings are frequently referred to as involved in six sets of institutions designed to organize more systematically the ways in which humans interact with each other. The lists vary across textbooks, but they generally talk about: (1) Economic institutions, that relate to the production and consumption of goods. (2) Social institutions, that relate to the interaction of family members, families, ethnic groups, genders, clubs, and other groupings, as well as to the training of young. (3) Technology and science institutions, that relate mainly to new inventions and products for being more productive or for understanding nature. (4) Political institutions, that relate to how decisions are to be made, interpreted, and implemented on behalf of society. (5) Inter-social relations, regarding how the society or collectivity of people are supposed to relate to other collections of people. (6) Legal institutions that relate to getting people to comply with rules on how they are supposed to interact with each other in the economic, social, technological, political, and inter-social realms. (7) Other institutions, such as art institutions designed to promote music, visual arts, and literature. If we are going to emphasize controversy, then art institutions become controversial by way of political institutions that try to repress or impose certain art forms.

Each of those sets of institutions corresponds to an important policy controversy. The six corresponding controversies might vary across policy studies people, but the list might generally include: (1) Prosperity, especially reducing inflation, unemployment, and poverty. (2) Merit treatment, especially in terms of abilities as they relate to different job opportunities independent of one's race, gender, age, or other groupings. (3) Technological improvement, especially in terms of encouraging useful technological innovation and dispersion while providing for displaced workers and firms. (4) Democracy, including majority rule with universal adult voter eligibility, and minority rights to try to convert the majority. (5) International interaction that involves nonviolent relations, buying and selling of goods, and free exchange of ideas. (6) Law compliance, including compliance with laws against violence, theft, consumer fraud, workplace abuses, and environmental pollution. (7) Other important public policy issues can be incorporated into the above categories; energy and health policy, for example, are largely matters of improving and spreading technology to provide less expensive energy sources and more effective forms of medical treatment.

These points are addressed in Table 1. The first column of the table lists the six general policy controversies corresponding to the six basic human institutions. Both conservative and liberals probably would agree that those policy issues are indeed quite important. They are, however, likely to disagree on the intermediate *goals* to seek in order to achieve their functioning on the basic institutions and issues. Both sides are especially likely to disagree as to what policy alternatives are best for achieving either the intermediate or higher goals.

Prosperity as a Specific Value

Column 2 summarizes the general conservative goals and alternatives on each issue. Column 3 summarizes the general liberal goals and alternatives on each issue. For example, on the issue of prosperity, conservatives tend to be oriented especially toward the goal of reducing inflation, with reducing unemployment as an important but secondary goal. Liberals tend to be oriented especially toward the goal of reducing unemployment, with reducing inflation as an important but secondary goal. Conservatives advocate increasing interest rates as a major means of reducing inflation. Liberals advocate decreasing interest rates as a major means of reducing unemployment. There thus is a conflict, or tradeoff, that tends to result in compromises on the setting of interest rates.

Column 4 refers to super-optimum solutions (SOS). These are win-win solutions, since all major sides gain, including conservatives and liberals in general. Such solutions are a special form of win-win solutions in the sense that the gain exceeds the best initial expectations of each side, and thus excludes a nonsubstantial gain. In the context of reducing inflation and reducing unemployment simultaneously, economic growth through increased productivity can be such a solution.Productive economic growth can come about through training, new technologies, competition, exports, and government capital where private enterprise is reluctant to get involved.

That five-part program can promote an increase in productivity, which in turn results in an increase in the gross domestic product. If there is a productivity growth in the GDP, then that means more goods are available. Inflation means too many dollars chasing too few goods. Thus, by having more goods available competitively, prices tend to go down. Increased production thus can reduce inflation better than can increasing interest rates, because increasing interest rates has the effect of reducing the GDP and increasing unemployment. Likewise, if there is a productivity growth in the GDP, then that means the population has more money available to spend. Increased national income means increased national expenditure. If the population does have more to spend, then the increased spending helps to create new jobs, thereby more than offsetting the previous unemployment or the unemployment that is caused by worker displacement as a result of productivity downsizing.

Other Specific Values

Turning to the second row and the issue of *merit treatment*, conservative talk about the importance of productivity and how color-blind and gender-blind hiring is relevant to having a productive economy. Liberals talk about equity, fairness in the allocation of jobs. To them, that may mean at least temporary preferences to address past overt discrimination, especially where those hired are qualified, where the tests are subjective, and where the gap is small between the score of the minority applicant who is given a preference over the competing applicant from the dominant group.

The win-win, or SOS, proposal that may be capable of achieving both high productivity and high fairness for minorities is a program of outreach training. That means seeking individuals who have potential capability, if given the proper intensive training, and who have not received adequate training previously due to lack of expenditures per student in the school systems that they attend. Such people would be hired or admitted to a certain university only if they score above the hiring threshold. There would thus be no preference in hiring, and there would be an ability test and a needs test for getting into the training program. The Reagan administration advocated outreach hiring, rather than outreach training, as a compromise between color-blind policy and preferences. Outreach hiring does not work so well, mainly because it assumes there are trained and qualified minorities available to be hired, which may not be so.

On *technological innovation*, conservatives are oriented toward increasing profits. Liberals want to increase competition. They both want to increase innovation. Conservatives want to preserve the patent system. Liberals want to replace the patent system with research grants. The SOS involves grants, required licensing, reasonable royalties, and the government as an issuer.

A key issue with regard to *democracy* is voter turnout. Conservatives are especially worried about double voting. Liberals are especially worried about eligibles not voting. Conservatives want to leave the system as it is, which has four elements that come up in the SOS. Liberals want to tinker, such as with postcard registration or motor voter laws. Some neutral approaches involve precinct registration or no purges of the voter rolls. The SOS is same-day registration, multiple precincts, multiple days, and the invisible ink security method.

World peace is in the context of United Nations peace-keeping. The conservative goal is to save U.S. dollars and lives. The liberal goal is to promote world peace, prosperity, and democracy. The conservative approach is minimum United States involvement. The liberal approach is substantial United States involvement. The SOS approach is to endorse a volunteer UN force.

The last is *law compliance*. Here we mainly are talking about what to do about drugs. The conservative goal is to reduce drug dealing. The liberal goal is to reduce the side effects of drug enforcement. That includes other crimes, corruption, great expenditure of dollars, health damage, poverty, and international competitiveness. The conservative approach is military action and police. The liberal approach is legalization. A neutral approach is traditional treatment and education or to separate marijuana from cocaine. The SOS is to deprofitize drug sales. That involves various parts, which are: (a) The treating addicts as sick people, (b) health-maintenance-organization (HMO) coverage for addicts, (c) no incentive to hook children, and (d) severe enforcement of illegal drugs outside of the HMO system.

Although the concept of superoptimizing is quite new, it is being increasingly popularized. This can be seen in the international dispute resolution of Jimmy Carter, or in some of the 1992 campaigning of Bill Clinton and Al Gore. What is needed is for scholars of public policy and public administration to develop further the theory, principles, and examples. Practitioners like Carter, Clinton, Gore, and others then can apply the ideas toward bringing about such universal values as prosperity, merit treatment, technological improvement, democracy, world peace, law compliance, and others.

Table-1: Universal Values and Win-Win Public Policy

ISSUES	CONSERVATIVE	LIBERAL	SUPER-OPTIMUM SOLUTIONS
1. Prosperity (esp. inflation& unemployment	– *Inflation* + interest rates	– *Unemployment* – Interest rates	Economic growth through 1. Training 4. Exports 2. Technology 5. Capital 3. Competition
2 .Merit Treatment (esp. race and gender)	+ *Productivity* 1. Color-blind hiring 2. Gender-blind	+ *Equity allocation* 1. Preferences 2. At least temporary	Outreach hiring 1. Enterprise zones 3. Equal opportunity employer 2. Advertising 4. Valid tests Out reach training 1. Needs test 2. Toward merit hiring & training

(Table : 1 Contd..)

ISSUES	CONSERVATIVE	LIBERAL	SUPER-OPTIMUM SOLUTIONS
3. Technology Innovation (esp. patents)	+ *Profits* 1. Preserve patent system 2. Abolish strict liability	+ *Competition* 1. Abolish patents 2. Research grants	1. Focused grants 2. Required licensing 3. Reasonable royalties 4. Government insurer
4. Democracy (esp. voter turnout)	– *Double voting* Leave as is	– *Eligible not voting* Tinker e.g. motor-voter postcard	1. Sample day registration 2. Multiple places 3. Multiple days 4. Invisible ink monitoring
5. World Peace (esp. role of UN)	*Save US $ & Lives* Minimum U.S. involvement	+ *World peace, prosperity, & democracy* Substantial U.S. involvement	1. Volunteer UN force 2. – Trade barriers 3. Trade + democracy

(Table : 1 Contd.)

ISSUES	CONSERVATIVE	LIBERAL	SUPER-OPTIMUM SOLUTIONS
6. Law Compliance (esp, drugs)	– *Drug dealing*	- *Side effects of drug enforcing* 1. other crimes 2. corruption 3. money 4. health damage 5. poverty 6. int. comp.	De-profitize drug sales 1. Confirmed addicts as sick people 2. HMO coverage 3. No incentive to hook children 4. Accept non-cures
	Military & police	Legalization	

NOTES

1. In the column on "issues," the concepts are goals that correspond to economic, social, technology, political, international and legal institutions - = Decrease + = increase
2. The items in italics are conservative or liberal goals. The items beneath the goals in roman type are conservative or liberal alternatives.
3. The alternatives or policies in the SOS column are capable of exceeding the goal-achievement of conservative alternatives on conservative goals and the goal-achievement of liberal alternatives on liberal goals.

NOTES & REFERENCES

1. For a discussion of win-win policy analysis in general, see Nagel (1995), "Win-Win Policy", *Policy Studies Journal, 23,* 1981-182.

2. For further details on each of the six values of goals, see the following: (1) (prosperity) Lee Bawden and Felicity Skidmore (Eds.), *Rethinking Employment Policy* (Urbana Institute Press, 1989). (2) (merit treatment) Norman Dorsen, Paul Bender, Burt Neuborne, and Sylvia Law (Eds.), *Political and Civil Rights in the United States: Volume II* (Little, Brown, 1979). (3) (technological innovation) Michael Goldhaber, *Reinventing Technology: Policies for Democratic Values* (Routledge & Kegan Paul, 1986). (4) (democracy) Charles Dunn, *American Democracy Debated* (Scott, Foresman, 1982). (5) (world peace) David Felder, *How to Work for Peace* (Florida A&M University Press, 1991). (6) (law companies) James Levine, Michael Musheno, and Dennis Palumbo, *Criminal Justice: A Public Policy Approach* (Harcourt Brace, 1980).

Chapter 7

Win-Win Public Administration

Stuart S.Nagel

Public administration is the study of methods for improving and understanding how governmental programs are implemented, especially in terms of personnel, financing, and accountability. This article systematically analyzes some recent developments in Chinese public administration. It uses a win-win or super-optimizing perspective which emphasizes methods whereby all major sides and viewpoints in a dispute or dilemma can come out ahead of their best initial expectations.

I IDEOLOGY VERSUS TECHNOLOGY

Table 1 analyzes the problems of ideology versus technology in Chinese public administration. From the establishment of the People's Republic of China to about 1980, the emphasis was on ideology in evaluating alternative ways to implement governmental programs. That meant referring to Mao, Marx, and Lenin or interpreters of them. The result in personnel management was to emphasize hiring on the basis of ideological loyalty and Communist party enthusiasm rather than technical skills. From about 1980, an increased emphasis was placed on knowledge of economics in administering a business program, engineering and physics in administering an energy program, or other substantive fields for other programs.

In terms of Table 1, the basic alternatives are ideology, technocracy, or a compromise between the two. Equity was the stated key goal of those supporting the ideology alternative; it was, however, often only a lip-service goal since personal status was the real goal. Efficiency and effectiveness was the stated key goal of those supporting the technocracy alternative. It too was often only a lip-service goal; personal status was actually the goal of those with technocratic skills.[1]

TABLE - 1: IDEOLOGY VERSUS TECHNOCRACY IN CHINESE PUBLIC ADMINISTRATION

CRITERIA ALTERNATIVES	C EFFICIENCY & EFFECTIVENESS	L EQUITY
C Technocratic	+	-
L Democratic & Equlitarian Ideology	-	+
N Compromise	0	0
SOS or Win-Win Both Simultaneously	++	++

NOTES :

C = conservative, L = liberal, N = neutral,
SOS = super-optimum or win-win solution

1. Public administration especially refers to personnel management and public finance.

2. In the context of personnel management, ideology in the 1970's emphasized Communist Party loyalty. In the 1980's, technocracy meant modern automation in tax administration.

3. In the context of public finance, ideology in the 1970's emphasized heavy taxes on the rich and on profit-making activities. In the 1980's, technocracy meant modern automation in tax administration.
4. The SOS alternative for personnel management might emphasize loyalty to worthwhile communist ideals like equity and merit in the distribution of government jobs, rather than irrelevant party loyalty or mathematical skills.
5. The SOS alternative for public finance might emphasize taxation to stimulate entrepreneurial development for the benefit of the economy, rather than confiscatory taxes or mindless automation.

In the late 1980's, more emphasis began to be placed on public administration as practised in the United States, Western Europe, and countries with American-trained professors and practitioners in public administration. That emphasis recognizes the importance of equity in governmental programs, including postal systems, elementary schools, urban transportation, and other governmental services that takes a loss in providing services to the poor and many other people in order to provide better access and equity. That emphasis also recognizes the importance of efficiency and effectiveness as manifested in the use of decision analysis, operations research, management science, and other such generalist techniques to supplement the substantive expertise that goes with business administration, engineering, physics, and other relevant substantive specialities.

Striving for both equity and efficiency simultaneously is associated with the super-optimizing idea of enabling both ideologists and technocrats to come out ahead of their best initial expectations. With regard to personnel, an enlightened public administration approach talks in terms of equality of opportunity to apply for and meet the entrance requirements in government positions. At the same time, high-quality standards, designed to promote efficiency and effectiveness, are set. The broadened perspective on public finance may emphasize income taxes to provide equity but sales and other consumption taxes as an efficiency way of collecting large sums of money.

II. PERSONNEL ADMINISTRATION

This more general analysis is applied in Tables 2 and 3 to personnel administration and in Tables 4 and 5 to financial management. (See Notes at the end of this article for clarification of letters, numbers, and symbols used in the tables.) Table 2 looks at a classic personnel recruitment problem. Applicant A does well on the first goal but not so well on the second goal although above a minimum threshold. Applicant B does well on the second goal but not so well on the first. The traditional recruitment approach might be to hire applicant C, who is compromise in the sense of falling in the middle on both goals. The super-optimizing solution (SOS) alternative might be to hire applicant A in order to obtain the benefits of his or her high quality on goal 1 but provide on-the-job training to raise applicant A on goal 2 to a level close to that of applicant B. Applicant B would be hired with on-the-job training if the nature of the skills were such that it is easier to train on goal 1 than on goal 2.

TABLE - 2 : SUPER-OPTIMUM SOLUTION APPLIED TO PERSONNEL RECRUITMENT

CRITERIA / ALTERNATIVES	G1 GOAL DECENT WAGES	G2 GOAL PREVENT OVERPAYMENT
G1 Alternative Applicant A	+	-
G2 Alternative Applicant B	-	+
N Alternative Applicant C	0	0
SOS or Win-Win Hire "A'ith OJT	++	++

NOTES:

1. Applicant A does the best on Goal 1, but Applicant B does the best on Goal 2. There is thus a tradeoff that needs to be resolved.

2. The usual way of resolving such a tradeoff would be to decide which goal is more important. One would then hire the applicant who does better on that more important goal.
3. The SOS alternative might be to hire the applicant who does better on the characteristic that is harder to train for. That might be the less important goal. That applicant would then be given on-the-job training to improve the other goal. The result might be that the applicant hired becomes the better person on both goals.
4. Another SOS alternative might be to hire the applicant on the more important goal but provide training on the other goal. The result might be that the one hired improves enough on the other goal so that his or her total score exceeds the applicant not hired, regardless of which goal is considered more important.
5. That is the essence of an SOS solution, namely to be the winning alternative regardless of whether one uses the goals and weights of any major groups, perspective, or ideology.

TABLE- 3: ELITISM VERSUS DEMOCRATIC SHARING IN REWARDING PERFORMANCE

CRITERIA ALTERNATIVES	C ELITISM	L DEMOCRATIC SHARING
C Reward High Performance	+	-
L Winners of Lower Goals	-	+
N Reward Moderate Performance	0	0
SOS or Win-Win Ask For Higher Performance But with Subsidized Facilitators	++	++

NOTES:

C = conservative, L = liberal, N = neutral,
SOS = super-optimum or win-win solution

1. The issue here is how to reward performing well in public administration.

2. The conservative approach is to mainly reward those who do especially well, thereby creating a small elite at the top. The liberal approach is to broaden the definition of doing well so there are more winners of rewards that are available.

3. If the conservative approach gives big rewards to the top 10% and the liberal approach gives small rewards to the top 50%, then the neutral approach might give moderate rewards to the top 30%.

4. The SOS approach might determine that the top 10% operates at a level of 8 on a 1-10 scale. The SOS approach might say that everyone who gets a score higher than 8 will be rewarded, but the SOS approach provides many facilitators to enable a high percentage of score better than an 8, may be even higher than 50%.

5. Facilitators especially relate to subsidies to upgrade the skills of public administrators so they can perform better than an 8 on a 1-10 scale. Facilitators might also include introducing new technologies that enable public administrators to be even more productive, especially if they are trained with the new skills needed to use the new technologies.

TABLE-4: A SUPER-OPTIMUM SOLUTION APPROACH TO TAX SOURCES

CRITERIA ALTERNATIVES	C STIMULATING INVESTMENT	L ABILITY TO PAY
C Sales Tax	+	-
L Income Tax -	+	
N Other or Both	0	0
SOS or Win-WIn Decrease Tax Rates But Increase Total Taxes with Well-Placed Subsidies	++	++

NOTES:

C = conservative, L = liberal, N = neutral,
SOS = super-optimum or win-win solution

1. Conservativestend to emphasize taxes on consumption such as the sales tax or the value added tax. Liberals tend to emphasize taxes on income especially progressive income taxes where the rates are higher on higher incomes.

2. The neutral position is to have both sales taxes and income taxes, but with the sales taxes rates lower than conservatives advocate, and the income tax rates lower than liberals advocate.

3. Both conservative and liberals recognize the need for some tax money to support the government activities they like. The super-optimum solution there is not to abolish all taxes. That would be undesirable to both conservatives and liberals if it means

abolishing the government activities they endorse. Likewise, the neutral position may result in a decrease in the government activities endorsed by conservatives and those endorsed by liberals.

4. The SOS alternative involves substantially decreasing both kinds of tax rates while at the same time increasing the total tax revenue by increasing the GNP tax base. That can be partly done by well-placed tax breaks and subsidies to encourage greater national productivity.

III. FINANCIAL ADMINISTRATION

Table 4 provides an SOS approach to tax source. The conservative alternative emphasizes sales taxes, which disappropriately bear on the poor. The liberal alternative emphasizes income taxes, which disproportionately bear on the rich. A compromise is to enact both taxes but with neither kind of tax bringing in as much revenue as might be needed. The super-optimizing perspective seeks to increase both kinds of taxes in order to have sufficient funding necessary for governmental programs. The key element in a super-optimizing approach (as reflected in the policies of both Ronald Reagan and Bill Clinton) is to try to have a system of well-placed subsidies and incentives so that total taxes will increase even if the tax rate is lowered.

Table 5 involves the important financial management problem of dealing with annual deficits and a large and possibly increasing national debt. The conservative alternative to dealing with a deficit tends to decrease domestic spending and increase consumption taxes. The liberal alternative tends to decrease defense spending and increase income taxes. The neutral alternative is electric. It seeks to increase spending, but spending designed to upgrade skills and introduce new technologies that will pay off in terms of a larger gross national product. It may use selective tax reductions with strings attached in order to reward productivity-increasing activities. This kind of perspective is especially associated with the public finance aspects of Japan and West Germany's industrial policy. It is also associated with newly industrializing countries of the Far East including: South Korea, Taiwan, Hong Kong, Thailand, and South China.

TABLE-5: DEALING WITH THE DEFICIT

CRITERIA / ALTERNATIVES	C DEFENSE AND INVESTMENT	L DOMESTIC AND CONSUMPTION
C - Domestic Spending + Taxes Poor	+	-
L - Defense Spending & + Taxes Rich	-	+
N - Both Spend + Taxes Both	0	0
SOS or Win-Win + Spending - Taxes	++	++

NOTES:

C = conservative, L = liberal, N = neutral,
SOS = super-optimum or win-win solution

1. A fuller statement of the conservative goal might be (1) have a strong national defense, and (2) stimulate through low taxes on the relatively rich. A fuller statement of the liberal goal might be (1) have strong domestic policies like education and housing, and (2) stimulate consumption through low taxes on the relatively poor.
2. The SOS involves a reduction of taxes in the form of tax breaks designed to stimulate greater productivity. Likewise, the SOS involves an increase in spending in the form of well-placed subsidies designed to stimulate greater productivity. The increased productivity means an increased gross national product which means an increased base on which to apply the national tax rate. Thus the tax rate can drop and still bring in increased tax revenue and thereby have more money available for government spending including defense, domestic policies, deficit reduction, and more well-placed subsidies.

This is a time of cataclysmic change in the People's Republic of China. Never before has the recognition of the values of public administration been keener. The country is now engaged in an effort to interact more widely with other countries. For this reason, it is incumbent upon the leadership to improve the competence and capability of the public service. Chinese scholars and observers of Asian public administration have described the underlying dilemma of an autocratic system of government coupled with the realization of the necessity for rapid change. Public administration is both a practice and a scholarly discipline. The primary emphasis of China is on improving the capacity of the public service. Scholars at the same time express a commitment to developing the field. Likewise with many other developing nations.[2]

NOTES & REFERENCES

1. The following points refer to Tables 1-5. They clarify the letters, numbers, and scoring of the tables :

   (i) Symbols in these tables include : C = Conservative, L = Liberal, N = Neutral, S = Super-Optimum, #1 = Group 1, and #2 = Group 2.

   (ii) The 1-5 scores showing relations between alternatives and goals have the following meanings : 5 = the alternative is highly conducive to the goal, 4 = mildly conducive, 3 = neither conducive nor adverse, 2 = mildly adverse, 1 = highly adverse.

   (iii) The 1-3 scores showing the relative weights or multipliers for each goal have the logical group, 2 = relatively middling importance, and 1 = relatively low but positive importance.

   (iv) A single asterik shows the winning alternative on this column before considering the super-optimum alternative. A double asterik shows the alternative that simultaneously does better than the conservative alternative, on the conservative totals, and better than the liberal alternative on the liberal totals.

2. For further details on win-win analysis, see S. Negel, *Super-Optimum Solutions and Win-Win Policy: Basic Concepts and Principles (Quorum, 1997)*, *S. Nagel, Public Policy Evaluation: Making Super-Optimum Decisions* (Ashgate, 1998), and S. Nagel, *Policy Within the Across Developing Countries* (Ashgate, 188).

PART - II

THE NATION-STATE, SOVEREIGNTY AND GLOBALIZATION

Chapter 8

Globalization and Public Policy : An Analytical Framework

Wolfgang H. Reinicke

This chapter develops a conceptual framework that links globalization and public policymaking. It is probably fair to say that the perception is widespread among policymakers and the general public that globalization has weakened the sovereignty of governments. Indeed, some have gone so far to state that globalization will lead to disappearance of states as primary organizing actors in the international system.[1] Given the powerful role that the nation-state has played in organizing social, economic, political, cultural, and other activities within its borders ever since the Industrial Revolution, the implications of such a withering away of the state, should it come to pass, would be profound to say the least. It is therefore inconceivable that states and governments will simply disappear from the landscape of politics in general, and of international relations in particular. States or not "up for grabs." After all, no viable alternative institutional form to organize contemporary political life has yet been put forward, however inefficient and ineffective the current form may have become.[2]

Yet some would argue that the significance of states relative to that of other social organizations such as institutional enterprises, nongovernmental organizations, and international organizations has been declining as a result of interdependence and globalization, leading to considerable tension between state and nonstate actors.[3] Others have taken the opposite track, suggesting that the metaphor of a powerless state is a myth and a convenient polity tool for politicians, left and right, seeking to justify politically difficult adjustments. As evidence that the state remains a powerful force, they point to the considerable and rising share of government spending as a percentage of GDP among the established industrial countries.[4]

Such a perspective, however, confuses the issue at hand. The state, by virtue of its formal powers, can raise taxes and increase spending and thus increase its weight in the national economy. But this by no means implies that its ability to conduct public policy for the economy and society at large has remained the same. On the contrary, it is an indication that, in order to maintain their operational capacity and fulfill their mandate to provide public goods and act in the public interest, governments in an increasingly open world economy need more resources rather than fewer.[5]

A more interesting and, from a policy perspective, more promising question is how states and governments might react to the phenomenon of globalization and any political challenge to their sovereignty arising from it. Just how does globalization challenge a government's sovereignty? How, if at all, does that challenge differ from the challenge of economic interdependence, which is also widely considered to dilute sovereignty? Will states – which, next to markets, remain by far the most powerful form of social organization in the modern world - resist being swept aside by globalization? Do governments have different options in responding to globalization? What are those options, how do they differ, and what will be their consequences? And if states were to disappear in the long run, what, if anything, would replace them?

Clearly, national governments will have great influence over the process by which tensions between public policies and globalization are resolved. Prior choices about how to organize and institutionalize political life limit the options available in the medium term. Thus, unlike a purely utilitarian or functional perspective, which would predict a withering away of state, a more realistic scenario posits that the implications of globalization for public policymaking - whatever the outcome - will be path-dependent andthus mediated by the primary form of political organization in the world today: the modern territorial and democratic state.[6]

Following from the empirical discussion in chapter 1, the analytical framework developed here also draws a distinction between interdependence and globalization. At the root of the distinction lies a differentiation between *external* and *internal sovereignty*. Both are relational concepts. But whereas the former focuses on a state's external environment and characterizes relations among states within the international system, the latter depicts a state's setting within its own territory, characterizing, for example, relations between a government and its citizens, the economy, or other, more narrowly defined groups and institutions. From the perspective of this study, public policy is defined as the principal instrument by which governments operationalize internal sovereignty both in a constitutive and in an executive sense.

Challenges to a state's external sovereignty have of course been the central force in the study of international relations. So far the same cannot be said of internal sovereignty, which has remained the focus of students of domestic politics. The globalization of industrial activity calls this conventional division of labour into question and suggests that the concept of internal sovereignty will become a central theme of the study of world political economy. The globalization of industry presents a fundamental challenge to states' ability to exercise internal sovereignty. Among other things this is reflected in the fact that, that is, matters of internal sovereignty, are being drawn into or reappear in discussion and deliberations on matters of foreign policy. When Theodore J. Low wrote his seminal article in the late 1960s, categorizing public policy into three functional areas, he stated that he did not include foreign policy in his categories because "in many ways it is not part of the same universe."[7] Such a rigid separation may have been possible at the time, but it is no longer possible today. Contemporary theories of international relations do not draw a distinction between internal and external sovereignty. As a result, these theories fail to appreciate the nature of the transformation that globalization entails for the international system, and in particular for the interests and motivation of its primary actors, the world's nation-states.

Interdependence: Challenges to External Sovereignty

The study of the increasing interdependence of national economies and the associated emergence of a world economy has become one of the core areas of research in the field of international relations. The popularity of interdependence as an analytical concept increased considerably with the publication of *Power and Interdependence* by Robert Koehane and Joseph Nye Jr.[8] They coined the term *complex interdependence* to characterize a condition in which independent states are connected by an increasing number of channels - political, social, economic, cultural, and others. They and other authors argued that complex interdependence led to a weakening of security issues, which had been the dominant set of issues defining the relationships among states in the international system.

Much has been written since then about complex interdependence, and the concept has been refined and even further redefined.[9] The central proposition, however, has remained the same: interdependence, or mutual dependence, implies sensitivity or vulnerability to an external force.[10] The units to be studied when examining and measuring interdependence are territorially bound, sovereign nation-states. International interdependence thus denotes a condition of mutual sensitivity and vulnerability among states in the international system. From the perspective of each state, the source of this sensitivity and vulnerability is *external*.

As discussed in the previous chapter, *economic* interdependence is characterized by an increasing flow of goods, services, and capital across borders. This increased flow is due to variations in countries' resource endowments, such as capital, labor, and natural resources, and differences in countries' stage of industrialization, among other factors. All these factors lead to an increasing international specialization and division of labor among national economies, which is then reflected in the pattern and composition of international trade and finance.

However, despite this expanded flow of goods, services, and capital across borders, national frameworks for policymaking under conditions of interdependence remain for the most part separate from the international arena. In other words, the increased interaction of national economies due to rising specialization leads to heightened interdependence, or, as is often argued, simply dependence, yet national governments remain the principal center of political and economic power as well as the locus of decisionmaking. Economic events in other countries are filtered through a set of policy boundaries, the effectiveness of which begins at, but does not reach beyond, the territory of the domestic economy.

It is helpful to introduce two distinctions that are often overlooked when considering the implications of interdependence on sovereignty. First, although it may be implicitly assumed, it is seldom spelled out that interdependence challenges not de jure or legal sovereignty, but de facto or operational sovereignty. In other words, it is not the legal concept of sovereignty that is being challenged, but the ability of states to practice that concept in the daily affairs of politics.[11] This distinction is important. If interdependence were to challenge the legal sovereignty of states, it would also by definition challenge the notion that the international system is anarchic (legal sovereignty being the basis for anarchy), a condition that lies at the heart to the dominant schools in international relations: realism and liberalism (these are discussed further below).

Second, and more important, it is helpful to distinguish between an internal and external dimension of sovereignty. Accordingly, sovereignty "combines a description of attributes with various emotive concerns for or against limitations on the *internal* and *external* discretion of the state."[12] Hedley Bull puts it succinctly in *The Anarchical Society*: "On the one hand, states assert, in relation to this territory and population, what might be called internal sovereignty, which means supremacy over all other authorities within that territory and population. On the other hand, they assert what might be called external sovereignty, by which it meant not supremacy but interdependence of outside authorities."[13] In each case, as John Ruggie has put it, "it[sovereignty] signifies a form of legitimation that pertains to a system of relations.[14] The concept of sovereignty did not start out with this double meaning attached to it. Rather, the term originated from the need to justify "the king being the master of new modern kingdom, absolute internally" and only later became "the justification of equality of such sovereigns in the international community ... a theory of sovereign states."[15] Going back to the fourteenth century, the concept almost exclusively referred to the internal dimension and initially served as a form of legitimation of central state authority against competing domestic claimants.[16]

Later this internal dimension also figured prominently in Max Weber's definition of the state as enjoying a monopoly of the legitimate use of force over a given territory and population.[17] It came to refer to a central legal and administrative structure, as well as its decisionmaking process, that forms a polity which defines a network of institutional ties, behavioral regularities, and values that bind together public and private actors, who participate in implementing authoritative decisions.[18] Put slightly differently, internal sovereignty refers to the formulation, implementation, and maintenance of a legal, economic, political, and social order that allows individuals to peacefully coexist and interact in a relatively predictable environment.

Over the years, the concept of internal sovereignty evolved into constitutional, democratic governance. "Subjects" became "citizens", and as far as internal sovereignty is concerned, the concept of citizenship and inclusiveness became central constitutive elements in shaping a state's identity. Internal sovereignty came to describe the relationship between a democratically elected government and society at large. Modern internal sovereignty refers to popular sovereignty. Internal sovereignty is bestowed upon the "rulers' at regular intervals through the electoral process and is thereafter subject to pluralistic and/or corporate structures of decisionmaking. As will be shown below, these links among internal sovereignty, democracy, and inclusive plurality are of great importance when analyzing the relationship between globalization and public policy.

In operational terms, internal sovereignty in today's modern democracy means the ability of a government to formulate, implement, and manage public policy. Thus, in terms of this inquiry, which focuses on the regulatory and rule-making dimension of public policymaking, governments exercise internal sovereignty when they make laws and regulations, decide on the best and most effective ways to implement those laws and regulations, and monitor compliance with them. A threat to a country's operational internal sovereignty implies a threat to its ability to conduct public policy. With respect to the economy, the legal dimension of internal sovereignty becomes operational when governments collect taxes or regulate private sector activities, assuming that the boundaries that define the relationship between the public and the private sector are both stable and symmetric.

The external dimension of the concept of sovereignty goes back to Thomas Hobbes. In contrast to internal sovereignty, external sovereignty implies the absence of a supreme authority and therefore the independence of states in the international system. External sovereignty is the logical consequence of Hobbes' position that there is no security in domestic anarchy. Thus Hobbes solved the problem of domestic anarchy by "exporting" it to the international system. External sovereignty is the central constitutive rule of the international system.[19] States are mutually exclusive and disjoined and follow the principle of self-help.[20] Identity formation by states (such as the development of interests, beliefs and expectations) in the presence of anarchy is primarily concerned with the maintenance of their own security. The internal system is competitive and individualistic, and security in the absence of central rule is the responsibility of each country individually.[21] External economic sovereignty is operationalized, for example, when countries collect tariffs or devalue or revalue their currencies.

It can now be seen that the two concepts of sovereignty are closely related. The rationale of external sovereignty would not exist in the absence of internal sovereignty. Indeed, it is unlikely that a state could exist for long relying solely on external sovereignty.[22] Suffice it to say here that, given the nature of the origin of external sovereignty, any threat to it would ultimately also affect its internal counterpart. Similarly, a sustained challenge to a country's internal sovereignty will eventually affect its external sovereignty.

As currently conceptualized, territoriality is central to both notions of sovereignty. External sovereignty is based on the principle of mutual exclusion, and it is this principle that defines territoriality in the international system.[23] With a few exceptions, such as global commons, the international system is fully determined. As far as the internal sovereignty is concerned, the assertion of final authority within a given territory is the very basis for its existence and legitimacy as well as its ability to be inclusive by generating a sense of identity and belonging.

But even though external and internal sovereignty are closely related and rely on the principle of territoriality as a common and defining characteristic, it is important to keep in mind that they are diametrically opposed, with respect to both the principles by which they operate and the purpose for which they came into existence. Any attempt by a single state to establish ultimate authority in the international system will be and always has been fiercely contested by others. But at home a government's authority is supreme and largely uncontested. Second, although states interact internationally with each other on the basis of mutually respected exclusion, inclusiveness is essential for both the effectiveness and the legitimacy of a government domestically. Third, whereas domestically the identity or purpose of government is to represent the collective interest, or the common or public good, internationally states need to fend for their own individual interests. Fourth, as a relational concept, external sovereignty refers to functional equivalents, namely, states, whereas internal sovereignty refers to functional opposites, namely, the public and the private domains. Fifth, the common attributes of territoriality individuates in the international system, but spatially delineates a collective at the domestic level. Given these two different roles or collective meanings attached to the two forms of sovereignty, it follows that states have a dual identity derived from their differing institutional roles at the domestic and the international level. Each of these roles generates different sets of interest and expectations, responding to a different environment and different actors. These roles have been kept separate even under conditions of interdependence.[24]

One of the major theoretical debates of the last decade between realists and liberals in the field of international relations has revolved around the concept of interdependence, in particular its meaning and significance for the interests, and subsequently, the behavior of states in the international political and economic system.[25] At the risk of oversimplifying this ongoing discussion, the two positions can be described as follows. Realists, or neorealists as they have been called in the most recent round of the debate, maintain that states' interests and behavior in the international system are shaped by the system's *structure*, which is characterized by the absence of a central power. The organizing principle is anarchy, which promotes competition and conflict among states and restrains their desire to cooperate with other states, even when there is a clear recognition that they have joint interests.[26] Liberals or neoliberals, on the other hand, while reorganizing and even accepting the inevitability of the anarchic structure of the international system, argue that *process* can under certain circumstances lead to cooperation among states. ("Process" here refers to interaction among states, which allows for learning by them - that is, by policymakers and bureaucrats - as a result of that interaction). In addition, the neoliberal perspective attributes to international institutions the ability to facilitate interaction and provide an environment conductive to both learning and reciprocity among states.[27]

In liberal theorizing, states seek to maximize absolute gains in the international system. That other states might gain as well is not an impediment to cooperation. The major impediment is cheating, which results in free riding in the international system.[28] Realists disagree, arguing that states do worry about the gains of other states. For realists, states perceive gains in relative terms: a state is unlikely to cooperate if another state is likely to gain more than it does, even if the first state would also benefit.[29] As a result, international institutions cannot have the mediating and facilitating effect on cooperation that liberals claim they do, and in a neorealist view of the international system one is likely to witness far less cooperation among states than the neoliberal approach would predict.

Yet as much as these two theoretical schools may differ on states' responses to increased interdependence, and thus on the promise of international cooperation and the role of institutions in facilitating cooperation, their approaches also - and this is central to the analysis - have a number of fundamental and important methodological and conceptual commonalties. Most important, both schools take a "rationalist" approach to international relations, which implies that the identities and interests of states are predetermined exogeneously and cannot change. Another shared concept is that states are unitary, self-interested actors coexisting in an anarchic environment. Hence, although the two schools differ on how states behave in an anarchic environment, they do not differ on the fundamental interests and identities of states in such an environment.[30]

This theoretical correspondence of neorealist and neoliberal views of states' interests, identities, and their anarchic surroundings also translates into a shared understanding of the nature and purpose of sovereignty in the international system, and how sovereignty is affected by economic interdependence. For both schools the origin of the challenge to a state's operational sovereignty is considered external, or "systemic," as it is often called. Interdependence describes the sensitivity of one nation to events occurring in another, and vice versa. The dynamic forces, the external pressures that states experience as a result of interdependence, originate in the international system, which is composed of other states. To what degree and in what form these external forces subsequently get refracted at national borders and are filtered into the domestic system - in other words, how vulnerable states are and how they respond to this vulnerability - is a source of dispute between the two schools.

Neoliberals, again, emphasize the absolute gains that can be derived from cooperation.[31] In the realm of economic interdependence, those gains are said to be achieved by reducing tariff barriers and capital controls - a reduction in the external dimension of sovereignty - in order to facilitate the free flow of goods and services so that intercountry specialization based on the principle of comparative advantage can be furthered. If common ground for a reduction of external barriers between two or more countries can be established, there is a basis for cooperation.

Cooperation will succeed and the gains from increased economic interdependence will be realized, in the neoliberal view, if other states do not cheat on previously agreed-upon arrangements to lower external barriers. Such an agreement to reduce and thus limit external sovereignty is rationalized by the principles of nondiscrimination and reciprocity - in other words, by a comparable reduction in the external sovereignty of all other states that are party to the agreement. Institutionalized forms of international cooperation are often referred to as international regimes, which are defined rather broadly as "sets of implicit or explicit principles, norms, rules, and decision-making procedures around which actors' expectations converge in a given area of international relations."[32]

Thus neoliberals acknowledge the neorealist claim that states compete in an anarchic international system, but suggest that they do so in a cooperative and reciprocal fashion, which alters their perception of risk and changes their incentive structure by reducing uncertainty, providing information, and lowering transaction costs. To the question of whether states do or do not lose external sovereignty in this process, the neoliberals answer would be "both." They do lose external sovereignty in absolute terms as economic borders are lowered, but they do not lose external sovereignty relative to other states, which lower their borders likewise, in line with the principle of reciprocity.[33] In substantive terms, this process, which will be called *cooperative competition*, is embedded in international regimes and evolves from each country's dominant domestic private sector coalitions, whose interests are projected by governments into international negotiations and the multilateral agreements that emerge from them.[34] Thus governments under conditions of cooperative competition do not necessarily represent the general public interest, but often only the dominant private sector interests in the international system, ensuring that those interests can be addressed once an agreement has been struck. This applies even to such cases as free trade, which, contrary to widespread perception, is not in itself a public good according to the standard Samuelsonian definition of nonexcludiability and joint supply.[35]

Neorealists, on the other hand, argue that the promise of absolute gains, although a necessary condition for cooperation, is not a sufficient one.[36] For these realists what ultimately determines whether or not states cooperate with other states is the relative gains to each, that is, how cooperation affects each state's position in the international system vis-a-vis other states. Because not all states can be relative gainers, realists argue, cooperation is unlikely to occur, and when it does is highly unstable and short-lived. For realists the international system is characterized by what is called here *adversarial competition*, which they argue is the only way to preserve external sovereignty.

Both schools acknowledge that states are structural and functional equals that compete in the international system and pursue similar interests. However, the terms on which that competition takes place and the ways in which states respond to a challenge to their external sovereignty vary. Neorealists see states as primarily adversarial, reluctant to concede external sovereignty. Neoliberals argue that states will cooperate if the potential joint gains resulting from greater economic interdependence can be realized, even though in absolute terms they will have to concede some of their external sovereignty. But while the two schools differ on the outcome of state interaction in the international system, they do not differ on the source. Both explain the success or failure of cooperation by pointing to external developments: changes in the position or behavior of other states in the international system.

This brief review sets the stage for a discussion of globalization and its implications for sovereignty and public policy. However, one cannot resist pointing to the empirical evidence of the world economy, which seems to confirm that individual governments, in relations to date involving both the real and the financial sectors, have by and large tended to follow a strategy of cooperative competition. They have relinquished some of their external sovereignty in absolute terms, while at the same time using international regimes to ensure that they do not lose external sovereignty in relative terms. Of course, this is not to say that adversarial competition has vanished from the field of international relations. Adversarial competition remains a policy option that states have on many occasions threatened to use, and in some cases have used, when cooperative competition has failed.

Globalization: Challenges to Internal Sovereignty

As was stated in the introduction, if there is no formal difference between interdependence and globalization, governments have little need or incentive to reassess their own role in view of globalization, or to reassess the purpose and principles of the institutions that have governed the world economy since the end of World War II. However, if such a distinction can be drawn, it provides the conceptual basis for a reassessment of the role of government and governance in an emerging global economy.

Chapter 1 described the characteristic feature of globalization from an empirical perspective.[37] Based on the discussion in the previous section, it is now possible to draw a formal, analytical distinction. According to one definition, globalization in its pure form is a process that subsumes and rearticulates national economies into the global economy through cross-national processes and transactions. These processes and transactions take on an autonomous role in a consolidated global marketplace for production, distribution, and consumption. According to this view, the global economy dominates national economies existing within it.[38] Although certainly helpful for comprehending the fundamental and historic transformation that the world political economy is undergoing, such broad macrostructural definitions do not capture the central difference between globalization and interdependence. Nor are they necessarily specific enough to allow for a comprehensive examination of the policy implications that globalization may entail for policymakers.

It was shown in Chapter 1 that globalization is an industry-level, microeconomic phenomenon. Cooperative competition among governments during the 1960s and 1970s - and its outcomes, liberalization and cross-border deregulation - were important preconditions for the strategic corporate decisions that now drive the geographic expansion of foreign direct investment and the rising incidence of intrafirm trade, international sourcing, and intefirm collaborative agreements. But increasing interdependence alone does not capture this process. Indeed, unlike in the case of interdependence, governments for the most part have not yet become involved in the dynamics of globalization. Recall that globalization was defined as a strategic decision to divide a growing number of functional aspects of the product life cycle, including R&D, production, marketing, and even disposal of a product, into different segments across a variety of structurally similar national economies, and that this decision often involves the internalization or quasi internalization into a single corporate entity of activities formerly conducted as market transactions across two distinct firms in distinct national economies. As an economic dynamic, therefore, globalization differs from interdependence in that it subsumes or internalizes into its own institutional structure economic activities that previously took place between national markets, that is, between distinct economic *and* political units. For a global as opposed to an international firm, foreign presence is no longer one of several elements in determining the firm's competitive advantage; it has become a precondition for participation in a particular industrial sector. Globalization has become an intrinsic structural characteristic of an industry.[39]

As national borders no longer encompass sufficient territory to function as self-contained markets for global companies, the spatial structure and dynamics that delineates the geography of private sector economic activities are becoming decoupled from the territorial structure and dynamics that define political geography, that is, the territorially bound nation-states and its power of decisionmaking within the economy. Territorially, the defining characteristic of internal and external sovereignty, becomes "unbundled."[40] Whereas the political geography that defines markets continues to be structured by mutual exclusion, the economic geography on the basis of which these markets function has become increasingly inclusive, defying the territorially fixed nature of the nation-state by creating its own, nonterritorial space. Keeping in mind the geographic and sectoral limitations of globalization discussed in chapter 1, national boundaries to an increasing degree no longer mediate market exchanges but instead merely register internal corporate flows. These off-market transactions are often misleadingingly treated as exchanges in such conventional measures as trade statistics and foreign exchange rates. To be sure, the management of interdependence was an important precursor to this development, but interdependence no longer adequately describes the structure of the international system or the challenges that emanate from it.

Quantitatively, this inadequacy of national markets manifests itself in the various empirical indicators of globalization examined in chapter 1. In the financial service industry it is probably best reflected in the fact that the financial intermediation of both credit and, more recently, market risk no longer takes places within national financial markets, but instead relies on a much broader and more fluid geographic space. The increasingly widespread phenomenon of parallel derivative markets is probably the most vivid example. The changing composition of international trade - caused by the rising importance of intrafirm trade and long-term supplier relationships, or the fact that global sales of the affiliates of multinationals have for some time exceeded world exports - reflects the increasing disjuncture between the economic geography of globalization and the political geography of a world economy structured by nation-states.

Qualitatively, this disjuncture, or mismatch, between political and economic geography does not challenge the external sovereignty of states. It cannot. Rather, by altering the spatial relationship between the private and the public sector, global corporate networks challenge the internal sovereignty of states. Specifically, since the organizational logic of globalization induces corporations to seek the fusion of multiple, formerly segmented national markets into a single whole, it generates an economic geography that subsumes multiple political geographies. As a result, a government no longer has a monopoly of legitimate power over the territory within which corporations organize themselves. The greater the mismatch between political and economic geography, the more difficult it will be for national governments to act in an inclusive manner, allowing individuals to coexist and interact in a relatively predictable environment. This leads to the heightened perception of risk and insecurity widely observed in our societies.

For example, a government's ability to provide such security for economic activity depends crucially on access to a constant stream of information about the activity of economic actors - a stream that is not always easy to maintain. Information asymmetries have always been one reason why policymakers find it difficult to keep up with the changing nature of the marketplace. But globalization has led to a sharp increase in these asymmetries, making it almost impossible for governments to maintain even a minimum amount of crucial information. Moreover, as far as regulatory and supervisory policies are concerned, globalization has led to an acceleration of the regulatory dialectic, in which public and private actors engage in a continuous contest, the former trying to constrain the latter while the latter tries to escape those constraints. This dialectic not only is fiscally wasteful but rarely achieves its goal. Similarly, as globalization progresses, governments will find it increasingly difficult to assess and collect taxes, since they lack crucial information about the activity of those they seek to tax.

In other words, the unbundling of political and economic geography brought about by globalization has created a structural imbalance, and possibly even a disjuncture, between the public and the private spheres of society. Governments and governance, which continue to be bounded by territoriality, can no longer project their policymaking capacity over the territory within which a global industry (on the supply side) and, to an increasing degree, a global community of consumers (on the demand side) operate. Globalization not only integrates along one dimension, the economic or private; it also fragments along another, the political or public.

This is not to say that private sector actors necessarily and always make a deliberate effort to circumvent and outrace government efforts to control them. Rather, each geography, the economic and the political, follows a set of fundamentally different operational logics. Political systems, at least in their contemporary form as nation-states, are boundary-maintaining systems. Indeed, their legitimacy is derived from their ability to maintain boundaries. Markets, although dependent for their creation on political power and local economic networks, do not depend, once in operation, on the presence of territorial boundaries.[43] Given the expansive nature of globalization, the spatial symmetry between the public and the private is disappearing. From the historical perspective this raises a number of important questions about the long-term future of the nation-state. After all, it was precisely the superior ability of the nation-state to establish internal sovereignty - to consolidate the public and private spheres into a single territorial entity - that allowed it to outmanoeuver institutional and organizational competitors such as city-states and city-leagues in the organization of political and economic life at the end of the feudal era.[44] The concluding chapter of this study will address this issue at greater length.

At this point it is important to recall the earlier distinction between legal and operational sovereignty. Like interdependence, globalization does not and cannot in any way challenge the *legal* internal sovereignty of a government. Globalization challenges internal *operational* sovereignty, and it is important for the subsequent discussion to keep this distinction in mind. Thus, just as states become increasingly sensitive and vulnerable to the actions of other states as increasing interdependence weakened their external operational sovereignty, so their internal operational sovereignty is being undermined by globalization, as territorially bounded governments can no longer project their power and policymaking capacity over the territory within which a global industry operates.[45]

Recall that the empirical examination of globalization in chapter 1 showed that the globalization of industry (financial services and manufacturing alike) is not necessarily equivalent to the globalization of the market economy. From the previous analysis of the divergent paths of political and economic geographies, this point can now be made at a more formal and general level. One can only confuse globalization with the rise of the global market economy if one understands a market economy (national, regional, or global) as an almost idealized arrangement in which rational, self-interested economic agents interact free of any constraints, political but also legal or of some other form, and are minimally affected by social relations, their history, traditions, culture, or other factors. In this atomized, undersocialized, and depoliticized conception of human action, the market economy and its geography would be a separate, differentiated sphere of modern society, unrelated to the broader historical, political, and social environment and their geographies, in which the market economy is embedded. Economic rationality would prevail over political, social, and judicial rationality.

Notwithstanding the fact that economic rationality is an essential component of a market economy, the latter is of course more than a loosely structured agglomeration of individual economic actors freely expressing their preferences in pursuit of their individual or private interests generating or, even Pareto-optimal outcomes for themselves. A market economy is a complex organization, based not only on the interaction of individual economic preferences but also on the presence of a collective or public interest that relies on relatively stable social relationships and patterns of behavior, legal norms and mechanisms, political forces and institutions, and, increasingly, ecological and resource constraints. All of these interact in a structured manner to produce the relatively consistent behavior characteristic of any large institution. Thus a market economy is a form of social organization - indeed it is the *principal* form of social organization that shapes industrial democracies. It is a highly complex system that forms a social whole but functions through a network of constituent parts.

It is true that economic interactions are the most visible of these constituent parts and the most closely associated with the wealth-generating potential of market exchange, that is, the pursuit of private interests. Economic interactions are the source of the spontaneity for which markets are well known. But the wealth-generating potential would not always be utilized, and indeed would be at high risk and would often fail, were it not for a broad set of legal and administrative parameters and a variety of social norms that give market economies a certain constructive character - a foundation, a collective or public good, that allows the market economy to perform its integrative function. For example, the institutions of a market economy and the transactions undertaken within them depend on the presence of trust - a collective good - which market process themselves cannot provide.[47] The social organization of trust is thus an important constituent element of a market economy and has to be developed by means other than economic exchange. If anything, it should be a precondition of economic exchange.

Markets are also firmly embedded in a network of organizations governed by legally binding administrative rules and regulations, which in turn are shaped by political forces. At the macrostructural level this network of organizations ensures the smooth and efficient interaction of participants in a market, and when necessary it employs legal means to enforce certain behaviors. At the macrostructural level organizations often perform the function of aggregating and intermediating the interest of persons and groups in the market, and representing these interests to policymakers. Chambers of commerce, labor unions, trade and business associations, and consumer groups are all vital elements of a modern market economy.

Thus the risk associated with the spontaneity of economic exchange and the pursuit of private interests would be too great without some constructive foundation and a stabilizing framework that can provide collective goods and meet the public interest. Similarly, the constructive foundation and the stability that these collective goods create would be of little tangible value unless one could point to the wealth and income generated by the spontaneous interaction of individual economic actors pursuing their individual interests. Societies can place too much emphasis on either of these constituent elements. Too much emphasis on the constructive aspects of a market economy is likely to stifle its dynamism, while an overemphasis on spontaneity can turn dynamism into turbulence and chaos. Managing such a complex organization and its constituent parts, that is, deciding which issues will be resolved by individual choice and decisionmaking and to what degree (the market being the principal mechanism), and which should be resolved by collective choice and decisionmaking, balancing public and private interests, and to what degree, is what public policymaking at the national level is all about. It presumes the ability of a government to exercise internal sovereignty.[48]

Following from the above, the unbundling of the political (legal, social, cultural) and economic geographies brought about by globalization has created an imbalance and possibly even a disjuncture between the two central constituent spheres of the market economy. Since the operational capacity of governments to exercise internal sovereignty depends on considerable correspondence between the two spheres, globalization has severely weakened the ability of governments to provide public goods and act in the public interest. Moreover, as has already been discussed, in many countries today sovereignty, in particular its internal dimension, is popular, legitimized at regular intervals through the electoral process. As a result, any threat to a government's internal operational sovereignty implies, by definition, a threat to the effectiveness of democracy itself. In other words, although individuals may exercise their legal right to vote, the power or influence of that vote in shaping public policy has decreased with the decline in operational internal sovereignty and will continue to do so. Ultimately, a persistent weakness and failure of internal sovereignty, therefore, will lead to a questioning of the institutions and processes of democracy itself.

Although this dynamic is certainly not the only explanation for the exhaustion of democracy and the declining trust in institutions of governance and political leaders in many countries, it certainly should be considered an important contributing factor.[49] In addition, it explains the increasing popular resentment against deeper economic integration, which ultimately threatens the process of globalization itself, as nationalism and the politics of identity provide a simplistic but easy, and therefore powerful, response to a complex, historic transformation of the economic (although not yet the political) landscape in which industrial societies coexist. In the words of one commentator, "Too much democracy kills the market, because the people, or an authority acting in their name, take all the decisions collectively, leaving nothing to the individual. But too much market may also kill democracy. If every choice is left to the market, the right to vote becomes meaningless, because the people you elect have no power to change anything."[50]

Taken together, then, the globalization of industry presents a challenge to the capacity of governments to govern. But this challenge to their ability to conduct public policy is not an external challenge. It does not emanate from another state, as usually conceptualized in the standard approaches to the study of international relations, and in a particular of international interdependence, which focuses on external sovereignty.[51] Rather, the challenge comes from within each country, as economic networks (legal and illegal alike) increasingly operate in a nonterritorial functional space that defies individual territorialities and thus internal sovereignties. Although this space has no center politically, it is highly integrated at the microeconomic level, creating what has been called a "*space-of-flows* operating in real time which exists alongside the *space-of-places*," also referred to as national but interdependent economies.[52] This space-of-flows, a growing part of which consists of cyberflows as electronic finance and commerce continue to gain in importance, is characterized by a set of mutually reinforcing cross-national networks pertaining to technology transfer, the processing and dissemination of knowledge and information, financial intermediation, transport, and, last but not least, research and development. These networks form the backbone of global corporate operations and thus of an emerging global manufacturing and services economy. Accordingly, the global economy is not located in another place or at a different level; it *is* another place.[53] Thus, although national boundaries have remained points of contact as well as points of separation between political systems, they no longer perform those functions in the strategies of global corporations or the consumption patterns of individuals, notwithstanding that there might be other factors that constrain their spatial horizon. Finally, given the close linkage between internal sovereignty and democracy, globalization not only undermines the effectiveness and efficiency of governments but weakens the legitimacy of democratic institutions and the democratic process itself.

How are governments to respond to this challenge? As the next chapter will show, they have a number of options. Global public policy, the pooling and collective operationalization of internal sovereignty, is one such option. But for global public policy to succeed, national governments have to agree to commit themselves to an unprecedented amount of cooperation. It is unprecedented because, contrary to the neoliberal vision of cooperative competition, where states lose some of their external sovereignty in absolute terms, there is no "space" for external sovereignty if global public policy is to succeed. More specifically, given the causal relationship between the two dimensions of sovereignty, external sovereignty ceases to exist among those states in those functional domains in which they agree to operationalize internal sovereignty collectively.

This need for cooperation among governments on a scale and depth not yet witnessed represents the central analytical challenge for global public policy and brings the discussion back to the debate between realists and liberals over the prospects for cooperation in the international system. However, given the focus of both on external sovereignty, neither realism nor liberalism can be very helpful in examining the policy implications of globalization, nor can either predict the prospects for cooperation under conditions of globalization. Indeed, the fact that the globalization of industry has transformed internal sovereignty from a domestic into a global policy issue has profound implications for this debate. As long as the internal system was characterized solely by the dynamics of interdependence, the preservation of external sovereignty was the dominant and singular interest of states in the international system, and shaped their identity. And even though neoliberals argued that the nature of the ensuing competition among states was likely to be cooperative, they had to concede the causal powers of anarchy to the neorealists, as the interests of states were exogeneously given and could not change.[54]

Globalization alters this one-dimensional constellation of state interests and identity in the international system. It introduces the possibility of change in the formulation and subsequent administration of those interests, neither of which was possible in neorealist or neoliberal thinking. By elevating internal sovereignty to the rank of a global policy issue, the international system, and with it the collectivity of externally sovereign states, is confronted with the management and resolution of this second, equally important determinant of states' overall identity. States no longer exhibit a singular systemic identity - the preservation of external sovereignty - but have to rely on the international system to achieve internal sovereignty as well. Given that for the foreseeable future the international system will continue to be characterized by exclusiveness, and thus anarchy (primarily of course to preserve legal external sovereignty, the only way for governments to achieve inclusiveness, and thus internal sovereignty, is to pool, and thus share, internal sovereignty in those sectors in which globalization has undermined the effectiveness and efficiency of internal sovereignty at the national level.

Therefore, the anarchic structure of the international system does not necessarily cause states to compete in order to maintain their external sovereignty, but it could induce them to cooperate to realize their internal sovereignty. It follows that state interests and identities in the international system are no longer determined a priori, as suggested by the neorealist approach and conceded by neoliberals, but instead may vary (cooperative competition versus competitive cooperation) depending on the issue under consideration. Neoliberals no longer need to concede the causal properties of anarchy to the neorealists. It is true that, under conditions of interdependence, anarchy causes competition among states seeking to preserve external sovereignty. But as shown above, under conditions of globalization, anarchy would be highly detrimental to a state's ability to realize one crucial aspect, if not *the* crucial aspect, of its identity.[55]

If the deeper integration of the world economy is to continue, cooperation is the *only* way to maintain internal sovereignty.[56] Cooperation thus becomes vital to the constitution of states, their interests, and their identities. Just as competition was rational for state engagement in the international system under interdependence, so the need to cooperate motivates states' behavior under conditions of globalization. *Anarchy is no longer just the outcome of, but also the cause of state interests in the international system.* The same reasoning that led neorealists to characterize the international system as competitive (internal sovereignty cannot be achieved under conditions of anarchy at the domestic level, and therefore anarchy must be "exported") now leads to the conclusion that the international system should be cooperative, because one central dimension, a state's identity, can only be achieved collectively.[57]

What is the role of external sovereignty in such a context? Can it still have any meaning? Is there still room for anarchy in the international system? Recall from the discussion at the beginning of this chapter that the principal rationale for the existence of external sovereignty was the desire to establish internal sovereignty in the territorially fixed geographic space - the state. The concept of global public policy, however, is based on a strategy whereby some dimensions of internal sovereignty at the operational level are territorially delinked and functionally desegregated. "Internal" thus no longer refers to territory but to the spatial extension within which global companies pursue their activities, cutting across a number of externally sovereign territories. Since "internal" no longer refers to territory, external sovereignty, as a heuristic device, loses its utility in the context of globalization.

Put differently, the purpose of external sovereignty was to ensure monopoly power over decisionmaking within a particular territory and to prevent outside interference. Its rationale was conditioned on the fact that internal sovereignty was operationalized territorially. Since internal sovereignty can no longer be achieved in a territorial context, external sovereignty becomes redundant. It has effectively lost its meaning. In fact, since external sovereignty is the central precondition for anarchy, it is to be avoided, as countries would then be unable to cooperate to achieve internal sovereignty. As will be discussed later, however, globalization remains a limited phenomenon. External sovereignty remains an appropriate conceptual tool. Even the collectivity of states that agree to pool their internal sovereignty on a particular policy issue remains externally sovereign (legal and operationally), with respect to each other in other policy domains and to third states in the same policy domain. How likely is it that countries would be willing to abandon their external operational sovereignty?[58] As will be shown in the first and last case studies, this is not as unlikely as one might at first be inclined to believe. The reason is obvious: the incentive for relinquishing external operational sovereignty is the hope of safeguarding its internal counterpart.

To sum up, the discussion on the debate between neorealists and neoliberals characterized the dynamics of interdependence as one of cooperative competition. States relying on the institutional and rule-based infrastructure of the world economy agreed to facilitate international economic exchange by reducing barriers to cross-border flows of goods, services, and capital. The behavior of states in the international system reflected the interests of the dominant domestic private sector coalitions. The goal was to enhance international economic competition, albeit in a reciprocal, that is, cooperative fashion.

Chapter 1 showed that the management of economic interdependence followed an agreed set of principles, emphasizing the reciprocal lowering of cross-border barriers to both real and financial flows. Managing economic interdependence in this way was considered an important precondition for globalization to occur. The mere presence of globalization thus confirms that cooperative competition has occurred. At the same time, however, cooperative competition has created new challenges for states, transforming their identity, interests, and thus behavior in the international system. To preserve the internal dimension of their sovereignty under conditions of globalization, states (barring other responses, which will be discussed in the next chapter) will *have* to cooperate to represent their own interests in the international system and thus preserve their own legitimacy and identity, and indeed rationalize their very existence.

In contrast to the case of interdependence, under conditions of globalization it is cooperation rather than competition that motivates states' global engagement and explains their behavior in the international system. However, given that countries differ over both what is and what is not in the public interest, as well as over how that interest can be best achieved (for more on that see 3chapter 3), the process or method by which states establish cooperation is likely to be on competitive terms. Whereas *cooperative competition* among states best captures the dynamics of interdependence, globalization inverts that formula and induces *competitive cooperation*. It is important to note, however, that "competition" here does not refer to the outcome of the interaction or to the type of order within which individual actors interact, but to the method or process by which a cooperative order is achieved.Thus competition here should be understood as a bargaining process, ultimately resulting in a cooperative agreement that defines global public policy, that is, the rules and procedures by which internal sovereignty is achieved and maintained in the global economy.

From a behavioral perspective, states' actions may not be all that different when they cooperate, in the case of interdependence, or compete, in the case of globalization. The crucial difference is the interests involved, their purpose, and the outcome of each process: private sector competition in the former, public sector cooperation in the latter. This change in purpose will have a profound impact. Take the case of the Bretton Woods institutions and the other international organizations originally designed to manage interdependence. Rather than promoting the progressive liberalization of cross-border economic flows, which within the established industrial economies has been quite successful, these institutions will have to address the consequences of that liberalization, following the principle of global public policy. This requires considerable change in their mandate and organization.

Given the nature of the challenge that globalization presents to national governments, it seems unlikely that they will not respond. But global public policy is not the only way in which government can regain or maintain internal sovereignty. On the contrary, as the next chapter will demonstrate, a variety of other strategies can achieve the same goal. However, they cannot do so without jeopardizing not only continued international economic integration but indeed the entire postwar international order.

NOTES & REFERENCES

1. See Jean Marie Guehenno, *The End of the Nation-State,* trans. Victoria Elliot (University of Minnesota Press, 1995); Kenichi Ohmae, *The End of the Nation-State: The Rise of Regional Economies* (Free Press, 1995).

2. Stephen Krasner, "Sovereignty: An Institutional Perspective," *Comparative Political Studies,* vol.21, no.1, (April 1988), p.76; see also Nicholas Colchester, "Goodbye, Nation-State, Hello ... What?" *New York Times,* July 17, 1994, p.17.

3. Jessica T. Mathews, "Power Shift", *Foreign Affairs,* vol.76, no.1 (January/February 1997), pp.50-66; Peter J.Spiro, "New Global Communities: Nongovernmental Organizations in International Decision-Making Institutions," *Washington Quarterly,* vol.18, no.7 (Winter 1995), pp.45-56; see also Raymond Vernon, "Transnational Corporations: Where Are They Coming from, Where Are They Headed?" *Transnational Corporations,* vol. 1, no.2 (August 1992), pp.7-35.

4. For a cogent summary of this view, see "The Myth of the Powerless State," *The Economist,* October 7, 1995, pp.15-16.

5. For an early exposition of this argument see David Cameron, "The Expansion of the Public Economy", *American Political Science Review,* vol.72, no.4 (1978), pp.1243-61; for a more recent exposition, addressing the rising popular resentment against globalization, see Dani Radrik, "Why Do More Open Economies Have Bigger GovernmentS? Working Paper 5537. (Cambridge, Mass.: National Bureau of Economic Research, April 1996); Dani Rodrik, "Trade, Social Insurance, and the Limits to Globalization," Working Paper 5905 (Cambridge, Mass: National Bureau of Economic Research, January 1997); and Dani Rodrik, *Has Globalization Gone Too Far?* (Washington: Institute of International Economics, 1997).

6. Krasner, "Sovereignty: An Institutional Perspective," pp.66-94.

7. See Theodore Lowi, "American Business, Public Policy, Case Studies, and Political Theory," *World Politics,* vol.16 (1964), p.689.

8. Robert O.Keohane and Joseph S.Nye Jr., "Power and Interdependence Revisited," *International Organization,* vol.41, no.4 (1987), pp.725-53.

9. For a general discussion see David Baldwin, "Interdependenceand Power: A Conceptual Analysis," *International Organization,* vol.34 (1989), pp.471-506; R.J.Barry Jones and Peter Willetts, *Interdependence on Trial: Studies in the Theory and Reality of Contemporary Interdependence* (New York: St.Martin's, 1984); P.A.Reynolds and R.D.McKinlay, "The Concept of Interdependence: Its Uses and Misuses," in Kjell Goldmann and Gunnar Sjostedt, eds., *Power, Capabilities, Interdependence: Problems in the Study of International Influence* (Sage, 1979). On complex interdependence see Robert O.Keohane and Stanley Hoffmann, "Institutional Change in Europe in the 1980s," in Robert O.Keohane and Stanley Hoffmann, eds., *The New European Community: Decisionmaking and Institutional Change* (Boulder, Colo.: West-view Press, 1991), pp.1-39; Koehane and Nye, "Power and Interdependence Revisited."

10. Robert O.Keohane and Joseph S.Nye, Jr., *Power and Interdependence: World Politics in Transition* (Little, Brown, 1977), pp.8, 12-19. The notion of increased national sensitivity to external (economic) development was first introduced by Richard N.Cooper, *The Economics of Interdependence: Economic POlicy in the Atlantic Community* (McGraw-Hill, 1968).
11. This distinction was first made by Bull, who calls the two concepts "normative" and "factual" sovereignty. See Hedley Bull, *The Anarchical Society: A Study of Order in World Politics* (Columbia University Press, 1977), p.8. The distinction has recently been elaborated by Koehane, who distinguishes between "formal" and "operational" sovereignty. See Robert O.Keohane, "Sovereignty, Interdependence, and International Institutions," Working Paper 1 (Harvard University, 1991).
12. Joel Krieger, ed., *The Oxford Companion to Politics of the World* (Oxford University Press, 1993), p.851.
13. Bull, *The Anarchical Society*, p.8.
14. John Gerard Ruggie, "Continuity and Transformation in the World Polity: Toward a Neorealist Synthesis," *World Politics*, vol.35, no.2 (January 1983), p.276. See also Ruth Lapidoth, "Sovereignty in Transition," *Journal of International Affairs*, vol.45, no.2 (1992), pp.325-46, for a good historical overview of the concept of sovereignty and its meanings.
15. Martin Wright, *International Theory: The Three Traditions*, edited by Gabriele Wight and Brian Porter (Holmes & Meier, 1992), pp.2-3.
16. The classic work here is Jean Bodin, *Six Books of the Commonwealth* (Harvard University Press, 1962). Bodin defined citizenship as subjection to a sovereign. See George Holland Sabine, *A History of Political Theory*, 4th ed. (Hinsdale: Dryden Press, 1973), chap.20; see also Max Adams Shephard, "Sovereignty at the Crossroads: A Study of Bodin," *Political Science Quarterly*, vol.45 (Columbia University, 1930), pp.580-603.
17. See Max Weber, *Economy and Society: An Outline of Interpretive Sociology*, edited by Guenther Roth and Claus Wittich (University of California Press, 19789).
18. Krasner, "Sovereignty: An Institutional Perspective," pp.66-94.
19. David Dessler, "What's at Stake in the Agent-Structure Debate," *International Organization*, vol.43, no.3 (Summar 1989), pp.441-74.
20. John Gerard Ruggie, "Territoriality and Beyond: Problematizing Modernity in International Relations," *International Organization*, vol.47, no.1 (Winter 1993), pp.139-74. As Ruggie correctly points out, in reality this exclusion cannot be total, for this would imply no contact among states. Over the years this contact has grown and developed into an extensive set of bilateral, plurilateral, and multilateral relationships that allow externally sovereign states to interact with each other.

21. Alexander Wendt, "Anarchy Is What States Make of It: The Social Construction of Power Politics," *International Organization*, vol.46, no.2 (1992), pp.395-421.

22. The distinction between internal and external sovereignty is also helpful in examining other issues in international relations. Yugoslavia provides an example. Although some progress has been achieved in establishing external sovereignty for the successor states of the former Yugoslavia, much work remains to be done to consolidate their internal sovereignty. If this fails, so will the ongoing efforts at sustaining external sovereignty for each successor state. At a more general level, it is probably accurate to assume that, in the evolution of the modern state in western Europe, internal sovereignty preceded the establishment of external sovereignty. In many of the former European colonies, on the other hand, external sovereignty, often imposed from without, was much more developed than its internal counterpart, which in many cases remains weak. See Robert H.Jackson and Carl G.Rosberg, "Why Africa's Weak States Persist: The Empirical and the Juridical in Statehood," *World Politics*, vol.35, no.1 (1982), pp.1-24; Robert H.Jackson, *Quasi-States: Sovereignty, International Relations and the Third World* (Cambridge University Press, 1990). See also Francis Deng and others, *Sovereignty as Responsibility: Conflict Management in Africa* (Brookings, 1996).

23. Ruggie, "Territoriality and Beyond," pp.139-74.

24. As Wendt points out, "the commitment to and the salience of particular identities vary, but each identity is an inherently social definition of the actor grounded in the theories which actors hold about themselves and one another and which constitute the structure of the social world." Wendt. "Anarchy Is What States Make of It," pp.395-421.

25. On this debate see, for example, *International Security*, vol.20 no.1, (Summar 1995), entire issue; Baldwin, "Interdependence and Power"; John Mearsheimer, "Back to the Future: Instability in Europe after the Cold War," *International Security*, vol.13 (Summer 1990), pp.5-56; Robert O.Keohane, *International Institutions and State Power: Essays in International Theory* (Boulder, Colo.: Westview Press, 1989); Joseph M.Grieco, "Anarchy and the Limits of Cooperation: A Realist Critique of the Newest Liberal Institutionalism," *International Organization*, vol.42 (Summer 1988), pp.485-507; Robert O.Keohane, ed., *Neorealism and Its Critics* (Columbia University Press, 1986).

26. The standard work on neorealism in Kenneth N.Waltz, *Theory of International Politics* (Addison-Wesley, 1979).

27. For the distinction between structure and process see Wendt, "Anarchy Is What States Make of It"; on the importance of process for cooperation see Robert Axelrod, *The Evolution of Cooperation* (Basic Books, 1984), and Kenneth A. Oye, ed., *Cooperation under Anarchy* (Princeton University Press, 1986).

28. This explains the liberals' frequent references to the prisoner's dilemma game.
29. Grieco, "Anarchy and the Limits of Cooperation," pp.485-507.
30. Wendt, "Anarchy Is What States Make of It," Wendt does acknowledge that a number of neoliberals have attempted to include theories of complex learning and adaptation in their writings, but argues that "they lack a systematic theory on how such change occurs," p.393.
31. For a distinction between absolute and relative gains see Grieco, "Anarchy and the Limits of Cooperation," pp.485-507.
32. Stephen D.Krasner, "Structural Causes and Regime Consequences: Regimes as Intervening Variables," in Stephen D.Krasner, ed., *International Regimes* (Cornell University Press, 1983), p.2.
33. Highlighting the difference between absolute and relative sovereignty should be the neoliberal rebuttal to the neorealist critique that neoliberals neglect to differentiate between absolute and relative gains - a critique eloquently advanced by Grieco, "Anarchy and the Limits of Cooperation." Thus neoliberals are concerned about relative notions of power, a concern that is embodied in the principle of reciprocity.
34. On "embedded liberalism" see John Gerard Ruggie, "International Regimes, Transactions, and Change: Embedded Liberalism in the Postwar Economic Order," and Stephen D.Krasner, "Structural Causes and Regime Consequences: Regimes as Intervening Variables," both in Stephen D.Krasner, ed., *International Regimes* (Cornell University Press, 1983); the importance of domestic coalitions and interest formation in the context of regimes literature has been demonstrated by Robert Putnam, "Diplomacy and Domestic Politics: The Logic of Two-level Games," *International Organization*, vol.42 (Summar 1988), pp.427-60.
35. John A.C.Conybeare, "Public Goods, Prisoners' Dilemma and the International Political Economy," *International Studies Quarterly*, vol.28 (March 1984), pp.5-22. If and to what degree individual governments use their internal sovereignty to ensure broad-based distribution of the gains is an open question. Rodrik also makes this point when he discusses the social implications of globalization, stating that trade not only increases income but also redistributes it among industries, regions, and individuals. "Therefore, a principled defense of free trade cannot be constructed without addressing the question of the fairness and legitimacy of these distributional `costs.'" See Dani Rodrik, "Sense and Nonsense in the Globalization Debate," *Foreign Policy*, vol.107 (Summar 1997), p.28.
36. Grieco, "Anarchy and The Limits of Cooperation," pp.485-507.
37. Holm and Sorensen also make such an effort. See Hans-Henrik Holm and Georg Sorensen, "Introduction: What Has Changed?" and "International Relations Theory in a World of Variations," in Holm and Sorensen, eds., *Whose World Order*? pp.1-17 and 187-206.

38. Paul Hirst and Grahame Thompson, "The Problems of 'Globalization': International Economic Relations, National Economic Management and the Formation of Trade Blocs, " *Economy and Society*, vol.21, no.4 (November 1992), pp.357-96; see also Paul Hirst and Grahame Thompson, *Globalization in Question: The International Economy and the Possibilities of Governance* (Cambridge, England: Polity Press, 1996).
39. Stephen J.Kobrin, "An Empirical Analysis of the Determinants of Global integration," *Strategic Management Journal*, vol.12 (1991), pp.17-31.
40. See Ruggie, "Territoriality and Beyond," pp.139-74. Ruggie adapted the use of this term from Friedrich Kratochwil, "Of Systems, Boundaries, and Territoriality," pp.27-52.
41. For more on the concept of information asymmetry, see the case studies.
42. The Internet and in particular electronic commerce have not only accelerated that process considerably, but have also given small individual consumers and small producers access to the global marketplace.
43. Kratochwil, "Of Systems, Boundaries, and Territoriality," pp.27-52.
44. See, for example, Hendrik Spruyt, "Institutional Selection in International Relations," *International Organization*, vol.48, no.4 (1994), pp.527-57.
45. Of course, this is not to say that, in a democracy, public policy has never been sensitive to the interests of competing groups, including that of the private sector. In a democracy, "voice" has been and should always be the principal instrument by which different interest groups, including the private sector, shape domestic policymaking. Thus, as discussed above, for example, the voice of the dominant private sector coalitions has been a central factor in determining the path of international economic interdependence and conditioning the positions of governments in international economic regimes. Globalization has changed this dynamic by making the option of "exit" not only a viable and sometimes more convenient option, but also in many cases the necessary, even the natural strategy. For more on exits, see Albert O.Hirschman, *Exit Voice and Loyalty: Responses to Decline in Firms, Organizations, and States* (Harvard University Press, 1970).
46. Marc Granovetter, "Economic Action and Social Structure: The Problem of Embeddedness," *American Journal of Sociology*, vol.91 (November 1985), pp.481-510.
47. James S. Coleman, "Introducing Social Structure into Economic Analysis," *American Economic Review*, vol.74 (May 1984), pp.84-88.
48. The balancing of public and private interests is, of course, not free of conflict. Yet all social actors are in agreement that a certain basic framework, be it of a legal, political, or even social nature, is not only compatible with but even desirable when operating in a market environment. Nowhere has this become more apparent than in the recent process of systemic transformation in the former Eastern bloc.

49. One commentator has taken the argument even further: "The nightmare for politicians is that they are held responsible for their national economies but have fewer ways of affecting the economy's direction. Responsibility without power can be as corrupting as power without responsibility." See E.J. Dionne, "All Politics is Now Global," *Washington Post*, July 13, 1993, p.A15. Another has linked it to the declining attractiveness of public service. "Thus [U.S.] congressional exodus may reflect a sense that what governments do matters less in a world than it is used to because the map of power is being redrawn; not the distribution of power among nations but between national governments on the one hand and non-governmental entities ... on the other. "See Jessica T.Mathews, "Exodus of Authority." *Washington Post*, January 22, 1996, p.A19.
50. Edward Mortimer, "Surfeit of Good Things: The right to vote can be meaningless if the real choices are left to the market and those elected are powerless to act," *Financial Times*, February 28, 1996, p.16.
51. The inability of the interdependence literature to focus on the internal dynamics that arise in response to increased interdependence has recently been acknowldeged. "Missing from this [interdependence] literature, however, was a systematic analysis of how interdependence affected domestic politics," Milner and Keohane, "Internationalization and Domestic Politics," p.7.
52. Ruggie, "Territoriality and Beyond," p.172.
53. The distinction between "somewhere else" and "another place" comes from Ruggie,, "Territoriality and Beyond," pp.139-74.
54. Wendt, "Anarchy Is What States Make of It," pp.395-421.
55. Recall the earlier point that external sovereignty is unsustainable in the longer term if internal sovereignty cannot be maintained, either by democratic or by other means. Historically, internal sovereignty has preceded external sovereignty and has been more important as a constitutive force during the process of state formation.
56. The argument presented here gives strong support to Wendt's analysis, which states that socialization, which is the interaction of states over time, will change states' identities and interests. Yet Wendt had to concede that the strength of his argument depends on "how important interaction among states is for the constitution of their identities and interests." Wendt, "Anarchy Is What States Make of It," p.423. As far as globalization goes, interaction is, of course, vital, since it is the only way to preserve internal sovereignty.
57. Keohane recently acknowledged that his and Nye's analysis in *Power and Interdependence* was limited to the international level, and thus that they "had to view interests [of states] as formed largely exogenously, in a way unexplained by our theory ... [yet] changes in the definitions of self interest ... kept appearing in our case studies." Keohane and Nye, "Power and Interdependence Revisited," p.739.
58. Note that this is different from the notion of declining external sovereignty under the neoliberal paradigm of cooperative competition. There sovereignty was said to decline in absolute terms but remain the same in relative terms. Here external sovereignty has lost its meaning. These are no longer interactions between separate territorial entities.

PART - III

ETHICS, POLITICS, AND PUBLIC ADMINISTRATION

Chapter 9

Accountability and Ethical Dimensions of Good Governance

T.N. Chaturvedi

I

EVOLUTION AND SIGNIFICANCE OF ACCOUNTABILITY

Accountability is today at the core of all democratic discourses. In a manner of speaking it has been the cause or the rationale, as well as the stimulus and accelerator of any people seeking freedom, whether from alien masters or from the holders of authority, whether legal or prescriptive, within the national frontiers. The British rule was from our viewpoint, irresponsible and unaccountable to the people and hence the various phases of attempts at transfer of power through constitutional reforms ultimately culminating in the attainment of Independence. In England itself, the nobles and barons had won the *Magna Carta*, a charter of rights, from King John in the 11th century. In colonial America there was the issue of "No taxation without representation". So, at the heart of the problem of accountability is the question of control of the purse, viz., raising and spending of public resources or the exercise of authority or the control of power. Thus, in a democracy, it is related to empowerment, participation and control of authority by the people.

However, even in a monarchical system, a certain modicum of accountability for actions was expected or prescribed, whether viewed conceptually or historically. So, negatively, the concept of accountability aims to prevent the misuse or abuse of power and authority, while, positively, it seeks to ensure the satisfaction of people's demands and a better order of things, which can be termed as good governance.

The concept of accountability revolves round the problem of administrative and political power. As James Madison remarked in one of the Federalist papers: "if men were angels, no government would be necessary. If angels were to govern men, neither external nor internal controls on government would be necessary."[1] Here in lies the significance of Accountability.

Accountability has various facets or aspects. As a concept it has a complexity of its own, and, naturally, as a consequence in implementation and even in enforcement. That is why it is often called an amorphous concept. We hear of diffused responsibility and that nobody can be held accountable for any acts of commission or omission. Thus one has to be clear not only about the locus and focus but also of the structures and different layers of authority. In practical terms, it is the question of a conscious design of the system to pinpoint accountability in specific individuals. But even otherwise, it may be said that like electricity, it may not be visible to the naked eye, but it is felt, can be realised and even perceived in the end result. It has been rightly said: "Accountability begins with individuals in simple societies. It ends with instructions in complex societies."[2]

With increasing political and social consciousness, there is a clamour for the need to demonstrate a sense of accountability on the part of not only individuals holding political and public offices but all public institutions, collectively exercising any power on the public, on its behalf or in its name. That is why there is public insistence that not only politicians and political parties but other sections of society like industry, business, trade and commerce, the judiciary and the legal profession, medical and academic or teaching professions, science and technology also have to be held to account for their activities and conduct as groups and individuals. It is strongly contended that even voluntary organisations, co-operative institutions or non-governmental movements and organisations which are considered to be a countervailing force to State power too cannot escape the imperatives of accountability. The mode of manifestation of accountability will naturally take different forms. A strong need for building an environment of accountability in society and in government is being felt. It is in this context that there has been all over the world, particularly in our country, and other developing countries, extensive discussion about the social responsibility of various segments or institutions of any influence. Apart from the legal framework, the emphasis is on the need to develop an effective code of conduct and professional ethics. If the widespread feeling in the people is allowed to grow that neither politics nor administration has adequate sense of responsibility, it is apt to endanger the very fabric of democracy and as concept it gets vulgarised.

Usually, the terms accountability and responsibility are used interchangeably. Sometimes a distinction is made between the two. Accountability is considered to be more external in character and responsibility as more concerned with the inner life or something within as an individual. Even in the case of such sophistry, one reinforces the other. It is the sense of responsibility which will pave the way for a 'responsible society' or a 'responsible government' and strengthen the climate of external or visible accountability and its operation in society. So, the two are inextricably linked and intertwined. It is the psychological dimension of accountability or responsibility which becomes important. Constitutional democracy is really based upon the political responsibility of individual citizens and enlightened citizenry as a whole. The philosophical and metaphysical element, thus, does have a relevance to the problem of responsibility and accountability. The entire concept is not simply mechanistic. The deeper nuances lead to the question of values and ethics in this wide spectrum of accountability. It is from this angle that we emphasise that accountability is threefold - to oneself, to the professional group or organisation that one may belong to, and to society at large. And it is the lack of harmonisation between these three that causes discontent, dissatisfaction and leads to confrontation and violence in society.

It has to be remembered that accountability begins when individuals or institutions are given tasks or power on behalf of fellow citizens, but it is demanded not of serfs but from autonomous or free citizens. Serfs in Greece and Rome were only ordered, by their masters to carry out task. No accountability was expected of them. It is wrong to juxtapose the two as opposing categories. There is no contradiction and conflict between the two. It is all a question of the delicacy and ingenuity of management. Accountability is not inimical to exercise of discretion and autonomy. Conceptually and operationally, the claims of autonomy and the compulsions of accountability have to be looked upon as two aspects of the same coin. The operationalisation of accountability depends upon the nature of the constitutional and political system of each country, its history and traditions and the framework of laws and regulations operating therein. The processes, procedures, institutions and instrumentalities, accordingly, develop and are conditioned. While in Athenian democracy or the village democracy of ancient India, the mode of accountability, its working and impact was simple, in a parliamentary democracy and federal form of government in today's international and complex society, the efficacy of the concept of accountability hinges on how carefully the mechanisms, institutions and instrumentalities are designed to ensure the goals of accountability. So, we can never be oblivious of the constitutional and political framework and its requirements.

While discussing the problem of accountability in a specific situation one has to deal with the problems of delegation, of discretion (how, why and in whose favour), of the relevance of formal law or even the relevance of natural justice to political and administrative responsibility, and the relative merits and feasibility of individual as opposed to collective forms of responsibility or accountability. We are aware as to how the concept of judicial review has expanded enormously in India during recent years through public interest litigation (PIL) by concerned individuals or social activist groups. This underscores its far-reaching implications and consequences for individuals exercising power and public servants required by the courts to pay compensation to aggrieved individuals personally or sometimes even to compensate the state exchequer. This obviously rests on the assumption that the errant individual office holder should be made to bear this burden as the constitutional democracy is designed for that very purpose of fixation of responsibility. As Herbert J.Spiro goes on to argue and link the process of accountability and responsibility with the fundamental question of legitmisation of political power under constitutional and democratic governments or why obey government: "It was achieved by dividing and subdividing the power once held by a unitary sovereign monarch, until all citizens have come to share it. Consequently, all share responsibility for the manner in which the one-time sovereign wielded. Politics is the process by which distribution of this responsibility throughout the political system is determined. Government is the structure of responsibility. And the problem of the citizen's responsibility for government has become at least as important as that of the jurisdiction of his obedience to government."[3] And those who are entrusted with authority or power under the Constitution cannot themselves claim to be beyond its purview!

Responsibility and Accountability

Some political philosophers and constitutional commentators have conceptually distinguished the meaning of responsibility in three different ways - (1) Responsibility as accountability; (2) Responsibility - as cause (explicit or implicit causal responsibility); (3) Responsibility as obligation. These are not really exclusive of each other either philosophically or practically. H.L.A. Hart in his *Punishment and Responsibility* gives a four-fold classification, viz. (1) Role-Responsibility; (b) Causal responsibility; (c) Liability - Responsibility; (d) Capacity - Responsibility. Another political scientist, Donald Wismithburg, distinguishes four uses of the term: mere obligation, responsiveness, accountability and legitimacy. It is not proposed to go into the philosophical foundations or parameters of accountabilities any further. All these shades of meaning or nuances of the term responsibility or accountability are mutually supportive and have practical connotation as has been evident in India during the constitutional and political discourse during the last few decades.

Political and bureaucratic or administrative accountability flows from their congruence. Responsiveness as a term was popularised in the context of citizen administration interface, decentralised decision-making and political processes, popularly called grassroots democracy. Responsiveness to whom and in what manner and with what intent, are the questions that arose. Responsiveness to popular will and public interest and law or submission to the interests and whims of fleeting political masters, has been a nagging problem in administration. Similarly, it has been seen in the recent politics of India as to how even constitutional legitimacy and authority become completely eroded due to the erosion of moral authority through allegations of graft, corruption, cronyism, favouritism, venality and similar moral and criminal misdemeanours in the higher echelons of political authority. There has been public insistence on the fixation of responsibility and enforcement of accountability as confidence in constitutional democracy has come to be questioned. In India we have adopted parliamentary form of government. The pattern of accountability is inbuilt into the system, though the grievance of the people is that it has got enfeebled in the course of enforcement due to the very deinstitutionalisation of the system which is supposed to take care of it. Our government is politically and constitutionally accountable to Parliament and thus to the people. Thus, this is the democratic concept of popular accountability and ministerial accountability. Ministerial or Cabinet responsibility can be subdivided into collective responsibility of the Cabinet and the individual responsibility of the minister. It is conditioned by the particular situation. Ministerial responsibility has also been looked at as moral responsibility or even punitive responsibility. It is in the context of public trust or a fiduciary relationship between the governor and the governed. Again, there is financial accountability. Accountability for probity is concerned with the avoidance of malfeasance and maximisation of resources for public good. It has really developed through ages independent of political accountability. It is here that the concept of independent audit comes in. In a manner of speaking,the need to fix responsibility or hold somebody accountable arises in cases of gross and callous inefficiency leading to public suffering, wilful attempt to cover mistakes, failure to take positive decision or required initiative despite discretion or authority and abuse or misuse of power and authority for some personal ends, direct or indirect, and not for public purpose. If there is persistent disregard of such lapses, the system gets into disrepute.

Concept of Independent Audit

The Indian Constitution has created the autonomous office of the Comptroller and Auditor-General of India, which is supposed to ensure the financial accountability of the government to the people through Parliament by submitting its report on financial transactions. Public audit is neither static nor negative in orientation. It is a developing function. Parliament has a permanent committee system to enforce responsibility. The Public Accounts Committee (PAC) and Committee on Public Undertakings (COPU) have done commendable work in this connection. Recently the system of subjects related standing committees has been inaugurated and has started well. Sometimes when any matter has become controversial or agitated the public mind, adhoc parliamentary committees are setup, such as those which examined the purchase of the Howitzer guns or securities scam. The committees function on the basis of directions of the Speaker or the conventions of the British Parliamentary system or as developed in the working of our own parliamentary system. The members of the committees are supposed to be nonpartisan in approach. The action taken reports are presented by the government to Parliament. The committees have no executive authority. They only make suggestions or recommendations and also criticise at times administrative functioning. But the effectiveness of the committee system depends on the responsiveness of the government itself and the pressure of public opinion as is exercised through Parliament.[4]

Ministerial Responsibility

It is through ministerial responsibility that control on bureaucracy or administration is exercised. Answerability of the minister for his department is the hallmark of democracy. In the U.K. and elsewhere a good deal of literature has been generated on the subject. This brings us to the vexed question of the relationship between the minister and his secretary. It is for the minister to hold his civil servants to account, but he cannot escape his parliamentary and ultimate responsibility for the acts of omission or commission of his department. It is sometimes referred to as constructive or moral responsibility. The public expects the minister to keep the civil servants in check. It may suffice to point out that Justice M.C.Chagla in the *Mundra case* said: "It is clear that a minister must take the responsibility for actions done by his subordinates. He cannot take shelter behind them, nor can he disown their actions". According to him, the assumption is that the policy once laid down by the minister is carried out by the civil servant, and if the latter feels that to do so he may be punished or dismissed, the responsibility of his action must be assumed by the minister. Similar views were expressed quite strongly by the Joint Parliamentary Committee set up to look into the securities scam in India. In England in the 1950s, Lord Carrington had to resign his office as minister in the wake of the Crichel Down affair though he was in no way personally involved in the scam, which was perpetuated by the civil servants of his department. As the minister responsible for the department, he was responsible for its actions, and he had to go.[5]

Nature and Ladder of Accountability

We have a written Constitution which enshrines the rule of law, and we come across the term legal or judicial accountability of the political as well as the permanent executive. This has come very much in focus recently due to some striking cases of political malfeasance. PIL has become fashionable as people nurse the grievance that politics and administration have both become unaccountable and insensitive. But one is not sure if it is the permanent remedy in the same way as antibiotics cannot be a substitute for efforts to live a healthy life. It is the enforcement of the rule of law that becomes of paramount importance.

From the viewpoint of democratic governance as J.D.Steward has done, we can look at the concept of public, popular or electoral accountability as a ladder of accountability;

Accountability for probity and legality.
Process accountability.
Performance accountability.
Programme accountability.
Policy accountability.

It is a ladder that leads from accountability by standards to accountability by judgement.[6]

In administrative vocabulary, the concept of accountability is directly related to the concepts of rule of law, right to information, transparency, administrative sensitivity and responsiveness, procedural and administrative reforms, value for money, result orientation, implementation and performance as well as long-term policy perspective and policy-making. This will also pave the way for macro-level as well as micro-level accountability.

In a democratic country, public accountability is an assertion that all authority is derived from the people. But the significance of authority as the right to call the weilders of power to account needs to be supplemented by the notion of power as the ability to call to account, through the exercise of control over performance: the principal element in accountability. Those who are entrusted with authority must be made to realise that for their allotted tasks, they have to work and they also must be made to realise that the authorities above mean it seriously. Accountability, in simple terms, means to render an account of one's action and so it relates to measures in terms of performance fully understood by accepted standards. It is this realisation that is the beginning of the ethos and culture of accountability. Though a complex concept, it must be understood that it is more than just an effort at fighting corruption. It really aims at and facilitates good governance, which can really ensure the credibility and stability of a democratic system. It is the effectiveness of enforceability of accountability that ultimately matters. If misgivings in the public mind develop about the willingness or the strength and purposefulness of the system in enforcing and ensuring accountability the possibility of good governance obviously recedes.

II

ETHICS IN PUBLIC LIFE

When the conduct of public business is shrouded in mystery and if the sense of accountability is at a discount in public affairs, many ethical dilemmas arise.

The maintenance of moral standards and norms in the conduct of public affairs in a democratic country tends to become a major problem for the people because of different levels of Government and the involvement of a large number of public functionaries in government. It is their perceptions on the presence of venality in public life, lack of integrity in government, and what is wrong and what is right in politics, which determine their faith in a democratic system. The ethical values that permeate the elected representatives, the executive, the legislature or negative influences exercised by political parties, pressure groups, lobbies and extra-constitutional authorities that very often spring up in the twilight zone of politics have a deep and lasting impact on the character, direction, dependence, credibility and the future of the system of representative government. The potential damage and threat to the political fabric of a system is not dependent on the character of government, i.e. whether it is an activist or limited in scope. History shows that neither a capitalist nor a socialist and communist nor a welfare State is immune to the corrosive evil of corruption. The standards of conduct and behaviour of people in political authority have their malignant influence in other walks of life in society. The ethical dimensions of how influential and powerful people conduct themselves in private life and the public domain set a precedent for the lesser human beings and groups in society to follow or to seek justification for their own self-seeking or even scandalous conduct. The perniciousness of ripple-effect encompasses all segments of society. It is not only the public systems that are under attack. The people harbour grievances against trade, industry, business, academia, medical and other professional groups and organisations in society. The evil within and outside the government circle is, thus, not limited to any narrow confines. Similarly, the influence of ethical conduct in positive terms is also not contained or concerned with only some specific sections and select groups but is relevant to the entirety of society and its wider network of relationships. As is often said, the moral basis for the unity and stability of society demands that ethical restraints must operate not only in respect of individuals but also organised groups - be they industrial, business and trade associations, labour unions, political parties, military and civil services, judiciary, non-governmental organisations, academic or professional associations, agriculturists organisations, etc. - apart from government itself. The all-pervading and inter-locking nature of ethics in public life is to be comprehended in all its manifestations and dimensions. This is borne out by history in different climes and ages and also by the progress of civilization today.

This problem is a continuing one and, therefore, a matter of continuing debate. It acquires a sharp edge and intensity in special circumstances and particular times. There is a widespread feeling that the present context all over the world, more so in our country, is such that the many facets of ethics in public life merit scrutiny. The scandals and cases of corruption, kickbacks, bribery, extortions, lying and deception by government all over the world, in both developed and developing countries at different times, are too many and too well-known to need any enumeration. In the wake of many cases of nepotism, influence-peddling, corporate bribery, corruption, wheeling-dealing, illicit operations, business malpractices, and unhealthy nexus between politics, administration and business coming to public notice at the time of the World War II, the US Senate set up a sub-committee under Senator Paul Doughlas, which submitted its report, commonly known as the Report on Ethical Standards in Government. This attracted attention all over the world and the various nuances of ethics in governance were discussed, researched and commented upon in various forums. The professional journals in social sciences, particularly those on public administration and political science, have devoted considerable attention to the issues of morality in politics and public life.

Defining the Morals or Ethics

The *Oxford English Dictionary* defines ethics as the science of morals or moral principles. It is very often used as a synonym or even an interchangeable expression for terms like values, norms, standards, morality, etc. In recent years, even the phrase 'social responsibility' has been used. Actually, the nuances merge despite the semantic distinctions.

No sophistry or analysis of philosophical implications is required for our purpose. There is convergence about the social and operational significance of the matter, even if there is lack of agreement in conceptualisation or rigorous philosophical definition. It has no narrow religious, sectarian or cradle implications. Ethics is again something like electricity, not apparent to the naked eye, but felt instantaneously in specific conditions and visible when power is switched on. It has something to do with the sense of right and wrong - what is permissible, what is not done.

Ethics has several attributes, some of which are universalistic in nature, while others are also bound by time and place. It may be specific to a particular task, situation, profession or area of responsibility, e.g. ethics of a doctor or a chartered accountant. Certain things are expected from everyone while there may be a few specific things expected according to the nature of groups or responsibilities. Ethics is something related to a state of mind, a way of looking at things which may develop into a pattern of behaviour or way of life and social conduct. One's values may indicate or reveal one's preferences, while norms identify social prescriptions or obligations which have a regulatory significance.

Ethics cannot be shaped and sustained in isolation. The heuristic process requires a supportive environment in which public opinion plays a significant part. In every field of activity, the components of ethical behaviour have to be identified and its dynamics worked out and appreciated. Efficiency, economy, effectiveness, equity and equality of treatment, and excellence, among others, are deemed to be commonly the ingredients essential to the conduct of public life and harmonious social relationships. Thus an entire culture or value system of ethical conduct is built up.

Application of Ethics

Its application and operation in specific situations become evident so that the generality of people recognise it. It is maintained and sustained by a sense of responsibility - not merely accountability to some external agency but also to something within. O.Glen Stahl, who did pioneering work in the area, especially in stressing the need for its study in the curriculum of Public Administration, rightly observed: "the problem of ethical conduct for public officials arises by virtue of the power and influence that he commands and the commitment that he undertakes of loyal and disinterested service to the public."[7] This has a number of operational implications, both in the case of elected as well as non-elected officials. The tragedy of the situation is that people feel that neither do elected public officials follow the constitutional oath administered to them, nor are public servants prepared to advise or act without fear or favour.

Another aspect to be kept in view is that ethical standards may transcend the narrow stipulations of law or rule book and code of regulations - many acts of omission or commission may not violate the law as such but may run counter to the norms of propriety, fairness, intellectual integrity, accountability and societal expectations. That is why in public life, be it politics or administration, the use, non-use, misuse and abuse of authority assume paramount importance for the public as well as the respository or wielder of that lawful authority. People are prone to believe that the information they are entitled as citizens to get from the government is withheld or access to authority is barred by gatekeepers. In such a milieu, the rightful publicity or public relations on the part of the government is looked at with considerable skepticism and disbelief. It is such a situation which has given rise to demand of the right to information and elimination of unnecessary secret in conduct of public affairs.

Faith of people in the ethical behaviour of public officials helps to narrow, and even bridge, this chasm. A similar note is struck by Cheseter I. Barnard, a well known management expert, when he characterizes moral behaviour or ethical conduct as "governed by beliefs or feelings of what is right or wrong regardless of self-interest or immediate consequence of a decision to do or not to do specific things under particular condition." Ethical behaviour is partly a matter of civilisation legacy, family inheritance, a fall-out of personal philosophy but, is certainly a social imperative if the society is to have an equilibrium conducive to social cohesiveness and good life. In the social perspective, it does become for an individual, at times, a matter of conscience or "inner voice" as Mahatma Gandhi called it. Efforts to remedy the pervasive malady of corruption has generally negative contours and connotations. Ethical conduct or ethics in public life has wider and positive dimensions and implications as well as possibilities.

Legislative and Electoral Reforms

As the legislature is the heart of the representative democracy, the legislature and legislative process become the starting point for any discussion of the subject. That is how the question of electoral reforms and fair and free electoral process came to the force. The quality, moral and intellectual, of legislators create misgivings in public mind. It becomes a matter for self-introspection as to why and how the words 'politics' and 'politicians' - even as popular representatives - should acquire pejorative connotations. Is public interest for them only factional or personal interest? Are legislative privileges meant for effective and honest public service or for self-aggrandisement? What kind of interest do they take in policy-making and law-making which are of prime importance in a democratic society? Do they become surrogates for some vested powerful interests or do they function conscientiously in honest discharge of their duties? The elected representatives are the chief instruments of promoting and defending the general public interest. On them squarely rests the responsibility of government, the responsibility to make public policy serve the general public rather than any special interest or particular group. And they cannot be allowed to evade or dilute it.

So far as the Government or the executive is concerned, it is supposed to be a repository of public trust. But is it even aware of the nature and sanctity of the trust? The scams and scandals, wheeling-dealing by power brokers, operations of economic buccaneers, and commissions and cutbacks epitomise only the betrayal of public trust. Public policy receives the lip service and public choice is determined by exceptions or deviations from the law and rules dictated by the impulse for personal enrichment or by the ostensible plea of filling the party coffers. With deviations from law or bending of rules, criminality breeds within and outside the system, and then it feeds on it. Distributive justice becomes a mere slogan to befuddle and confuse the common man. People are almost convinced that first in the name of socialist planning and then in the process of unwinding it or of disinvestments in public sector or liberalisation of the economy, the public domain continues to be a grazing pasture for the predatory politicians and their freebooting cohorts. The change in the models of development makes no difference to the keptomanic impulses that move those who run the government. Moral amnesia continues to prevail and any concept of accountability is considered to be an unmitigated nuisance. Even the idea of constructive accountability and moral responsibility is being ridiculed, whatever the unanimous report of the Joint Parliamentary Committee on Securities Scam may say or however much the intellectuals may hark back to the cannons of ministerial responsibility as laid down by Chagla Commission on Mundra case in the time of our Prime Minister Jawaharlal Nehru. Very often, the political executive provides either protection for collective self-aggrandisement and political skullduggery to public servants or tries to pulverise and politicise the permanent services, adding to the pathology of administration which the common man daily bewails but to which he helplessly submits. The administrative machinery is occasionally misused to settle political scores. At certain times public servants doing their duty become the plaything of factional politics. At other times public servants establish cosy relationship with politicians to seek their own selfish ends. Criminalisation of just administration at a point of time is curable but when it inundates the entire machinery of the State it poses a grave threat to democracy. The rampant corruption, growing indiscipline, lack of sensitivity and allergy to the very word accountability in administration have vitiated the relationship between the governors and the governed - indeed the servants and the masters in democracy. Nehru invariably exhorted the public servants and political masters on all possible occasions to beware of the pit-falls in this regard. But things have gone from bad to worse during the years.

Politicization and Commercialisation of Crimes

The feeling is growing that the Rule of Law is only a camouflage for double-standards and doublespeak. There is the usual talk of politicization of crime and criminalisation of politics. It has assumed the form of commercialisation of both crime and politics. Development, which was geared to solve social tensions and bring about social harmony, has given rise to fresh tensions due to distortions and inequities in the developmental process. The development of land for providing housing to people has become playground for mafia and real estate sharks. What was for long known and believed has been authenticated by the Vohra Committee Report. But such is the penumbra of distrust in public that the Supreme Court had to ask for its authenticated version and a report on action taken thereon.

In the corridors of power, the charlatans and Rasputins continue to strut majestically to the utter dismay of the common man. People ask as to how in India only one minister has gone to jail for corruption since Independence despite a plethora of inquiry commissions, committees, judicial pronouncements, parliamentary disapprobation and public clamour. According to a political analyst S.Andresk, 'unhindered plundering at top reduces democracy to kleptocracy'. This undermines people's faith, even all development efforts. People are aware of the Lockheed scandal in Japan in the 1970s and its consequences when the Japanese Prime Minister was unseated and jailed. The exposure of corporate payoffs and 'lubrication' payments have tainted international government -business relations leading to distrust of multinationals. This is also apparent from many contributions to this issue. In Japan, Prime Ministers and Ministers are punished for graft. US President Richard Nixon had to resign after the Watergate scandal. In Italy, many politicians are in prison for corruption and their links with the mafia and two former Prime Ministers are being prosecuted. In France, recently investigations have been ordered against Prime Minister Alain Jupee, and at least three former ministers. But sweet reasonableness and all-quiet on our front creates disquiet in the public mind. Mafias in every walk of life seem to flourish and parallel channels of settlement of disputes are cropping up when even laws' delays become chronic. The parallel economy seems to dictate the matter of policy and society inspite of occasional moral indignation.

People perceive a widening hiatus between promise and performance, policy and practice, and plan and implementation. Hypocrisy is the last refuge of many power-wielding sections in society. Trade, business and industry continue to organise seminars, invite ministers and officials to discuss the role and responsibility of business and their ethics in the context of globalisation, liberalisation and free-market economy. Can democratic government withstand the pressure of market forces, if so how? People suspect that such gatherings are aimed more to show either political clout or cultivate men in seats of authority. Such is the incredulity! Scarcity continues to raise its head to the distress of the common man. Liberalisation, to many, raises the question of the social cost to the vulnerable sections in society. Quality continues to be at a discount; productivity is low. Nowhere is there evidence of self-regulation. Inventing and hunting for alibis and pretexts is the usual ploy. As a perspective writer puts it: "This unseen, often used but more often abused term `system', holds the country in its paralytic grip. It is the favourite *alibi* for sloth, indolence and non-performance. It is the table at which the buck - of corruption, non-accountability, negligence and inefficiency - stops. What is egregious is not just the use of this word `system' as a convenient *alibi*, but in fact that its widespread usage has elevated it to a status of its passive acceptance on the part of one and all - it is almost as if everyone waits with bated breath for the result of most inquiries at the door of the system. It is the universal appeasement for everyone and then nothing is heard of the issue till another crisis occurs leading to the reopening of all old cupboards to pull out nostalgic skeletons."[8]

When the government and administration abdicate their responsibility and are insensitive to their duties or indifferent and callous to public good, there is no alternative but to approach the judiciary, the custodian of liberties and rights. If the discretion of men who have power cannot be trusted, the only recourse left is to limit it by law. But at a time when the judiciary is also under stress of various kinds and is overburdened, its reach cannot be a substitute for administrative fairness, responsiveness and sensitivity. It can lead to further administrative rigidity and even administrative paralysis. It cannot administer on behalf of those who are supposed to govern in terms of the Constitution. Judicial activism cannot, in a big country like ours, be the substitute for an effective political system and efficient administration. It only adds to social and economic 'inefficiency' unless the different wings, as envisaged in the Constitution, activate themselves and act in harmony with due sense of dilatoriness, responsibility and restraint. The dilatoriness of judicial processes is itself becoming proverbial. Much is expected from the Press and the non-governmental or voluntary organisations as in default of political leadership they do represent the collective conscience and the will of the people. In the recent past, they have also fallen under a deep and dark shadow of suspicion and deviation from the path of rectitude. Many in the Press have succumbed to allurements and blandishments of the government as was reported and commented upon recently with reference to a few states. This fortunately has initiated a process of self-critical and inward look in the media. Some of the NGOs have been officially censured for feathering their nests and other malpractices, while people look upon them as countervailing power to the arrogance of authority of maladministration in civil society. Idealism in the common man is not dead and it is the voluntary power and the might of the Press which can arouse and awaken it for constructive task of nation-building. But it is not difficult for them to redeem themselves for the redemption of the country from the morass which seems to have engulfed the country. Only four days before his assassination Mahatma Gandhi thus warned the country during his prayer meeting: "The subject of corruption referred to by the correspondent is not new. Only it has become much worse than before. Restraint from without has practically gone. Corruption will go when the large number of persons given to the unworthy practice realise the nation does not exist for them but they do for the nation. It requires a high code of morals, extreme vigilance on the part of those who are free from the corrupt practice and who have influence over corrupt servants. Indifference in such matters is criminal. If our evening prayers are genuine, they must play no mean part in removing from our midst the demon of corruption" (M.K.Gandhi, Delhi Diary, 26 January 1948). Unfortunately the warning went unheeded. Gandhi's uninvolved and reverberating voice of truth and compassion can still help to galvanise the country if the common man asserts himself. In democracy, it is the collective will of the people that would matter ultimately and to this fact History is an eloquent witness.

Stopping the Moral Decay

The need for organisation, activation, articulation and assertion of public opinion and enlightened citizenship is the life-breath of any vibrant democratic system. Public apathy leads to moral decay. Public vigilance and public awareness of its role and responsibilities provides a safeguard to the sustenance of ethical conduct of public affairs. The politics of governance in a democratic set-up cannot be allowed to degenerate into political self-aggrandisement and political chicanery. It is well to recall here that what the then United States Secretary of the Interior, Harold Ickes said during the hearings of the Ethics Committee: "Within my knowledge, no public officer has bribed himself", and he went on to emphasise the fact that official morality is more than a political problem. "By all means let us consider how to assist in the establishment of higher moral standards in the official conduct of the Government, but at the same time let us realise that we cannot hope to assist the Government in this regard unless we are willing to assist ourselves and each other in the establishment of higher moral standards as between `man and man in private life'. Politics is an important part, an integral part, but only a part of the whole pattern of life".[10]

Inspite of the encircling gloom, it is wrong to think that all is lost and the decay in political system is irreversible. There is an intellectual churning. There is a questioning of many assumptions and practices. Very often, there are successful expressions of moral indignations. Despite trenchant critique, and castigation of the dismal scenario, the scholars come out with a number of constructive suggestions which are pregnant with possibilities. It is neither feasible nor necessary to discuss them in detail. By way of illustration, we may mention a few such as the need for moral education, electoral and parliamentary reforms, campaign ethics, transparency in functions, improved parliamentary practices, setting up of Ethics committee in legislatures, demystification of governmental processes, greater public awareness of public issues, strict enforcement of Rule of Law, scientific method of reward and punishment in public services, fairness and firmness in public dealings, better understanding of both rights and duties by citizens, measures for improvement in functioning of political parties, disclosure of assets by people in authority, stress on accountability, promotion of professional ethics, greater emphasis on efficiency, responsiveness and sensitivity in administration, expeditious investigation and early disposal of court cases, appointment of *Lokpal* and so on. They are not pious cliches or platitudes. They can and are to be institutionalised and operationalised. But a ritualistic approach will only breed further disenchantment. It is the inner check within the individual citizen enlivened with moral temper of society that can reinforce institutional and legal checks. As Senator Paul H. Douglas said in his famous Hodkin Lectures at Harvard: "Since the state is but the individual writ large, perhaps the disclosures of the past years may reawaken within us a sense of our individual failure to live upto the standards we inwardly cherish. The faults we see in the government are all for often the reflection of our moral failures. All this may dawn upon us, so that we will not only help to reform government but also to reform ourselves. If it does, the regenerative power both of democracy and of the human spirit will have another great victory in the continual moral struggle which goes on within each of us and within society."[11] Does it have for us a contemporary ring and relevance?

It is a pity that during the last decades, many institutions which facilitate the working of democracy and ensure accountability, were deliberately denigrated. They have to regain their resilience and vitality so as to fulfill the functions they are supposed to perform. Building of institutions and their credibility is a difficult but creative task in democracy. When all institutions function, as enshrined in the Constitution or set up according to law, with elan and in harmony with utmost intellectual sincerity and with public interest as the sole guiding star, it is only then that the governance of men acquire a moral legitimacy which temporary aberrations cannot destroy. Transparency in politics and public affairs is one of the powerful instruments to accomplish. Mahatma Gandhi gave us the well-known talisman for decision-making in our day-to-day work as to how a particular action or a decision affects the poorest of the poor whom we may have seen. Is it not of universal significance and relevance today? Our scriptures have also always emphasised the moral imperative to do to others the same as we want to be done to us. Is it not practical wisdom of ethical behaviour in public life? Having adopted the national moto of *Satyameva Jayate* (Truth always triumphs), people legitimately expect that the governance of the country will be carried on some moral principles and ideals as embodied in the Constitution. This is the matter of soul-searching. It is the moral legitimacy of the political regime which is the bulwark of a democratic and representative government. Like that Apostle of Truth Mahatma Gandhi, Thomas Jefferson provides a guideline for men concerned with public affairs so that there is no deviation and departure from rectitude in public affairs. this is as follows: "Whenever you are to do a thing, though it can never be known but to yourself how you would act were all the world looking at you, and act accordingly."

NOTES & REFERENCES

1. Alexander Hamilton, James Madison, and John Jay, *The Federalist*, Harvard University Press, 1961.
2. Patricia Day and Dudelf Klein, *Accountabilities: Five Public Services*, Tavistock, London, 1987.
3. Herbert, J. Spiro, *Responsibility in Government*, Van Norstrand, New York, 1969.
4. K.S.Ramchandran (ed.) : *Watching Over a Watch Dog - Public Accountability - Role of CAG*, Ashish, Delhi, 1991.
5. C.P.Bhambhri, *Bureaucracy and Politics in India*, Vikas, Delhi, 1971.
6. Anthony Hopwood and Cyril Tomkins, (ed.) *Issues in Public Sector Accounting*, Heritage, Delhi, 1985.
7. Srivats Krishna, *The Hindustan Times*, 15 Oct., 1995.
8. M.K.Gandhi, *Delhi Diary*, 26 Jan., 1948, Allahabad, Navjivan Press.
9. George A. Graham, *American Politics*, Louisiana University Press, 1952.
10. Paul H. Douglas, *Ethics in Government*, Harvard University Press, 1953.

Chapter 10

Ethics in Public Life and Corporate Governance in the United Kingdom Today

© *Rosamund Thomas*

1. Modern ethics in public life: where it began and why?

The British Civil Service, together with that of France, were reported in 1986 by Mr.Christopher Tugendhat, as being "the two best" in the European Community. The British Civil Service was "very much admired" for its objectivity, fairness and impartiality.[1] Why, then, the emphasis in the 1990s on a need for `Ethics in Public Life'?

The modern issue of 'Ethics in Public Life' began in the United States with the Watergate scandal in the early 1970s. The conduct of Federal public servants - both careerists and political appointees up to the top echelons - was examined by experts in political science in the post-Watergate era and led to a number of changes: the enactment in 1978 of the Federal *Ethics in Government Act*[2] (amended in 1989 by the *Ethics Reform Act*); renewed attention in major US universities to education and training for the Public Service; and internal reforms within the Federal bureaucracy. The first *Ethics in Government Act* of 1978, which created new criminal and civil offences for the misuse of power, position and information by public servants in the Federal Executive Branch of Government, was extended Government-wide by the 1989 *Ethics Reform Act* to cover Congress and the Judiciary.

Canada felt the impact of Watergate in so far as during the 1970s the Federal *Conflict of Interest Code* for Ministers and civil servants was strengthened several times. Canada concentrated at Federal level, then, mainly on financial conflicts of interest in contrast to today's world interest in wider issues of 'Ethics in Public Life'.

State Governments in the United States followed the Federal law with variations of ethics and conflict of interest statutes. Although the Canadian Federal Government kept to non-statutory Code covering financial and other conflict of interests, Provinces in Canada passed laws in these respects.

In other countries institutional developments were put in place to combat corruption, such as the setting up of Independent Commissions Against Corruption: for example, in Hong Kong to combat corruption among, for example, police officers and seek to make constructive progress in reducing types of behaviour in public life which threaten progress in socio-economic terms and in international trade.

'Ethics in Public Life' in its modern form emerged in the 1970s with the above-stated developments ranging on a spectrum, or scale, from measures to deal with a former public official who retires with valuable government contacts which he/she may seek to exploit for personal gain - to criminal offences of corruption within, say, the police or other parts of a public bureaucracy.

2. The United Kingdom approach to ethics in public life: before and after Nolan

The post-Watergate reforms in North America of ethics legislation and anti-corruption institutional measures in the Far East and elsewhere largely passed the United Kingdom by. The British Civil Service, founded on the principles of the Northcote-Trevelyan Report of 1853, espoused the convention of political neutrality, which was upheld by 'on the job' training, and later by the establishment of the Civil Service College in 1969, as well as by a disciplinary Code.[3] Criminal laws had existed to cover offences of corruption and unauthorised disclosure of information from the turn of the century, namely the *Prevention of Corruption Acts* (1889-1916) and the *Official Secrets Acts* (1911-1939). The 1960s and early 1970s saw some instances of corruption in English local government particularly in respect to the awarding of contracts for public building works which oversplit into British Central government. A Royal Commission on Standards of Conduct in Public Life, under the Chairmanship of Lord Salmon, reported in 1974, but the Report remained largely unimplemented.[4] Breaches of trust arose especially during the 1980s when civil servants, such as Clive Ponting and Sarah Tisdall, were prosecuted under the *Officials Secrets Acts* for unauthorised disclosure of official information and in 1989 the *Official Secrets Acts* were amended.[5] In the main, however, the British Civil Service continued to be renowned for its lack of corruption. 'Ethics' was not a word being used in the context of public life: rather, the term was 'standards of conduct'.

The 1990s brought change in the British Civil Service: privatisation of a growing number of State functions had taken place from 1979; contracting out of numerous other government services; a renewed emphasis on financial efficiency and reductions in the numbers of civil servants, together with the separation of Executive tasks into Executive Agencies: the Civil Service College, for example, became an Executive Agency in June 1989.[6] At the same time Parliament was experiencing increasing pressures from the growth of professional lobbyists and a lack of clarity about the acceptance of gifts, hospitality and outside employment by Members of Parliament and Ministers of the Crown. Citizens, too, were becoming more aware through media coverage of issues of public and private behaviour by their elected representatives. The consumer-led society of the 1990s in Britain was voicing opinions about the standards they expected of those in public life. A minority number of individual cases involving unacceptable behaviour of Ministers and Members of Parliament led the then Conservative Minister,

John Major, MP, to set up the Nolan Committee, under an independent Judge, Lord Nolan (replaced in 1997 by Sir Patrick Neill, QC and now known as the Neill Committee) to inquire into 'Standards in Public Life'. Now in the late 1990s an 'ethics explosion' has arisen worldwide, coupled to an anti-corruption drive, with governments, businesses, universities, and professional bodies like those of Accountancy and Law, seeking to teach and practise 'Ethics in Public Life and Corporate Governance'. The term 'ethics' has been adopted now in Britain alongside that of 'standards of conduct'.

3. The positive approach in Britain to ethics in public life: 7 key elements or pillars

Ethics is the *positive* side of seeking to uphold standards of conduct and behaviour in Public Life and relies in its modern form upon (i) codes and laws and their regulation/enforcement; (ii) institutional changes/reforms; (iii) audit, public accountability and openness; (iv) guiding principles and motivation to encourage good conduct; (v) external and internal education and training for public life; (vi) democratic trends including the views of the public in respect of their calls for greater trust, honesty and integrity in public and business life; and (vii) the culture and values prevailing in a country.

The weight given to these seven elements varies from country to country and traditionally the United Kingdom has given less weight to a legal approach to ethics than, say, the United States. Each of these seven elements or pillars will be examined briefly:

3 (i) Codes of Conduct and Laws in Britain

* Codes of Conduct

a. Central government

Codes of conduct have existed for decades in many countries, including Britain to set standards in public, business and professional life. In Britain, the Treasury and Civil Service Committee of the House of Commons (now the separate Treasury and Public Administration Committees) was well advanced in proposing changes to the *Civil Service*

Code when the Nolan Committee issued its First Report in 1995:[7] the Nolan recommendations were integrated into the new *Civil Service Code*. The Code of the 1990s is more decentralised than before, with the centre - the Cabinet Office - setting the guidelines and Departments of State supplying the details.

In Britain, Codes of Conduct have been extended government-wide, with a new Code of Conduct having been introduced post-Nolan for Members of Parliament and another Code for Ministers of the Crown: replacing the old *Conduct and Procedures for Ministers Guidelines*. Appendix Two at the end of this work summarises the post-Nolan Codes of Parliamentarians, Ministers and civil servants.

h. Local government

At local government level, in respect of the *elected* members, known as Councillors, the Nolan Committee in its Third Report[8] of 1997 has recommended a radical new ethical framework whereby Parliament approves a statement of the "General Principles of Conduct for Local Councillors"[9] *and* a "Model Code of Conduct for Local Councillors" prepared by representatives of *local* government, and also approved by Parliament. The Nolan Committee proposes that each Local Authority should be required to adopt a local Code of Conduct which incorporates the general principles *and* achieves the same effect as the approved model Code. The above structure intends to place upon each Local Authority a firm responsibility to adopt a Code within the *national* framework, which meets *local* needs. This structure is likely to provide consistency in Codes for Local Authorities. The Nolan Committee has recommended Local Government Tribunals in England, Scotland and Wales, each as an independent arbiter with the power to hear appeals from Councillors and to require a Local Authority *inter alia* to alter its Code of Conduct, when necessary.[10] However, since the Nolan Committee's Third Report on local government (1997), *devolution* of certain powers to Assemblies in Scotland and Wales has been voted with a Devolution Bill now having been prepared. Devolution will require careful thought as to how an ethical framework is implemented in Scotland and Wales.

In respect of officials, known as Officers, in local government in England, Scotland and Wales, the Nolan Committee decided against a formal framework similar to that for Local Councillors. Instead the Committee proposed that the work done by the Local Government Management Board and by individual Local Authorities in establishing Codes of Conduct for Officers should be built upon. The Nolan Committee calls for a procedure for whistelblowing in every Local Authority which provides clear routes for staff working within the organisation to voice confidentially their concerns, as well as a publicised complaints system for people who receive services from, or through, a contractor to the Local Authority.

Another key cause of concern identified by the Nolan Committee in regard to local government was the potential for improper behaviour if the normal professional relationship between the Councillor (the elected member/ politician) and Officer (the official) became unsatisfactory - for example, "too cosy or too combative".[11] The Nolan Committee recommended that a formal protocol setting out the relationship between members and officers should be adopted throughout local government.

* **Laws and proposed laws in the United Kingdom in respect of anti-corruption and misuse of public office**

a Updating the offence of corruption

Britain is in the process, like certain other countries in response to its own and OECD initiatives, of reforming its *Prevention of Corruption Act* 1889 to 1916. In December 1996 the Home Office published a consultation paper on the law relating to bribery of, or the receipt of a bribe, by a Member of Parliament.[12] It has been unclear as to whether an MP would be prosecuted under the *Prevention of Corruption Acts* or disciplined under Parliamentary law.

In March 1997 the Law Commission published draft proposal for a modern law on bribery. The Law Commission proposes the abolition of the distinction between a *public* and *private* organisation but did not deal with the bribery of a Member of Parliament.[13]

In June 1997 the Home Secretary announced his intention (1) to take forward the Law Commission's proposals for a new offence of corruption covering both the public and private sectors and (2) to legislate to bring bribery of MPs - in respect of their official Parliamentary duties - within the scope of statute law, once reconsideration of reports of relevant Parliamentary Committees had been considered. These proposals are deemed to be more effective against bribery and corruption in a wider range of circumstances. The Nolan Committee, however, believes that the responsibility of *public* office holders should continue to have special emphasis in statute and recommends also a new offence of misuse of public office.

b. Proposal for a new offence: misuse of public office

Whereas the US Federal Government enacted ethics legislation in the aftermath of the Watergate scandal in the 1970s, the United Kingdom has not legislated in this area. However, in 1997 in its Third Report the Nolan Committee recommends a new statutory offence of 'misuse of public office' to cover serious misconduct which does *not* entail bribery or corruption. In recommending such an offence the Nolan Committee does not envisage frequent prosecutions. Nonetheless, the Committee deems it important in Britain that such an offence should exist to cover the gap in the existing statutes; to signal clearly the special terms on which all *public* offices are held; and to achieve consistency across all public bodies. The new offence should apply to Ministers and civil servants, local government Councillors and Officers, the police, magistrates and the judiciary, and to non-departmental public bodies. It is even envisaged, after consultation that the offence applies to other bodies which the Nolan Committee considered in its Second Report - for example, further the higher education institutions and possibly fully *privatised* companies, such as the utilities.

The new statutory offence proposed by the Nolan Committee, which covers punishment for misconduct by those in Public life which does not involve corruption, develops the existing *common law* offence of 'misuse in a public office' and prosecutions are still undertaken under the common law from time to time. However, the Law Commission noted in its consultation paper on corruption, that the common law offence is 'wide-ranging and ill-defined'.The offence involves, for example, dishonesty which extends beyond misconduct in a public office. The proposed new *statutory* offence of 'misuse of public office' would give some clearer indication of the circumstances in which an offence might occur. The Nolan Committee recommends that consent to bring criminal proceedings under this new statute law should be vested in the Director of Public Prosecutions. A defence to criminal proceedings should be that the office holder has acted in good faith.

At local government level, the Nolan Committee proposes the abolition of '*surcharge*' and, subject to consultation, the new statutory offence of misuse of public office would apply to all holders of public office.[14] Surcharge, which in England and Wales can be imposed by the District Auditor, applies to elected local Councillors and paid Officers of local government who may be liable to the penalty of surcharge in the event of losses to the local taxpayer. No such liability or penalty applies in any other area of British Public Life: for example surcharge does not apply to Government Ministers or civil servants, although it applied to Accounting Officers of central government Departments - Permanent Secretaries - until 1981. After the date, surcharge was abolished largely on the grounds that the potential sums involved were too large to be recouped from a single individual.

c. Official Secrets Acts 1911-1989

It was noted earlier that in 1989 the Official Secrets Acts of the United Kingdom 1911-1989 were amended - particularly the offence relating to the unauthorised disclosure of official information - or leakage of government information.[15]

d A range of other laws affecting conduct and behaviour in both the public and private sector exists

Company law - for example - covers the role and duties of company Directors and there is a law relating to insider dealings. Information on these laws is available elsewhere.[16]

3(ii) Institutional changes/reforms for an ethical framework in Britain

Parliament

Codes and laws to be effective need appropriate regulation and oversight. In Britain a new Office - the Office of the Parliamentary Commissioner for Standards - has been introduced. Akin in some respects to the role of the Auditor General at the National Audit Office, who oversees the financial standards and efficiency of Executive Departments of State, the Office of the Parliamentary Commissioner for Standards is a new innovation, separate from but co-operating with Parliament, to advise Members of House of Commons who have dilemmas about procedures of conduct. Sir Gordon Downey, the first Parliamentary Commissioner for Standards, has investigated and reported upon, as is his role, the behaviour of a number of Members of Parliament, including Ministers of the Crown who appear to have breached Parliamentary standards. A case in point is Jonathan Aitken, former MP and Minister.

Improved declaration and registration of Members' interests have been devised as part of the new ethical framework for Parliament. The Parliamentary Commissioner for Standards advises Members of the House of Commons about any uncertainties or concerns they may have in respect of the new procedures for declaration and registration.

Another development at Parliamentary level has been to rename the House of Commons Privileges Committee the 'Committee on Standards and Privileges' to extend the Committee's remit to oversee the work of the Parliamentary Commissioner for Standards. Also, the Committee considers any matters relating to the conduct of Members, including specific complaints about alleged breaches in any Code of Conduct which have been drawn to its attention by the Parliamentary Commissioner. These improvements to Parliamentary procedures and machinery have been made as a result of the Nolan Committee's First Report of 1995 and Parliament's own response.[17]

* **Executive**

Institutional changes and reforms in the Executive Departments of State at central government level in Britain in the postNolan era include the appeal process, referred to earlier, whereby the Civil Service Commissioners provide the ultimate appeal for a civil servant who has a dilemma to propriety or ethical standards. See Appendix Two to this paper.

* **Local government**

At local government level, the Nolan Committee in its Third Report of 1997 - not yet implemented - recommends that Councils should set up a Standards Committee, composed of senior local government Councillors (that is, elected members or politicians) who have the power to examine allegations of misconduct by Councillors and to recommend disciplinary action. Greater clarity was called for at local level not only in respect of Local Authority Codes of Conduct but also in regard to the rules of registration and declaration of interests and action to be taken by Councillors when faced with a potential conflict - for example, all relevant interests should be declared at meetings. If a Councillor fails to abide by these rules, the Nolan Committee proposes that the Standards Committee would be able to recommend to the full Council that the Councillor should comply or be disciplined.[18]

Another key concern at local government level found by the Nolan Committee is still abuses of the planning process and the granting of planning permission. The foregoing recommendations relating to Codes of Conduct and conflicts of interest at local level are deemed to be of particular importance in their application to the planning process.

In any country, institutional machinery, or reforms, need to accompany Codes and laws to ensure their effective implementation, oversight and amendment. The foregoing demonstrates the machinery operating at central and local government levels in the United Kingdom. Other relevant machinery includes the system of Ombudsman in Britain.

An appropriate ethical framework means devising Codes or laws suited to a country's available staff and other resources. They should not be too complicated or detailed. Similarly, institutional machinery like an Office of the Standards Commissioner or Committees and/or formal procedures for whistle blowing need to be simple and clear. In Britain, the Nolan Committee in its reports has warned that:

- attempting to enforce good conduct through detailed rules can itself contribute to wrong-doing - especially if these are based on the presumption that people will naturally misbehave;
- a lack of clarity and consistency in rules and procedures is unhelpful;
- awareness of the codes or laws needs to be a part of any ethical process.

3(iii) Audit, public accountability and openness

Financial audit of central and local government is crucial to ethical government. Indeed, so many cases of misconduct in public and business life stem from opportunities faced, or sought, to 'get rich quick'. At central level the National Audit Office, under the Comptroller and Auditor General, fulfills the *external* monitoring role. Select Committees of Parliament in Britain also provide external accountability and report upon the performance of Executive Departments of State. In addition, Departments each have an internal Accounting Officer.

Open government in the United Kingdom at central government level is upheld by the Code of Practice on Access to Government Information (rather than a statute law).

At local government level the Audit Commission undertakes the traditional role of external audit and, unlike central government, a statute law provides access to information. However, new rules on openness to allow planning agreements to be subject to discussion by elected members of the Local Authority *and* the public are recommended by the Nolan Committee, rather than restricting access to supporting documents.[19]

3(iv) Guiding principles in British public life and motivation to encourage good conduct

No ethical framework of itself can yield 'good conduct' without underlying principles designed to underpin behaviour from the top to bottom of an organisation. Seven key principles of public life were advanced in 1995 by the Nolan Committee to support good conduct in

British central government. These seven principles have been carried forward in 1997 by the Nolan Committee to local government in England, Scotland and Wales but, as noted earlier, devolution will require their clarification in Scotland and Wales.

* **The Seven Principles of Public Life**

The seven guiding principles of British public life put forward by the Nolan Committee are:

* Selflessness
* Integrity
* Objectivity
* Accountability
* Openness
* Honesty
* Leadership[20]

To nurture Ethics in Public Life, fundamental principles to guide human behaviour need to be identified, as above. But ethical conduct also requires 'motivation' and example: the development of the *will* of individuals who will wish themselves to serve the public and/or their shareholders, employees and clients with integrity and to make sacrifices, where relevant, in the public interest. Suitable personnel management policies and their implementation can help to uphold morale and develop motivation but leadership and example from the top are prerequisites. Ethics in public, business and professional life is the antipathy of self-interest, greed, jobs for the boys, corruption and selfishness.

3(v) External and internal education and training for public life

Centre for Business and Public Sector Ethics, Cambridge, has concentrated on developing, through research, knowledge and ideas, suitable for higher education, training and 'best practice'.

Dr. Rosamund Thomas, Director of the Centre, has provided written evidence to the United States' Ethics Law Reform Commission (1989);

the UK Nolan Committee (1994/5); the UK Law Commission's inquiry into *Fiduciary Duties* (1996) and to the House of Lord's special inquiry into the British Civil Service (Session 1996-97), and to others.

Centre for Business and Public Sector Ethics has held seven International Conferences in Cambridge, England, since 1989 which have brought together government officials from home and abroad, businessmen, academics and professionals to explore ethics - based on an agenda devised by the Centre. After nearly ten years' research the Centre is publishing its findings for international use in a book series called 'Teaching Ethics'.[21]

Centre for Business and Public Sector Ethics uses a *comparative* research method which unites theory, or 'best ideas', with 'best practice' and is able to provide advisory/consulting services to governments; curriculum design for courses in universities, college and training institutions on Ethics in Public Life and Corporate Governance; and other initiatives.

In the United Kingdom, universities are only recently beginning to teach ethics as a modern subject, although it is now a *compulsory* subject in some other countries. Again, Centre for Business and Public Sector Ethics is working with certain UK universities putting an 'ethics' input into their courses, based on earlier research. The Centre has devised, a 5-module course on Ethics in Government and Business, which is available for a fee, on request.

The British Civil Service College is introducing certain elements of ethics into its courses. Centre for Business and Public Sector Ethics is working with the British Council and the Crown Agents, as well as the Foreign and Commonwealth Office, in regard to education, training, and policy advice for Ethics in Public Life at home and abroad.

Education and training - both in universities/colleges and within the Public Service - help to create an understanding of why ethical conduct is necessary to promote sound government and business practices; to prevent corruption; to make staff aware not only of Codes and laws but also of the consequences of their actions should they not follow 'good practice' and to examine, through case-studies, ethical dilemmas.

3(vi) Democratic trends involving the views of the public in respect of their calls for renewed trust, honesty and integrity in public, business and professional life

The extent of the public's role in creating ethical government and an ethical society depends on a country's democratic or non-democratic status. In a number of Western democracies, including Britain, Canada and Spain, a loss of *trust* in those persons holding public positions has been the cause of the modern reforms to strengthen government rather than endemic corruption.

The Nolan Committee enlisted information from the British public during its three enquiries by placing advertisements in the local press calling for members of the public to write to the Committee with their concerns about 'Standards in Public Life'. The forgoing seven principles which have been formulated bear in mind the views of the British public and their calls for greater integrity, honesty and openness in public life.

3(vii) Culture and values: their reflection in British policy

Ethics reflects the culture, values and norms in a society: these may be synthesised into Codes of Conduct, laws and principles governing behaviour. This work has set out the British approach to a framework and principles for Ethics in Public Life.

Each country has to formulate its own fundamental Ethical Principles for Public Life to create the kind of society, government and businesses it requires. However, it is possible to learn from international developments. Any educational and training programme, for example, needs to take into account culture and values and seek to strengthen those values held in esteem by that society, as well as the traditional skills which a country does not wish to lose in the process of development and modernisation.

In Britain ethical foreign policy has been formulated more overtly than in the past by the new Labour government elected in 1997. Yet, ethical dilemmas face all countries and have to be resolved: can a reduction in the trade of arms from the West, including Britain, be held to when many countries are competing towards greater export sales and increased trade? Can environmental conservation and the protection of endangered species and forests be adhered to in the spirit and practice of the Rio Treaties signed by many nations on Environmental Conservation, against pressures for development to create enriched markets or personal gain? Can violence in society be minimised when global drug trafficking is taking place and individual and organised crime proceeding apace, alongside new developments in electronic and it communications?

These types of ethical dilemmas face many nations. Appreciating the culture and values of one's own country and seeking to uphold them through ethical policies - as well as grappling with the dilemmas and pressures which arise - are all part of the process of Ethics in Public Life and Corporate Governance.

4. Corporate Governance in Britain Today

4(i) The London Stock Exchange

The London Stock Exchange is the UK's major Stock Exchange and provides an essential marketplace where companies can raise finance for expansion and investors share in their growth.[22] By the end of 1966 there were 2,704 companies in the main market, (known as the Official List), - 2171/UK and 533 international and 252 on the Alternative Investment Market (AIM), which is for smaller, young and fast-growing companies.

The London Stock Exchange regulates both capital raising and trading markets, assessing applications of companies wishing to join main market (Official List), monitoring listed companies' ongoing compliance with the rules, and dealing with any breaches. It is responsible also for supervising the conduct of the 300 member firms which deal on its markets. Regulation takes the following 6 forms:

* Recognised Investment Exchange
* Competent Authority for Listing

* Creating the rules of the Exchange
* Monitoring members compliance with rules and vetting new applicants
* Regulating companies' compliance with continuing obligations
* Investigating abuse of its markets.

In 1986 'Big Bang' took place which brought about wide-ranging changes in the rules of the Stock Exchange, such as abolition of the system of minimum commission and the rules concerning membership. There were changes also in the UK's system of regulating investment business with the introduction in 1986 of a new regulatory system under the *Financial Services Act*. The Stock Exchange has always had responsibility for overall regulation of its member firms but the *FSA* added a new *statutory* dimension designed to protect investors. The Act divided responsibility for regulation and supervision of the securities market into two: the supervision of an investment business's conduct in its relation with its clients; and the regulation and operation of the marketplace. A new organisation - The Securities Association (now The Securities and Futures Authority) - was created to take on the first of these roles and has been recongised as a Self-Regulating Organisation (SRO) under the Act.

The Stock Exchange continues to regulate the operation of the marketplace as a Recongised Investment Exchange (RIE). In order to carry out business on the London Stock Exchange today a firm needs to have gained authorisation from an SRO as well as membership of the Exchange. The Stock Exchange also regulates listed companies, as the UK's Competent Authority for Listing.[23]

The number of individual shareholders in the UK has fluctuated during the 1990s but the former Conservative Government's privatisation programme - for example British Gas, Trustee Savings Bank, and BT3 issue in 1993 - with the tax encouragement given to employee share ownership, led to increase in the number of individual (that is, private) investors as distinct from institutional ownership. 60% of shares in listed UK companies are held by UK institutions - pension funds, insurance companies, unit and investment trusts. Of the remaining 40% about half are owned by individuals and half by overseas owners (mainly institutions). Discussions about the role of shareholders in corporate governance, therefore, mainly concerns the institutions, particularly UK institutions.

4(ii) The Cadbury Code on Corporate Governance

The Cadbury Committee set up in the early 1990s was a private sector initiative, under the Chairmanship of Sir Adrian Cadbury. The Cadbury Code which ensued became a benchmark in thinking in Corporate Governance in Britain and abroad.

The Cadbury recommendations were publicly endorsed in the Uk and incorporated in the Stock Exchange Listing Rules. The Cadbury Code defined 'corporate governance' as 'the system by which companies are directed and controlled'. It put the Directors of a company at the centre of any discussion on corporate governance, linked to the role of shareholders, since they appoint the Directors.

It has been pointed out that this is a restrictive definition of corporate governance and excludes many activities involved in managing a company. Bodies like the Institute of Directors in the United Kingdom argue that British business has been labouring under the burden of excessive regulation for many years and that over-zealous implementation of the Cadbury Code has added to this burden.[24]

4(iii) The Greenbury Code on Director's Remuneration

Both the Cadbury and Greenbury Reports were responses to things which appeared to have gone wrong. The Cadbury Report was a response to corporate failures at the time in the UK and the Greenbury Report to unjustified rewards - or compensation packages - in the privatised utilities. Both Committees concentrated largely on the prevention of abuse.

The Greenbury Committee, chaired by Sir Richard Greenbury, was not about controlling board remuneration (although some believe there is such a need) but its primary aim was full disclosure. The new corporate governance requirements for full disclosure of Director's emoluments and for a remuneration committee report have led to companies' annual reports carrying a disproportionate amount of information on these subjects. In the main, the larger listed companies have implemented both Codes fully, while smaller companies find it harder to comply.

4(iv) Preliminary Report (August 1997) of the Committee on Corporate Governance (the Hampel Committee)

In November 1995 the Committee on Corporate Governance, under the chairmanship of Sir Ronald Hampel, was established on the initiative of the Chairman of the Financial Reporting Council. This development followed the recommendations of the Cadbury and Greenbury Committees that a new Committee should review the implementation of their findings. Among the Committee's sponsors are the London Stock Exchange, the Confederation of British Industry and the Institute of Directors, as well as the National Association of Pension Funds.

The Committee's remit was agreed with the sponsor organisations, as follows:

> 'The Committee will seek to promote high standards of corporate governance in the interests of investors protection and in order to preserve and enhance the standing of companies listed on Stock Exchange. The Committee's remit will extend to listed companies only.'

Among its tasks the Committee will conduct a review of the Cadbury Code and:

* keep under review the role of Directors - executive and non-executive - recognising the need for board cohesion and the common legal responsibilities of all Directors;
* be prepared to pursue any relevant matters from the report of the Study Group on Directors' Remuneration, chaired by Sir Richard Greenbury.
* address, as necessary, the role of shareholders in corporate governance issues;
* address, as necessary, the role of auditors in corporate governance issues.

While there is evidence that the Cadbury Code led to higher standards of governance and greater awareness of their importance, there has been a lack of guiding principles underpinning the detailed rules and a heavy emphasis on management accountability in contrast to business prosperity. The *Preliminary Report* of the Committee on Corporate Governance[25] seeks to correct this imbalance, as do some of the responses to that Report.

4(v) The Principles of corporate governance

The Hampel Committee identifies broad principles of corporate governance under four main heads:

A.	Directors:	6	principles of corporate governance relevant to Directors
B.	Directors Remuneration:	3	principles
C.	Shareholders:	4	principles
D.	Accountability and Audit:	4	principles[26]

There are noticeable differences between the Principles of Public Life recommended by the Nolan Committee and the above Principles of Corporate Governance. The Nolan Committee concentrates on ethical principles like selflessness, integrity and honesty. By contrast the principles underlying corporate governance focus narrowly on the role and responsibilities of company Directors and 'good management practice'. Indeed, the section on the need for standards of conduct contained in the earlier *Cadbury Report* has been omitted from the Hampel Committee's *Preliminary Report*. There is common agreement, however, that over-detailed and excessive regulation does NOT create ethical conduct. Ethics in Public Life and Corporate Governance need to be founded on all seven pillars set out in Appendix One to this work.

4(vi) The duties of company Directors

The Hampel Committee sets out in its *Preliminary Report* the duties of Directors as being:

* the basic legal duties of Directors are to act in good faith in the interests of the company and for a proper purpose, and to exercise care and skill (derived from common law);

* The duties are owed to the company, meaning generally the shareholders collectively;
* These duties are common to all Directors - executive and non-executive alike - (although the English courts tend to take into account such factors as whether a Director is full-time and the type of company).

4(vii) Audit, accountability and disclosure/openness

Most of the Cadbury recommendations were well received and acted upon by the accountancy profession, the Auditing Practices Board and the Accounting Standards Board. However, the primary responsibility for good corporate governance rests with the Directors. The statutory role of the auditors is to provide the shareholders with *independent* and *objective* assurance on the reliability of the financial statement and other information provided by the company - it meets the special position of the auditors under the *Companies Act*.

In addition, both the Cadbury and Hampel Committees have made recommendations concerning internal audit and controls.

Section B of the Greenbury Code has been implemented under Section 12.43(x) of the Stock Exchange Listing Rules, which requires companies to include in their annual report details of the 'remuneration packages'. Remuneration disclosures have led to excessive detail being reported to the point of obscuring essential features. Recent changes to the *Companies Act* are designed to avoid duplicating the Stock Exchange Listing Rules and are welcomed by the Hampel Committee.

4(viii) Training

Training for Directors in their responsibilities is advocated by the Hampel Committee, particularly on relevant new laws and regulations and changing commercial risks.

No reference is made by the Hampel Committee to training Directors in Business Ethics and/or Standards of Conduct in Business Life. The Centre for Business and Public Sector Ethics, Cambridge urges that these be added to the training and broad principles relevant to Corporate Governance.

The Committee on Corporate Governance in Britain warns that it is not just a matter of prescribing particular corporate structures and complying with a number of detailed rules. Nor is it a matter of 'box ticking' components of the Cadbury Code. Indeed, the Committee notes that it would not be difficult 'for lazy or unscrupulous Directors - or shareholders - to arrange matters so that the letter of every governance rule was complied with but not substance'. Furthermore, the Committee believes that the requirement to disclose details of individual Director's remuneration has been more 'intrusive' in Britain than in some countries, proving a disincentive to foreign nationals to accept appointment to the boards of UK companies.

The true safeguard for good corporate governance, the Committee urges, is the application of independent judgement by experienced and qualified individuals - executive and non-executive Directors, shareholders and auditors.

It could be added that education and training in these aspects of judgment and Business Ethics is required also. Business Ethics covers wider matters of conflicts of interest, the stakeholder principle and culture and values in a business corporation. On occasions, Ethics in Public Life and Business Ethics merge: for example, in the case of Lord Simon of Highbury who, on accepting a Ministerial posting in the new Labour Government formed by Prime Minister, Tony Blair, faced a *potential* conflict of interest. Lord Simon gave up his post as Chairman of British Petroleum Plc (BP) to work unpaid for the new Labour Government. It appears that, from the time he became a Minister, Lord Simon placed certain shares he owned in the blind trust administered by his bank. However, he retained in his own name some 270,000 BP shares as well as some pound 14,000 Grand Metropolitan shares. The reasons reported for his retention of shares in his own name in commercial companies - while at the same time, serving as Minister for Trade and Competitiveness in Europe - was that, in respect of his BP shares, insider trading laws prevented him selling them. In the case of his Grand Metropolitan shares, it was stated that delays in paperwork accounted for these shares still being in his name.

Profits rose on Lord Simon's BP shares: some 18% increase since 7 May 1997 when his Ministerial appointment was announced. Conservative critics of the new Labour Government argue a 'U turn' by Lord Simon, since it was declared initially that he would not review his shareholding until early 1998. Nonetheless, in August 1997 Lord Simon announced that he was to sell his 2.3 million BP shareholding, donating to charity the pound 350,000 profit which has accrued since he became a Minister.

In the Federal Government of Canada, there is an Ethics Counsellor to Ministers[27] - including the Prime Minister - who provides guidance and advice to new and existing Ministers on potential and actual conflicts of interest. In the UK, the interface between business and Government, including conflicts of interest issues, needs further consideration, as does the stakeholder principle[28] and other aspects of Business Ethics. A point of particular interest in the above-stated case is that, as Chairman of BP, Sir David Simon CBE, (later Lord Simon of Highbury), was a member of the Committee on Corporate Governance (Hampel Committee) from its establishment in November 1995 until his resignation on 7 May 1997 when he became a Government Minister. It is clear that the Hampel Committee needs to extend beyond the narrow issues of Corporate Governance to address wider issues of conflicts of interest, as well as to consider the seven pillars of propriety set out in this work - (Appendix One).

5. Conclusion

There are noticeable differences between the reforms for Ethics and Governance in Public and Business Life. This distinction stems perhaps from the culture of *service* traditionally built into Public Life. The Nolan Committee in the United Kingdom, for example, concentrates on *positive* guiding principles like selflessness, integrity and honesty, as does the work of Centre for Business and Public Sector Ethics, Cambridge. By contrast, the principles of Corporate Governance focus mainly on the roles and responsibilities of company Directors and 'good management practice'. The latter still tend to be concerned primarily with accountability.

Although the Hampel Committee in its *Preliminary Report* has sought to redress the imbalance between business prosperity and accountability, work still needs to be done to emphasise broad principles of Business Ethics and standards of conduct in Corporate Life.

There is common agreement in Britain that over-detailed rules and excessive regulation do not create ethical conduct. Ethics in Public Life and Corporate Governance need to be founded on all seven pillars set out in Appendix One to this work. These pillars form the rock on which good conduct may be built in any fast-moving society and include ethical principles (not simply 'good practice' principles) to uphold standards and the *will* of individuals to create - not only trust in a society, government, company or profession - but also a worthy and compassionate society.

Finally, it should be confirmed that the majority of those who serve in Public Life in Britain and direct our companies operate to high standards. But, there have been instances of corruption and misbehaviour. No country can afford to be complacent in these matters - and with fast-moving changes, such as privatisation and building societies converting to banks, as well as instant communications globally, new safeguards for ethical conduct have to be devised, implemented, revised and upheld. This work presents the reforms in Ethics and Corporate Governance in Britain today.

NOTES & REFERENCE

*. This is the text of the Address made by the author at the Indo-British Round Table Conference on Public and Private Sector Ethics at Indian Institute of public Administration, New Delhi, in November 1998.

1. See Rosamund Thomas ed. Chapter 1, Appendix 1 in *Government Ethics* (Second edn. London, HMSO 1996; Third edn. Cambridge, Ethics International Press Ltd. forthcoming 1998).

2. Ibid *Government Ethics*, Chapter 7, p.121.

3. See House of Lords Select Committee on the Public Service *Special Report* - written evidence in the form of a Memorandum by Dr.Rosamund Thomas, Director, Centre for Business and Public Sector Ethics, Cambridge pp.268-275. HL Paper 68 Session 1996-97 (London, The Stationery Office 18 March 1997).

4. Royal Commission on Standards of Conduct in Public Life (1974-1976): Chairman, the Rt.Hon.Lord Salmon *Report* (London, HMSO Cmnd. 6254 July 1976). Lord Salmon is now deceased.
5. Rosamund Thomas *Espionage and Secrecy: The Official Secrets Acts 1911-1989 of the United Kingdom* (First edn. London, Routledge, 1991; 2nd edition Cambridge, Ethics International Press Ltd. forthcoming 1998).
6. See Select Committee on the Public Service: *Special Report op.cit.* See also Rosamund Thomas ed. *Government Ethics op.cit.* and *Supplement to Government Ethics* (Cambridge, Ethics International Press Ltd. forthcoming 1998).
7. See *First Report of the Committee on Standards in Public Life* (Chairman Lord Nolan: London, HMSO CM. 2850 - I & II Vol.I Report and Vol.II Transcript of Oral Evidence).
8. See *Third Report of The Committee on Standards in Public Life: Standards of Conduct in Local Government in England, Scotland and Wales* (Chairman Lord Nolan: London, The Stationery Office Cm. 3702 - I & II Vol.I Report and Vol.II Transcription of Oral Evidence).
9. The new proposed statement of 'General Principles', as a document to be approved by both Houses of Parliament, is intended to replace the present National Code of Local Government Conduct, which is widely viewed as being confusing, unhelpful and constrained by too many detailed rules.
10. The proposal is for a Local Government Tribunal to be set up under the *Tribunals and Inquiries Act.*
11. See Summary of the Nolan Committee's *Third Report on Standards in Public Life: Local Government.*
12. *Clarification of the Law relating to the Bribery of Members of Parliament: A Discussion Paper* (London, Home Office, December 1996).
13. *Legislating the Criminal Code: Corruption: A Consultation Paper*, Law Commission Consultation Paper No.145 (London, The Stationery Office 1997).
14. The Nolan Committee proposes, as an interim measure, pending the introduction of a new statutory offence of misuse of public office, that surcharge should be abolished and replaced with remedies of compensation and disqualification from office.
15. Rosamund Thomas *Espionage and Secrecy op.cit.*
16. For example, the Institute of Directors publication on Guidelines on Legal Responsibilities of Company Directors (London, Institute of Directors).
17. See Appendix Two to this work.
18. The Nolan Committee proposes at local government level a public register of interests covering pecuniary interests of a Councillor and his/her close family/household, as well as non-precuniary interests which relate to the Councillor's service on bodies with which the Council is associated. As stated, all relevant interests should be declared at meetings.

19. See *Summary* of the Nolan Committee's Third Report on Standards in Public Life: Local Government.

20. See Appendix Three to this work for further details of the seven guiding principles of British public life.

21. Centre for Business and Public Sector Ethics, Cambridge, England, can be contacted at Lilac Place, Champney's Walk, Cambridge CB3 9AW: fax +44(0)1223 461514. The 'Teaching Ethics' book series is published for the Centre by Ethics International Press Ltd. of Cambridge. Orders for books may be placed by fax to the above number or any other enquiries to the Centre.

22. The London Stock Exchange is one of the top three exchanges globally.

23. In 1986 the London Stock Exchange became a private limited company under the *Companies Act* 1985. In 1991 the Exchange replaced the governing Council of the Exchange,with a Board of Directors drawn from the Exchange's executive and from its customer and user base.

24. The Stock Exchange is preparing to introduce SETS (Stock Exchange Electronic Trading Service) in October 1997 which is based on an 'order book' system. See *A History of the London Stock Exchange: London Stock Exchange: Fact File 1997* and *London Stock Exchange Annual Report 1997* (London, Stock Exchange Ltd.).

25. *The Preliminary Report* was replaced in January 1998 by the *Main Report. The Institute of Director's Response to the Preliminary Report of the Committee on Corporate Governance* (London, Institute of Directors, September 1997).

26. See Appendix Four to this work for the full list of broad principles of corporate governance in Britain.

27. Although the UK has a new Parliamentary Commissioner for Standards, who gives advice to *elected* Members of the House of Commons (including MPs who also are Ministers of the Crown), there is no similar Counsellor for Ministers *appointed* to Government from business. The Cabinet Secretary, who holds the dual role of Head of the Civil Services, has attempted to advise and comment - for example, in the case of Jonathan Aitken, former Conservative Minister, but it is not a very satisfactory arrangement. New machinery in the UK, similar to that in Canada, would be advisable.

28. The 'Stakeholder Principle' and 'Stakeholder Relationships' are dismissed in the book ed. by Rosamund Thomas *Environmental Ethics*, Ch.11 by Professor Bernard Cary, (Cambridge, Ethics International Press Ltd., 1st edn. Nov.1996).

APPENDIX ONE

7 Pillars of Ethics in Public Life and Corporate Governance

Codes and/or Laws on Ethical Standards and anti-corruption, etc.	 1
Institutional Changes, Reforms to create an ethical framework	 2
Audit, Accountability and Openness	 3
Guiding Principles and Motivation through leadership/example, encouragement, and appropriate personnel procedures	 4
External and Internal Education and Training	 5
The Views of the Public and the retention of their trust	 6
Culture and Values of the society identified as important and reflected in the codes/laws/principles/education/ training and in ethical policies made by government(s) and business corporations for a fair, objective and compassionate society.	 7

APPENDIX TWO

Revised Westminister Model of Parliamentary Government (Post Nolan)

EXECUTIVE

Civil Service

- The *Civil Service Code*
- Open Government (Code of Practice on Access to to Government Information)
- Decentralisation of responsibility for many aspects of the *Civil Service Management Code*
- a new appeals procedure for civil servants concerned about propriety or ethical standards (staff should be able to raise concerns in confidence with an individual outside their normal management line. Where he/she believes the response is not reasonable, he/she may report the matter to the Civil Service Commissioner)

Ministers

- Adoption of Code of Conduct for Ministers
- Ministers also bound by the new Code of Conduct for Members of Parliament

LEGISLATURE (PARLIAMENT)

House of Lords	*House of Commons*
– 2 principles	– Adoption of 7 Nolan Committee principles in a Code of Conduct for Members of Parliament
– Registration for first time of the interests of Members the House of Lords	– Improved declaration and registration of Member's Interests
– Extension of guidance to Lords in relation to declaration of interest (when taking part in a debate or vote etc.)	– Setting up of the Office of the Parliamentary Commissioner for Standards
	- Committee on Standards and Privileges

APPENDIX THREE

The Seven Principles of Public Life

Selflessness

Holder of public office should act solely in terms of the public interest. They should not do so in order to gain financial or other material benefits for themselves, their family, or their friends.

Integrity

Holders of public office should not place themselves under any financial or other obligation to outside individuals or organisations that might seek to influence them in the performance of their official duties.

Objectivity

In carrying out public business, including making public appointments, awarding contracts or recommending individuals for rewards and benefits, holders of public office should make choices on merit.

Accountability

Holders of public office are accountable for their decisions and actions to the public and must submit themselves to whatever scrutiny is appropriate to their office.

Openness

Holders of public office should be as open as possible about all the decisions and actions that they take. They should give reasons for their decisions and restrict information only when the wider public interest clearly demands.

Honesty

Holders of public office have a duty to declare any private interests relating to their public duties and to take steps to resolve any conflicts arising in a way that protects the public interest.

Leadership

*Holders of public office should promote and support these principles by leadership and example.**

* See First, Second and Third Reports of the Nolan Committee and Summary to the Third Report *op.cit.*

APPENDIX FOUR

The Principles of Corporate Governance in Britain

The Hampel Committee on Corporate Governance identifies in its *Preliminary Report* (August 1997) the principles of corporate governance under four main heads:

A. ***Directors*** — 6 principles of corporate governance relevant to Directors:

1. *The Board* — Every listed company should be headed by an effective board which should lead and control the company.

2. *Chairman and Chief Executive Officer* — There are two key tasks at the top of every public company - the running of the board and the executive responsibility for the running of the company's business. How these tasks are carried out should be publicly explained.

3. *Board Balance* — The board should include a balance of executive Directors and non-executive Directors (including independent non-executives) such that no individual or small group of individuals can dominate the board's decision-making.

4. *Supply of Information* — The Board should be supplied in a timely fashion with information in a form and of a quality appropriate to enable it to discharge its duties.

5.	*Appointments to the Board*	There should be a formal and transparent procedure for the appointment of new Directors to the board.
6.	*Re-election*	All Directors should be required to submit themselves for re-election at regular intervals and at least every three years.
B.	***Director's*** *Remuneration*	3 principles relating to Director's remuneration are as follows:
1.	*The Level and Make-up of Remuneration*	Levels of remuneration should be sufficient to attract and retain the Directors needed to run the company successfully. The component parts of remuneration should be structured so as to link rewards to corporate and individual performance.
2.	*Procedure*	Companies should establish a formal and transparent procedure for developing policy on executive remuneration and for fixing the remuneration packages of individual Directors. No Director should be involved in fixing his or her own remuneration.
3.	*Disclosure*	The company's annual report should contain a statement of remuneration policy and details of the remuneration of each Director.
C.	***Shareholders***	4 principles in respect of shareholders are as follows:

1.	*Shareholder Voting*	Institutional shareholders should adopt a considered policy on voting the shares which they control.
2.	*Dialogue between Companiesand Investors*	Companies and institutional shareholders should each be ready, where practicable, to enter into a dialogue based on the mutual understanding of objectives.
3.	*Evaluation of Governance Disclosures*	When evaluating companies' governance arrangements, ... institutional investors and their advisors should give due weight to all relevant factors drawn to their attention.
4.	*The AGM*	Companies should use the AGM to communicate with private investors and encourage their participation.
D.	***Accountability and Audit***	These 4 principles apply to both listed companies and auditors.
1.	*Financial Reporting*	The board should present a balanced and understandable assessment of the company's position and prospects.
2.	*Internal Control*	The board should maintain a sound system of internal control to safeguard shareholders investment and the company's assets.
3.	*Relationship with the Auditors*	The board should establish formal and transparent arrangements for maintaining an appropriate relationship with the company's auditors.

4. *External Auditors* The external auditors should independently report to shareholders in accordance with statutory and professional requirements and independently assure the board on the discharge of their responsibilities under D.1 and D.2 above in accordance with professional guidance.

Auditors have a dual responsibility - the *public* report to shareholders on the statutory financial statements and on other matters required by the Stock Exchange Listing Rules; and additional *private* reporting to Directors on operational and other matters.

APPENDIX FIVE

Governance of the Financial Services Industry in Britain

The Securities and Investment Board (SIB), set up under the *Financial Services Act* of 1986, recognises a number of principal regulators in the financial services industry which are:

* the Securities and Futures Authority (SFA) responsible for regulating firms involved in the securities and futures sectors of financial services
* the Personal Investment Authority (PIA)
* the Investment Management Regulatory Organisation (IMRO)

The Securities and Futures Authority (SFA) is responsible, for example, for regulating firms involved in dealing or advising in securities or derivatives - that is, in shares, funds traded options, financial futures and commodities futures on metals, oil, cereals and others. The SFA's regulatory process consists of:

* authorisation	the vetting of a firm to ensure it is suitable to be permitted to conduct investment business
* investor protection policy	the relationship between regulated firms and their investors is of key interest to the SFA. Rules are developed to govern the conduct of business between both parties.
* financial risk	The financial health of a firm is a cornerstone of the regulatory regime.
* surveillance	routine inspections/visits to firms made without warning to check on

	their compliance rules and the monitoring of trading patterns to watch for irregularities.
* investigation	where a serious breach of rules is suspected, a more focused investigation ensues - sometimes involving other UK and overseas regulatory bodies.
* prosecution	serious breaches of the rules are considered at a more formal level and sometimes by an SFA Tribunal. Penalties range from a warning to a fine, constraint on trading, or de-authorisation. Individuals can be disciplined also.
Complaints and Arbitration	Where a customer - that is, an investor - is unable to resolve a dispute, the SFA Complaints Bureau will attempt to resolve it or arbitration procedures are also available.
Complaints	An independent Complaints Commissioner oversees the work of the Complaint Bureau.

In 1996 the Securities and Futures Authority in Britain dealt with disciplinary proceedings arising from Barings, as well as others, like unauthorised trading in Sumitomo, concerns over trading in Skynet stock, over trading in the case of Morgan Grenfell Asset Management and problems in Fidelity Brokerage Services, which came to notice as a result of a surge of complaints to the SFA from their customers.

These regulatory bodies assist to prevent national and international fraud and 'white collar' crimes.

NOTE:

All the UK financial services regulators are involved in both prudential supervision and protection of investors. The 1986 *Financial Services Act* - notwithstanding its strengths - has created a complicated and duplicative system, criticised by regulators, practitioners and others. The Chancellor announced on 20 May 1997 that the UK should have a *unitary* system of regulation of financial services, and radically this is to include banking regulation. Details of the unitary regulator and the repeal of the *Financial Services Act* 1986 are not yet fixed.

APPENDIX SIX

Professional Standards of Conduct

The example of the Law Society is used here to illustrate professional regulation and standards. The Law Society is the professional body for solicitors in England and Wales.

The Law Society seeks to enhance the status of the legal profession by controlling and setting standards for solicitors. The Law Society has various powers and duties accorded to it consolidated in the *Solicitors Act* 1974 (as amended by the *Administration of Justice Act* 1985 and the *Courts and Legal Services Act* 1990).

The Law Society exercises its *statutory* functions, which include:

* education and training (including post qualification continuing education)
* ethics and guidance/advice on conduct
* remuneration (the issuing of Remuneration Certificates)
* records (keeping the Roll and the issuing of Practising Certificates to Solicitors)

The Law Society is an independent body, membership is voluntary, although ALL solicitors come under its jurisdiction.

Solicitors have certain responsibilities to their clients, which include a 'duty of care'. The Law Society has a complaints handling arm, known as the Solicitors Complaints Bureau, through which complaints can be made if this and other duties of solicitors appear to be in breach.

One of the responsibilities of the Law Society is to take action against an offending solicitor.

APPENDIX SEVEN

Some Organisations/Committees/Commissions in Britain Concerned with Ethics in Public Life and Corporate Governance

1. *Centre for Business and Public Sector Ethics, Cambridge*

Founded in 1988 as a national and international educational body having charitable purpose, some six years before the Nolan Committee, and specialising in research and dissemination of ideas, knowledge and practices on ethics/ standards of conduct.

Other centres and universities in Britain are now beginning to develop ethics.

2. *Professional Bodies*

   - including those of accountancy, law, banking, and most of the Chartered bodies which govern the professional standards/ behaviour of their members and have addressed, or are addressing, 'ethics';
   - the Institute of Chartered Accountants in England and Wales, for example, which has placed 'ethics' on its examination syllabus;
   - the Law Society;
   - the Institute of Bankers.

3. *Cadbury Committee on Corporate Governance* (superseded by the Hampel Committee)

4. *Greenbury Committee: Study Group in Director's Remuneration*

5. *The Committee on Corporate Governance* (Hampel Committee)

   - includes review of the implementation of the findings of the Cadbury and Greenbury Committees

6. *Regulatory Bodies in the Financial Services industry and other regulatory bodies*

The Securities and Investment Board (SIB), set up under the *Financial Services Act* of 1986, recognises a number of principal regulators in the financial industry which are the Securities and Futures Authority (SFA); the Personal Investment Authority (PIA) and the Investment Management Regulatory Organisation (IMRO).

7. *Committee on Standards in Public Life*

Set up in October 1994 as independent body (known as the Nolan Committee, now Neill Committee).

8. *The Law Commission*

Concerned with Law Reform in the UK and indirectly with 'ethics' in respect of its Consultative Documents on *Fiduciary Duties* and the *Law on Bribery*.

9. *Government Institutions*

Most institutions of British government at central and local levels take account of aspects of 'ethics' and standards - for example, the National Audit Office, the House of Commons Committee on Standards and Privileges and to an extent other Select Committees of Parliament; the Ombudsmen, etc.

It is hoped that the more 'compassionate' society spoken about by British leaders in 1997, following the death of Diana, Princes of Wales, is ushered into our modern societies, including Britain.

NOTE:

Codes have been created in Britain to deal with many aspects of government, business and professional behaviour - for example, for financial dealings in the City of London and elsewhere in respect of the operations of financial markets; the selling of pensions and the new Codes for Mortgage Lenders.

It is easy to create new Codes and yet still to have unacceptable behaviour operating beneath and behind them.

The seven pillars of Ethics in Public Life (and Corporate Governance) need to be put in place for ethical conduct to be realised.

LIST OF DOCUMENTS

Standards in Public Life
First Report of the Committee on Standards in Public Life (Nolan Committee)
Report: Cm. 2850-1;
Transcripts and Oral Evidence Cm. 2850-11

Local Public Spending Bodies
Second Report of the Committee on Standards in Public Life *Report:* Cm. 3702-1;

Transcripts and Oral Evidence Cm. 3702-11

Standards of Conduct in Local Government in England, Scotland and Wales

Third Report of the Committee on Standards in Public Life
Report: Cm. 37021-1;

Transcripts and Oral Evidence Cm. 3702-11

and

Summary of the Nolan Committee's Third Report on Standards in Public Life

'Misuse of Public Office: A New Offence?': A Consultation Paper from the Nolan Committee (London, The Stationery Office)

All available from The Stationery Office, London; their agents and through good booksellers.

ed. Rosamund Thomas *'Government Ethics'* (Cambridge, Ethics International Press Ltd. 2nd edn. 1996) in the 'Teaching Ethics' series. To order: Fax +44 1223 461514.

ed. Rosamund Thomas *'Environmental Ethics'* (Cambridge Ethics International Press Ltd. 1st edn. Nov. 1996 in the 'Teaching Ethics' series. To order. Fax +44 1223 461514.

Clarification of the Law Relating to the Bribery of Members of Parliament: A Discussion Paper (London, Home Office, December 1996).

Legislating the Criminal Code: Corruption: A Consultation paper (Law Commission Consultation Paper No. 145 London, the Stationery Office 15 January 1997).

House of Lords Select Committee on the Public Service *Special Report* with Evidence HL Paper 68, Session 1996-97, (London, The Stationery Office 18 March 1997).

Committee on Corporate Governance (Hampel Committee)
Preliminary Report, August 1997.
Main Report, January 1998.

The Institute of Directors Response to the Preliminary Report of the Committee on Corporate Governance. September 1997. Obtainable from the Institute of Directors, 116 Pall Mall, London SWIY SED. London Stock Exchange Ltd., London EC2N IHP June 1997).

The Securities and Futures Authority *Annual Report 1997 An Outline of SFA* (London, The Securities and Futures Authority Ltd., Cottons Lane, London SEI 2QB).

Press Cuttings

Times 29.07.97

Times 06.08.97

Times 13.10.97

GLOSSARY OF TERMS

Business Ethics (of which Corporate Governance and Standards are a part)

Compliance/Regulation

Conflicts of Interest

Corporate Governance/Company Law

Corporate and Social Responsibility for the Environment by Government and Business

Ethics in Government/Government Ethics

Governance/Good Governance/Good Government

Legal Ethics/Banking Ethics/and other variants of ethics

Standards of Conduct in Public and Business Life

Chapter 11

Administrative Corruption : Causes and Cure

U.C. Agarwal

One of the most worrisome problems facing the country is the widespread prevalence of corruption among its public men and officials - high and low. In fact, this menace of political and administrative corruption has greatly accentuated our other socio-economic difficulties.

All pervasive corruption has considerably reduced the efficiency and credibility of all institutions and instruments of governance. They inspire little public confidence for rendering any worth while public services. The general belief is that large amounts of money earmarked for development and public welfare purposes are misappropriated and misapplied or wasted by the concerned public officials, that sizeable portions of Government revenue from various taxes and duties are also intercepted by dishonest persons in power or their agents. As a result even though people are made to pay increasingly heavy taxes and all kinds of other levies, not much surplus funds are left after meeting the salary, etc. of public servants for any long term development works. In fact, practically all State Governments, local bodies and the Central Government have become financially bankrupt during the last one decade or so. Most of them now depend on borrowed money even for normal revenue expenditure. This keeps their debt burden and interest payment liabilities rising year after year. The country is practically in a debt trap.

The latest Union Budget for the year 1999-2000 revealed the sorry state of the Central finances in very clear terms. The "Fiscal Deficit" or excess of government expenditure over its revenue is shown in the Budget to be more than Rs.91,000 crore. The interest payment liability for the year provided in the budget is Rs.75,000 crore. This single item of expenditure accounts for 46.3% of the total estimated annual revenue of Rs.1,62,000 crore. Thus nearly half the annual Central revenue goes towards unavoidable interest payment on accumulated debt. The fear is that this will go on rising further every year. The pity is that even after knowing this grim financial picture there is little evidence of any concern for economy or avoidance of wasteful expenditure. The top politicians holding high offices are seen to be living in royal style at public expenses. All healthy norms and values have been thrown to the winds. There is mercilessly spending of public money for keeping false social status and lavish life style The guardians of the state, barring some exceptions, have become undependable in safeguarding public interest and money.

Unabashed corruption among top political leaders and higher officials has also vitiated the general climate of honesty and integrity in the country. This has cast its evil influence on most other sections of the society in keeping with the saying - "Yatha raja, tatha praja". If the moral level of the higher ruling class goes down, the moral conduct of others down the line goes down too. As a result we now find many industrialists and businessmen not to have moral hesitation in making poor quality goods and selling at high prices; shopkeepers too feel no sense of guilt in selling fake medicines or life endangering adulterated food stuff like, edible oil, dal etc. for illegitimate money making. The evidence of fall in the ethical standards of our people in general could also be seen in the questionable conduct of many professionals like doctors and lawyers. They grossly over-charge their patients and clients and at times do not hesitate to betray their trusts. There are increasing number of complaints of wrong treatment of patients with the sole intention of fleecing them. We appear to have lost our moral base and consider money making to be the all and end all of life. There are no leaders left to set higher moral standards. It may be worthwhile to ponder over as to how and when corruption became so serious a problem in India and what measures were taken in the past to curb it and why have these not worked so far? The remedy may lie in identifying the basic or root-causes of corruption and to devise effective ways to eliminate them. The fight against corruption and illicit money making may not be futile if genuine and determined efforts are made. Obviously, there can be no instant remedy for the cancer of corruption an evil that has been neglected for so many years. Multi-pronged strategy of reforming the existing political, economic and administrative systems would also be necessary after identifinly the various causes of corruption. Necessary preventive, detective and punitive measures would have to be initiated for corruption free administration.

Corruption had started showing its ugly head during the second world war years of 1939-45. Dr. Radhakrishnan, in his speech, following the famous "Tryst with destiny" speech of Pandit Jawaharlal Nehru on the mid-night hours of 15th August 1947 had warned the government and the nation about the new problem of corruption. He had said "unless we destroy corruption in high places, love of power, profiteering and black marketing which have spoiled the good name of this great country in recent times, we will not be able to raise the standards of efficiency in administration as well as in the production and distribution of the necessary goods of life". He had laid emphasis on the emergence of corruption in "high places". Before independence corruption was generally confined to lower level functionaries, barring few rare cases of high level corruption. Even among the lower levels, corruption was prevalent only among the staff of a few departments like PWD, Excise, Forest, Civil Supplies and the Police. The higher civil services were generally free from corruption. The Second World War time scarcities, controls, rationing, numerous war related civil works and supply contracts sowed the seeds of corruption in the concerned departments of the Central and State governments. When these transactions increased in number and size involving crores of rupees the level of corruption also went higher bringing even some senior officers within its clutches. Soon after independence, political power also started corrupting many elected leaders. The Santhanam Committee Report of 1964 stated "we heard from all sides that corruption has in recent years spread even to those levels of administration from which it was conspicuously absent in the past". The report further observed `there is a wide spread impression..... that some ministers, who have held office during the last 16 years have enriched themselves illegitimately, obtained good jobs for their sons and relations through nepotism, and have reaped other advantages inconsistent with any notion of purity in public life." The nature of corruption in those days was generally confined to allotment of plots of land, cinema sites, petrol pumps, awarding of government contracts for construction works or supply of goods and services etc.

Some seriousness was undoubtedly shown by government in those early years to deal with the problems by enacting the Prevention of Corruption Act 1947 and by setting up an anti-corruption police organisation known as the Delhi Special Police Establishment (DSPE) in 1946. This organisation later became part of the CBI with some enlargement of its functions and role. A number of other legal and administrative measures were also taken to ensure integrity among public officials. These included amendment of the anti-corruption law by placing the burden of proof of honesty on an accused officer found in possession of assets disproportionate to his known sources of income. Under our normal laws, an accused is presumed to be innocent unless proved guilty by the prosecution. This legal position was reversed for those public servants accused of having disproportionate assets. In their cases the accused government servant had himself to prove that his assets were legitimate. All government servants were also required to submit annual property returns to ensure that these property transactions were bonafide and legitimate. The fundamental civil service rules were amended to provide for premature retirement of government servants of doubtful integrity as charges of corruption could not always be proved beyond reasonable doubt in a court of law.

Unfortunately inspite of such legal powers and constitution of the CBI, corruption continued to grow and has now reached such heights that the Santhanam Committee on corruption could not have visualized it in those years. The many scams and scandals of the nineties revealed most glaringly that the persons accused of graft and other wrong doings were no longer ordinary ministers and officials but some former Prime Ministers, some Chief Ministers and many high profile Cabinet Ministers, as also Governors and top officials of PSUs and government. The suspected transactions of very high level corruption related to purchase of Bofors guns, HDW submarines and other costly defence equipments; there were also the Bank Security Scam, the telecom scam, the hawala transactions, the urea purchase deal and the fodder scam. The list of such scams and scandals is quire large. These have caused huge losses to the public exchequer. These have also amply revealed that the affairs the country are no longer in safe hands. With corrupt persons heading the government and administration the sufferings of the people has increased. Democracy is becoming a curse rather than a boon for them.

When high level public men and officials have fallen victim to temptations and are found to be abusing their powers and offices, how could their subordinate law enforcement agencies like the CBI check their misdeeds? Laws, rules, regulations, procedures and methods of transaction of government business, however, sound and excellent cannot by themselves ensure corruption free administration if the top leaders and senior civil servants entrusted with their enforcement fail to do so but instead abuse official positions for personal gains. When the top becomes unclean, the bottom seldom feels any sense of guilt in making illegitimate money in whatever manner possible. This is one of the important factors in making the entire government machinery not only corrupt, but also slow moving, and unhelpful. Therefore, the general complaint based on sufferings of the people is that no paper moves in most government offices unless chased from office to office and from seat to seat by an applicant with the help of "speed money". Corruption in public dealing offices has now become normal, accepted and open. People find no alternative but to comply with the demands of the lower level officials of government and local bodies for getting their work done. Even for payment of government dues, taxes and levies or for filing of sale-tax or income-tax returns, there are reports that bribes need to be paid to keep the last date or to avoid hours of unnecessary waiting. The concerned public servants keep gossiping and sipping tea without attending to the work of the waiting public to compel them to offer bribes to avoid further waiting. All occasion and opportunities of public dealing are said to be utilised by the lower officials to harass the people and extract illegal money without any fear or feeling of guilt. Corruption of this type has almost acquired a kind of legitimacy and people have little choice but to live with it. The near total breakdown of discipline and sense of public duty among public servants is indeed a matter of serious concern. Already government irrespective of its party label, has lost credibility and confidence of the people. They very much wish to avoid any contact with the corrupt government machinery. Generally there is also reluctance to approach the police in times of need for the fear of undue harassment. As a result many crimes like theft, robbery, dacoity, etc. go unreported to the police as people generally believe, however, unwarranted this may be, that the police itself may be hand in glove with the criminal elements. It is unfortunate that all categories of public dealing officials and the police have acquired such poor and contemptuous image. It is some what anachronistic to call them "Public servants" when they are generally looked down upon by the public for their rude behaviour and greed. Even medical and educational institutions run by government have allegedly become dens of corruption in diverse ways. The word "government" is becoming synonymous with corruption.

To effectively deal with administrative corruption, a three pronged action plan comprising preventive, detective and punitive measures needs to be devised and systematically implemented. Even though widespread prevalence of corruption in administration has been sufficiently highlighted all these years and also decried by all concerned but remedial action so far has been sporadic, unsystematic and lukewarm. Due to lack of strong will and resolve in fighting corruption it has continued to spread like cancer and has discredited administration. To check corruption undue emphasis has been given to individual cases of corruption and that too of smaller fries mostly rather than in eradicating its basic causes. The real solution to eliminate or minimise corruption lies in removing its main causes. As malaria cannot be eradicated by merely killing some mosquitoes here and there but by attacking their breeding grounds. Curbing of corruption similarly needs removal of its root causes and not by merely catching some individual culprits alone.

As is well known, corruption became widespread after independence due to large-scale involvement of government in economic activities in addition to its earlier role of maintenance of law and order. The new economic role of Government provided vast opportunities for corruption to officers and employees. With their low salary structure in those years, on the one hand and the new tempting opportunities of illegal money-making on the other hand, many public servants fell victim to greed and illegal money making. Emphasis shifted to "making" rather than "earning" money by them. This fall from grace was further facilitated due to lack of vigilance and policing. Some political bosses who themselves wanted to get rich by abusing powers also encouraged corruption. In due course some kind of unhealthy nexus got established between the corrupt officials and the corrupt political bosses.

That proved not only financially costly for the public sector undertakings and turned many of them into losing concerns but also damaged the climate of integrity in the public services. With the spread of corruption in the public services and among politicians, the number of honest individuals has very much come down. Over the years honesty has largely been devalued and corruption has become a way of life. Many ministers in the states, as is the common talk among officials, want money before clearing any file including those of postings, transfers, promotions of officials. Some central ministers too are now said to be doing the same thing. Accordingly it is time to reflect on the desirability of reducing the role of government in the economic and commercial areas. Even its regulatory functions ought to be minimised to control and prevent corruption. While admittedly government has still some role to play in the vital infrastructure sector e.g. power generation, petroleum production and other strategic industries, it should selectively withdraw from such other economic activities which could be safely entrusted to the private sector to improve the climate of integrity in the public services. The on going "economic reforms" need to be pursued further with speed. In the regulatory field also government appears to have gone too far by enacting numerous unwarranted laws to regulate the day to day life of individuals and impose all kinds of economic, political and administrative restrictions on them. While some laws and regulations are essential to ensure stability, peace, order and harmony in society and for the protection of life, liberty and property of the individuals over-regulation of the type we have, often results in avoidable harassment of the people and rise of corruption among public servants particularly at the points of public contact or the cutting edge of administration. This low level corruption directly affects the common people. It increases with every new law and regulation by providing new opportunities of illegal money making for relaxing these laws and regulations at a price.

The requirements of all kinds of certificates like birth, death, marriage, family planning, caste, medical, residential, etc. for different purposes are proving to be fertile grounds of corruption among the concerned public officials. While the wrong and dishonest claimants of such certificates always manage to get them through bribery, the deserving and honest applicants have to run from pillar to post. They are harassed until the appetite for corruption of the officials is satisfied. It is therefore time to review the essentiality of many of these certificates. Should not a solemn statement of facts by the applicant himself with suitable warning of penal prosecution if found false suffice? The warning may include the risk of withdrawal of benefit secured through false statement at any time. Is it not preferable to trust the people more than the public officials when many of them have become utterly corrupt and the certificates given by them are no guarantee of correctness?

Similarly the need for production of ration-card for many purposes like getting passports, registration of vehicles, issue and renewal of driving licences or for opening of bank accounts appear to be unnecessary and uncalled for. The bureaucracy has spread its tentacles far too much. The only purpose served by these needless requirements is to allow illegitimate money making by dishonest officials. Unfortunately, the elected representatives of the people too have developed vested interests in these corruption-prone regulations. It is alleged that in some states MLAs and other elected members of local bodies too have started collecting "haftas" from field officials to protect them from unwanted transfers or complaints of corruption. They have joined hands with corrupt public officials and are thus betraying the trust of the people. Power has corrupted them and they want to regulate the life of the people more and more for money making.

Licence, permit, quota raj is said to have ended but even the remnant government clearances required in the industrial sector, in export-import areas, regulatory functions like inspection of mines and factories etc. provide enough scope for corruption to some categories of lower officials. Even now there are far too many categories of Inspectors meant to enforce laws like Weights and Measures Act, Prevention of Cruelty to Animals Act, Shops and Establishment Act, Food Adulteration Act, Factories Act, etc. To ease corruption some such numerous regulatory functions could be combined and handled by one agency. Some of these could also be entrusted to various reputed associations of commerce, industry, trade unions or associations of the consumers and shopkeepers etc. Non-Government., and voluntary bodies (NGOs) need to be associated in regulatory work as much as possible to avoid harassment by and corruption of the lower government officials. Hordes of Inspectors only vitiate the climate of integrity. Over-regulation has unduly increased the work-load of the judicial magistrates and courts also. 30 million cases are reportedly pending presently in our courts. Many of these could have been avoided through more imaginative and purposeful enforcement of laws and rules. People need to be directly associated in regulatory functions.

Some years back, a study of the case work-load of the magisterial courts of Delhi to consider their request for more magistrates was entrusted to me. This study disclosed that nearly 95% of the case-work related to various miscellaneous laws and only 5% work related to serious criminal offences like theft, robbery, dacoity, rape, murder, etc. falling under the IPC. Many of these minor Act offences were also of a technical nature involving minor breaches of laws. These could have been best handled on the spot by mobile courts in a summary manner rather than through regular courts adopting the long drawn out judicial procedures. That provides scope for corruption to the lower staff like Peskars, police and process servers. In a large city like Delhi, cases of public nuisance for obstructing free movement on roads and pavements, traffic offences and other offences like late closure of shops, and establishments using unauthorized loud speakers, etc. could run into several thousands on any single day. These ought to be handled on the spot by mobile courts for the sake of economy, speedy justice and prevention of low level corruption. The study concluded saying that the existing number of magistrates was more than sufficient provided the law enforcement work was done in a more imaginative and rational way. Unfortunately in many areas of our public administration the emphasis is more on the quantitative aspect of work and much less on its qualitative aspect. Administration has accordingly spread out too much and has become more uneconomical and less productive. No wonder that more than 97% of the government employees presently are of categories D and C and hardly 3% belong to higher 'B' and 'A' categories. As a result we have a large army of "public servants" but little of public service from them. The smaller the administrative machinery the better may be its efficiency and integrity.

There is urgent need to bring about greater openness and transparency in administration. Since undue secrecy breeds and hides malpractices and corruption, government transactions should be sufficiently open to public scrutiny, barring of course the sensitive areas like defence and state security, etc. A well planned Freedom of Information Act ought to be enacted to enable people to obtain, on payment of reasonable fees, copies of all government records barring of security nature. That should disclose that all sales and purchase and other transactions were bonafide. On many occasions, it has been found that large unwanted stocks of materials were purchased at the behest of sales agents by offering attractive commissions to concerned officials. There were cases of electric cables having been purchased in DESU at a time to last for 10 years or more. Unwanted medical stores too have been purchased in large quantities neglecting the purchase of more essential medicines. Good machines have been sold as scrap and their replacements purchased at high prices. Greater openness in these transactions should reduce malpractices. Unfortunately, lack of administrative supervision and general indifference to public interests have encouraged many types of malpractices. Public gaze of government functions through openness should activate official supervision as well. The present climate of apathy and neglect of public duties by senior officials calls for greater public watch on administration by opening public records for public scrutiny. Official machinery alone can no longer be depended upon fully as it has lost public faith and trust.

Many important electoral reforms need to be introduced to check the increasing infiltration of criminals into politics. Reportedly large number of criminals are presently holding high political offices and have damaged the climate of integrity in administration to a very large degree. According to figures made public by one of the Election Commissioners of India in 1997 as many as 700 of the 4000 odd MLAs in the country at that time were "history-sheeters", 40 MPs were of similar unsavory character. It was also revealed that in 1996 General Elections 1500 of the 13,952 contestants in nine States were "persons with criminal records" which include cases of murder, dacoity, rape, theft and extortion. It is the general belief that while initially political parties used criminals to capture booths and win elections now the tables have turned. The criminals have started using different political parties to get themselves elected by infiltrating into them in large numbers. Democracy is thus getting subverted by criminal elements to serve their own interests through money and muscle powers.

Corrupt political elements reportedly provide support to corrupt administrative personnel. Curbing of administrative corruption therefore first requires curbing of political corruption. Politics and administration are inseparably interwoven in any democracy. If the political environment gets criminalised and corrupted, administrative environment is bound to get polluted too. Corrupt ministers generally dislike and sideline honest officers. They prefer to work with more pliable individuals and like to have them as their aids and advisors.

To protect honest officials and promote fairness in administration management of the civil services should be made the responsibility of statutory Civil Service Boards comprising senior civil servants only. The political heads and leaders should have minimum role to play in deciding the postings, transfers and promotions of officers. Any types of politicisation of the civil services would reduce their role and utility in a parliamentary democracy. It would also hinder punitive action against corrupt persons as they would invoke political protection of one party or the other. The breakdown in the internal control and command system of the civil services has undermined their morale, discipline and integrity as well. Good and honest persons feel insecure and unsure of getting their due on the basis of their merit and performance alone. Many accordingly perforce adopt one or the other unscrupulous politician as their God-father. Often the senior and superior officers are afraid of their own juniors and subordinates who may be having high level political support. They feel diffident to prevent the wrong doings of such subordinates. This unfortunate situation could be corrected by minimizing the role of politicians in the management of civil services.

Another important cause of corruption in administration is due to the excessive discretionary powers given to ministers in matters like allotment of plots of land, houses, shops, agencies of various PSUs like petrol pumps, telephone booths, supply contracts, gas, electricity and telephone connections, reservation of seats in the railways and airways, all types of discretionary grants etc. These powers need to be drastically reduced and subjected to proper guidelines. Names of all beneficiaries of any discretionary favours ought to be compulsorily published in national press to detect and discourage cases of abuse, if any. Free and complimentary passes for travel in the Railways, Airways ought to be abolished. Privileges of any kind should be anathema in any democratic system.

To deal with high level administrative corruption, the Sanathanam Committee had recommended setting up of an independent Central Vigilance Commission (CVC), keeping ministers out of its purview, but bringing all public servants of the Central government and its PSUs within its jurisdiction. This Commission was to be headed by a high level CVC with the same measure of autonomy, independence and status as the Comptroller and Auditor General of India and the Chief Election Commissioner. The Central Vigilance Commission was to be given statutory status by a suitable parliamentary legislation. The Commission was to be legally empowered "to initiate, conduct and complete such action as may be considered appropriate, including prosection against a public servant found guilty" after preliminary investigation of the complaints by the Commission. Power to decide to initiate disciplinary action or prosecution was to be vested in the Commission itself by withdrawing these powers from government.

Unfortunately, the CVC scheme finally accepted and notified by government by a Resolution of 1964 fell far short of the Santhanam Committee's recommendations. The basic weakness of the scheme, was that it had no statutory basis. It was the creation of a government Resolution which was liable to frequent changes at Government's sweet will. This had in fact, been happening, affecting adversely both the nominal independence of the Commission as also its jurisdiction from time to time. The arrangement was of an administrative nature lacking the force of low.

The Commission had also not been given the ultimate power as was recommended, to decide on initiation of disciplinary action or prosecution of any corruption accused public servant. This power continued to rest in the government but was only required to be exercised after obtaining the Commission's 'advice'. Cases of disagreement with the Commission on its advisory functions however could only be included in the Commission's Annual Report to Parliament and no more. Such annual reports were, also, not to be sent directly to Parliament by the Commission but only through the Ministry of Personnel and Training - the designated administrative ministry. The reports were often placed before Parliament, after much delay and were rarely discussed being out of date. Thus, cases of non-acceptance of the Commission's advice by government even in important matters hardly caused any worry or embarrassment to government. For purposes of investigation of any complaints made to the Commission, it had no investigating agency of its own but had to depend on the government controlled CBI or the departmental vigilance units of the concerned ministries.

The latest CVC ordinance of 25 August 1998 with its amendment of October, 1998 had attempted to confer the long delayed statutory status on the Vigilance Commission. These also empowered the CVC to exercise supervision over the CBI in corruption related cases. Some of the earlier weaknesses of the Central Vigilance Commission scheme were thus attempted to be removed.

Unfortunately this ordinance lapsed on 5th April 1999 since Parliament could not find time to approve it within the time limit allowed under Article 123 of the constitution. Political turnmoils, walkouts led to frequent adjournments of both Houses of Parliament disrupting all legislative business. As a result even though the CVC ordinance had been passed by the Lok Sabha, it could not be passed by the Rajya Sabha and its life expired. The Vigilance Commission once again has now been kept alive through a fresh Govt Resolution of 5th April 1999. One has to wait and see if the CVC Bill, incorporating the provisions of the Ordinance and still pending in the Rajya Sabha is passed to become law and if so how soon. Past experience is not quite hopeful. For the Lokpal Bill even though first introduced in the 4th Loksabha in 1968 was allowed to lapse and other successive Lokpal Bills of 1971, 1977, 1985, 1989 and 1996 too lapsed, without becoming law. The seventh Lokpal Bill of 1998 of the BJP coalition Government is now pending in the Loksabha. This coalition Government has already been defeated in the Loksabha on the 17th April 1999. As political circumstances look at present, the 1998 Lokpal Bill too has little chance of being enacted into Law. The Lokpal legislation has jurisdiction over central ministers and MPs to scrutinise complaints of corruption against them. There is remote chance of any political groups viewing the Lokpal Bill kindly. Unfortunately even the Central Vigilance Commission Bill, dealing with Central Government officials too is likely to go the way of the several Lokpal Bills. In that eventuality the Central Vigilance Commission may have to continue to be an administrative, rather than a statutory body. The pity is that the new 1999 Resolution replacing the Ordinance for the continuance of the Vigilance Commission has further diluted its powers and functions than the 1964 Resolution. It has now no powers to act suo-motto, or to suggest changes in administrative procedures, practices and systems to check corruption and improve the climate of integrity. It has also no power to deal with complaints of misbehaviour, arbitrariness etc. of Government servants unless there is any corruption angle in them punishable under the Prevention of Corruption Act. The commission is not left with any supervisory role over the CBI, the anti-corruption police. In brief the fight against corruption may again become a casual and non-serious matter. The CVC would be nominally independent but lack legal teeth. The people, the media, and the academic community have therefore to continue to raise their voices more vigorously against the problem of corruption and the need to fight it. There cannot be any good governance until the administrative machinery in cured of corruption. Unfortunately our democracy appears to have developed vested interest in corruption and therefore the elected leaders of the people merely shed crocodile tears over corruption but are luke-warm in setting up powerful statutory anti-corruption bodies like the Lokpal and CVC. They only shout from the house top to "wage war" against corruption but do little else. There is more rhetoric than real substance in these populist slogans. A time may come soon for the people to take the bull by the horn by resorting to some kind of "direct action" against corrupt persons. That may lead to more chaotic situation and ought to be averted by taking sound legal measures.

PART - IV

PARADIGMS OF DEVELOPMENT

Chapter 12

Approaches to Development Policy

Noorjahan Bava

Eversince man became self-conscious, he has been fascinated by the phenomenon of 'development' and growth around him. "Societal development" is one of those issues in social sciences raised thousands of years ago and is still pondered. It belongs to those great and important concepts around which number of social science theories have been organised. Abandoned and rejected in the past the idea of societal development and its theories have revived with the emergence of the Third World.

Approaches to Development :

Approaches to development are many and varied. One comes across as many as five distinct approaches to development.[1] These are:(1) Theories of social change (2) Theories of motivation (4) Theories of economic and political development and (5) Theories of modernisation. To this must be added (6) the Third World perspective which has to be given weightage in any study of development, (7) sustainable development and (8) Human Rights approaches.

1. Development as Social Change

Among social scientists, to the sociologists who have shifted their focus from the 'more dangerous' concept of development to the 'less dangerous' concept of social change, if development is anything it is an aspect of social change. In the words of John G. Gunnell, social change refers to "a significant transformation of social image and the corresponding alterations in behaviour",[2] and denotes "awareness on the part of those involved". According to this perspective development is not primarily a set of diverse characteristics to be recorded, but a pattern of thought and action to be understood. Theories of social change fall under two broad groups: one, the "linear" or evolutionary and two, the 'cyclical' theories. According to the formar (also known as the evolutionary, or organisonic, histio-sophic approach) social change is evolution and social progress. Change occurs in "levels" or "stages" one unfolding itself to the next. "Each stage is an improvement upon the other"[3].

Marx, Comte, Spencer and Hobhouse are the most significant theorists of linear type of social change.[4] Marx viewed development as the dialectic, historical (evolutionary), inevitable, unilinear process of societal transformation involving various stages. It is an on-going process of growth in a sequential transformation involving various stages. It is an on-going process of growth in a sequential transformation which leads spirally from lower to higher stages of matter, substance and organization resolving in the process the contradictions, especially those of class struggle through revolutionary changes and resulting in the perfection of the mode of production and the self-perfection of man himself. As societies develop, the dominant mode of production emerges either the slave, the feudal, the capitalist, or the socialist. Every new and higher mode of production signifies a new and higher level in the history of man's development.[5] In Marxian perspective, development also means an on-going expansion of production i.e., continuous or sustained economic growth arising out of increasing application of functional rationality and scientific knowledge. Marxism asserts that development is goal-oriented, that is a historical inevitability and that political development can not take place independently of economic development.

If development consisted of intellecutual and moral self-perfection of man and his increased humanization according to Comte, Spencer identified development with evolution and characterized the processes which led to new types of structures (biological and social) as 'unilinear, spontaneous and continuous growth', and Hobhouse regarded mental development as the source of social development.

Based on various approaches[6] such as socio-cultural, repeated process, causal-functional, oscillations and fluctuations, linear theories attribute social change to both "endogenous" and exogenous"[7] factors like decisions of individuals, influence of material factors and ideas, cultural contact, conquest, revolution, growth of knowledge, technological inventions, industrialization, social conflicts etc.[8]

When societies became more complex on account of industrialization, mechanization and structural differentiation, the concept of evolutionary social change was challenged and cyclical change was advocated by many including Pareto, Sorokin and Arnold Toynbee.

2. Development is Growing Systemness

The emergence of the Third World nations witnessed renewed attempt at theory building in the sphere of societal development. Realizing the preoccupation of the new nations with the twin issues of economic development and nation building, the Western world advocated a spate of theories, known under the rubric the "system" theories. The influence of the dominant Western mode of social analysis, viz structural-functionalism,[9] ecological approach[10] and behaviourialism is writ large on the system theories.

System theorists have conceptualized development in two ways. Some view development as growing systemness. Others look upon it as continuum from traditionalism to modernism or transition from agricultural to industrialized society. Development as growing systemness refers to the irreversible on going process of change and continuity involving increasing differentiation and interdependence of the system. While growing interdependence manifests itself in declining self-sufficiency and growing complementation of the units of the system, the on-going differentiation reflects itself in the proliferation of specialized roles and goal directed organization. Industrialization with all its consequences constitute the turning point into process of the growing systemness.[11]

Using the Parsonian paradigm of pattern variables[12] some functionalists viewed development as a continuum and contrasted the characteristics of traditional or "underdevelopment" societies with "developed" or modernized societies. Thus Hoselitz observes, "Economic development may then be considered as being associated with a transformation of social behaviour from a form which in its economically relevant aspects is oriented toward ascription, partcularism and functional diffuseness to a form of social behaviour oriented toward achievement, univesalism and functional specificity"[13]

Among Public Administrationists Fred W. Riggs, the most innovative of model builders who first developed the Agraria – Industria' typology later rejected it in favour of his "fused-prismatic and diffracted" models of societies[14]. He termed the functionally diffused societies as a "fused" and the functionally specific ones as "diffiracted" and the nodal society intermediate between the two polar types as "prismatic" or transitional (developing) societies. Using the Parsonian paradigm, Riggs hypothesized that "a diffracted system would rank high in terms of universalism and achievement orientation and fused model high in particularism and ascription with prismatic model intermediate in these scale".[15]

3. The Motivational Approach

Motivational theories explain the causes rather than the meaning of development. Max Weber thought that Europe became the cradle of industrialization because of the spirit of capitalism fostered and nurtured by the Protestant Ethic.[16]

Everett Hagen's theory of "Status withdrawal"[17] too stresses the point that "development or modernization can occur only where natural conditions can be found and where the society as a whole and the individuals in it have a burning need for change and innovation."[18]

David Mc Clelland[19] sought an explanation for economic development in the 'achievement syndrome'.[20] Mc- Clelland says:

"The higher and wider the spread of the achievement, (achievement motivation) the more likely that economic development will be intense"[21]

Robert Linton and others think that the quest for security is the most common important enough motivation of man leading to economic and social development.

4. Economic and Political Development Approach

The theory of development has always remained in the center of scholarly interest in Economics and Political Science.[22] Theoriesof economic and political development far from treating development as a spontaneous evolution, view it as a goal-oriented activity.

Economic Development

Whereas among the classical economists Adam Smith and others who were the champions of laissez-faire equated economic development with capital formation, and Marx identified it with the socialist system, the neo-classical economists namely Alfred Marshall, Pareto and others identified it with the stability and continuity of the capitalist system and the positive role of the state in the regulation of economy.

Joseph P. Schumpeter who, like Marx, predicted the decline of capitalism and its succession by socialism distinguished between 'economic growth' and economic development'. A product of the cumulative changes brought about by the material and immaterial forces of production, 'Growth' is steady, continuous and slow, whereas 'development' which is the effect of technological and social factors and to some extent growth, is discontinuous, disharmonious, uneven, cyclical and unstable. Technological change is the determining factor and the entrepreneur the propelling force of economic development.[23]

Most of the development theories of the nineteen fifties and sixties were based on the experience of the Western developed countries. Following the 'stages' approach which is essentially an adaption of the classical dialectical logic from the study of history to evolutionary economic development these theories attempt to categorize the growth process in terms of different "stages" through which all countries are expected to pass.[24] Thus Richard Gill speaks of the movement of the 'barter' economy to 'money' economy and then finally to credit economy'.[25]

Walt W. Rostow who regards the technological innovations as the crucial variable of economic development distinguishes five basic stages of economic growth, viz., the "pre-Newtonian" or "traditional", "transitional", "take-off", "maturity" and "massconsumption". stages.[26] After reaching the mass consumption stage, a society has several choices: pursue international power, develop a welfare state or further increase in consumption.[27]

When development became the center of politics in the emerging countries the neoclassical economists interpreted development as economic development and economic development as increase in national income or Gross National Product (GNP) per capita. In other words the output of the economy of a nation (i.e. GNP) was determined by the input (say, capital) as multiplied by its productivity or efficiency (as measured by the input-output ratio).[28] The classical model of development may be expressed thus:

$$\underline{O} = \frac{(O)}{I} \times I$$

In which $\underline{O}$ designates output (GNP)

I inputs

$\underline{O/I}$ Productivity or efficiency.

Classical economists further thought that economic development should be left to the market mechanism which should be allowed to guide the economy to reach to optimum point and the role of the government in development should be minimum. In this model, the administrative, technological and other factors are assumed as given and per capita national income becomes the indicator of economic development.[29]

In the 1970's the classical economist's view that development means economic development and economic development means increase in the GNP per capita was no longer accepted. Because of the inherent limitations of the per capita national income approach[30] students and scholars of development have gradually edged away from a purely economic definition into considering it as "multi-faceted" and as including social and political development.[31] Today an increasingly equitable distribution of wealth and income, full utilization of manpower, better utilisation of natural resources and protection of the human environment are included as the major development objectives. Social development is now recognized as an integral part of development. It is closely related to economic development and refers to the improvement in the general well-being of the people, which, in the final analysis is the ultimate objective of development. It is measured by the level of welfare including not only the reduction of disease, poverty, but also the state of physical, mental and social health and the level of living (i.e. level of satisfaction of the material needs of the population in terms of per capita goods and services available at a given period of time).[32] A country with a lower GNP per capita but with an equitable distribution ensuring that no one would die of starvation should be considered as having a higher level of social development than one with a higher GNP per capita which is not equitably distributed. Participation of individuals in the development effort is also an important element in modern social development.

As Malcolm Adiṣeshaiah observes: "Development is measured by the extent to which the skewed distribution of factor ownership is corrected by the number of people who are lifted over the poverty line, by education, health facilities and housing provided to them, by the range of employment generation, by economic growth, price stability, political participation of the unorganized and disinherited majority and by cultural progress.[33]

Political Development

In the burgeoning [34] literature on political development developed between 1960 to 1976 by American political scientists, the term 'political development' was largely used to perform a 'legitimating' rather than an 'analytical' function. As Huntington and Dominguez, observe, it has been used in four different general ways: geographical, derivative, teleological and functional. In the geographical sense, the term has been used to describe the politics of developing nations of Asia, Africa and Latin America. The derivative usage links political development with political modernization. In the teleological sense, the term denotes the movement towards one or more goals for the political system. The goals which may be simple or multiple include 'democracy, stability, legitimacy, participation, mobilization, institutionalization, equality, capability, differentiation, identity, penetration, integration, bureaucratization, security, welfare, justice, and liberty. As Ferrel Heady says. there is no commonality among these goals but they indicate the value preferences of the political scientists who selected them.[35] The functional approach is a movement towards "politics characteristic of a modern industrial society".[36]

Theories of political development show three distinct approaches viz; the structural-functional approach, the social process and comparative history approach[37]. Commenting on the three approaches, Huntington makes the ignificant statement that the structural-functional approach was weak in change, the social process approach was weak in politics, and the comparative history approach was weak in theory.[38]

Applying the "comparative history" approach, Lucian W.Pye, a pioneer in the field, has interpreted the term political development (1) as political requisite of economic development (2) as the politics typical of industrial societies (3) as political modernization (4) as the operation of nation state (5) as administrative and legal development (6) as mass mobilization and participation (7) as the building of democracy (8) as stability and orderly change (9) as mobilizaiton and power and (10) one aspect of a multi dimesnsional process of social change.[39] His development syndrome consists of 'equality, capacity and differentiation'.[40] Within the system approach, Gabriel Almond, the most ardent advocate of the structural-functional framework, along with Powell views political development as increase in the capabilities of the political system for successful adaptation to meet challenges such as state and nation building, participation of organized group in decision making and welfare which may emanate either from the international environment or from the domestic society or from political elite within the political system itself. The authors conclude that political development is a comulative process of (1) Structural and zonal differentiation. (2) Subsystem autonomy and (3) secularization of political culture, the significance of which lies in the effectiveness of the political system and its increased capabilities."[41]

Samuel Huntington who challenged the stages or linear view of political development and liberated the concept from socio-economic modernization, identified political development with "Institutionalization of political organizations and procedures".[42] He observed that a well institutionalized polity would be marked by high levels of adaptability, complexity, autonomy and coherence. The strength of political organisations and procedures varies with their scope (the extent to which they encompass social activities) and their level of institutionalization (the process by which they acquire their value and stability).

While social scientists like Lerner[43] and Karl Deutsch[44] identify political development with social processes like industrialization, Westernization, commercialization, mass education and social mobilization etc., the comparative historical approach of Eisenstadt, Barrington More and Reinhard Bendix sought to compare the nature of evolution of two or more societies through both space and time. Theories of political change viz., componential change, crisis change and complex change view political development as political change. Huntington whose name is associated with componential change believed that the relationship between political participation and political institutionalization should be taken as the central focus of political change. A political system, according to Huntington, consisted of five components: culture, structure, groups, leadership and policies. In order to understand the totality to political change, one has to study changes deeply in cach one of the five components and the relation between changes in one component and changes in another.[45] While Almond and Rustow, the followers of crisis change emphazize the choices to be made by the political leadership, Ronald Brunner and Garry Brewer speak of political change as complex amalgam of a number of significant demographic, economic and political variables that could open before policy makers a vast field of choice for achieving the objectives which they regarded as desirable.[46] To Helio Jauguribe, political. development is political modernization and institutionalization put together.[47].

A latest study by Leonard Binder reaffirms its faith in the 'development syndrome' development earlier by Lucian Pye, consisting of "equality, capacity and differentiation".[48] Binder says that development polities are confronted with five type of crises of political development namely identity, legitimacy, partcipation, penetration and distribution.

5. The Modernization Approach

Development has been equated with modernization by many scholars.[49] Some members have thought of it in terms of society as an entity while others have segmented it into phases such as economic or political. While Daniel Lerner, Alex Inkles, Monte Palmer, to mention only a few, have thought of it as a societal transformation involving complementary changes in the demographic, economic, political, communication and cultural sectors of a society, others like David Apter, Myron Weiner, C.E. Black, Dankwart Rustow and Welch, Jr. have segmented it into political modernization[50] and Alfred Diamant[51] and Edward Shils[52] equated modernization with Westernization. Scholars attempting to give the term more specificity with reference to the national state have included as defining features of modernity such manifestations as "mass education, urbanization, industrialization, bureaucratization, rapid communication and transportation",[53] a high rate of growth in national GNP, manipulation technology and social mobilization.

(6) The Third World Perspective

The highly 'ethnocentric' developmentalist theory woven around the American paradigm of behaviouralism, structural-functionalism and systems approach evolved by the exclusive efforts of Western scholars at a time when, the American social science, had reached its 'intellectual arrogance' as Ralph Braibanti puts it, together with its assumptions is being questioned today. The Third World rejects the view that the

Western experience is the only consummated development experience and therefore, the only possible road to development today. While Satish K. Arora[54] questions the 'selflimiting approach' which over-looks history prior to the eighteenth century and outside of the Western world and its assumption that there was no political development prior to eighteenth century and the process began particularly after the political revolution in France and the industrial revolution in England, Nathan Shamuyarira[55] and Inayatullah[56] challenge the Western presumption that all history is exorably moving towards the same destiny, same goals and same value system as the Western man has and takes the West to task for conveniently ignoring the vast span of technological development before this period which the traditional societies had developed and transmitted to the Western society. Huntington also joins issue when he raises the pertinent question: "If political development was merely to reflect the present state of Western societies and it was assumed that all societies were to move in the same direction what could one think of the Chinese, Greek, Roman and Indian and other highly developed political systems in ancient times?"[57]

Many scholars question the wisdom of applying the theoretical framework of the Western developmental model to the politico-economic scenario of the developing world. Whereas D.L. Sheth[58] focusses on the basic inadequacies of the systems approach and calls for a comparative theory of the state and nation-building, Nathan Samryarira draws attention to the dysfunctional consequences of factionalism, instability and chaos produced by increasing 'differentiation' and 'institutionalization' in the ethnic pluralist societies such as Nigeria and Zaire and the failure of the international dimension in Afro-Asian states and government'.[59] Even as he accepts that modernization is a powerful model of historical growth, equally shared by the liberals and Marxists, and by contemporary sociologists, Rajni Kothari thinks that its major weakness lies in its 'historicist', 'teleological' and 'apolitical' nature and gives a clarion call for the 'linkage model' for the fulfillment of values like freedom, justice and democracy an approach which will enthrone politics in the process of social change and calls for regional and international cooperation among Third World nations.[60] Questioning the 'equilibrium, stability and homeostasis' assumptions and exposing its empirical, methodological and epistemological shortcomings of modernization theory, Jose A. Silve Michelena rejects the model for its incapacity to be an explanatory and predictive theory of development and calls for the study of historical processes with an integral perspective.[61] Since a developing society is involved in a network of internal and external 'linkages' with the capitalist countries, C.P. Bhambhri urges the political leaders and political movements of Third World 'to delink' themselves from the capitalist order.[62] In their attempt to overcome the 'Eurocentric' bias and the limited explanatory capabilities of both modernization and imperialism theories, Latin American scholars like Andre Gunder[63], Marcos[64], Kaplan and Bernstein[65] have advanced the 'theory of dependence' as a new interpretation of the process of under-development and apply the theory to both capitalist and socialist powers. Nathan Shamuyarira observes a Third World country that is dependent on a socialist power is no better off than one dependent on a capitalist power. He observes that the Soviet Union's extension of its hegemony over Eastern Europe, over some Asian countries, and over Cuba has had more or less the same effect of domination, penetration and exploitation as the African nations' dependence on European states and their multinational corporations..[66] The central feature of African economies, according to him is that have become integrated with the world capitalist system.[67] In his opinion, ' self reliance', 'full participation of citizens in the political system' and 'growth of the national consciousness among the citizenry' constitute the three basic indicators of political development.[68] Development in the Third World, write R. Gosh and Kurian, requires fundamental change in attitudes, values and institutions which have to be planned and organized. Conflict and struggles are inherent in the process[69], and both the people and the state must play their parts. Thus while modernization may be considered an integral part of the development process, it is not necessarily the reverse, because ethical considerations and normative judgements are implicit in the concept of development[70].

As seen above, there is no agreement on one single, universal meaning of development, despite debates over a variety of theories advocated by social scientists over the centuries. Explanations of development have been characterized by particular ideological focus, set of values, goal priorities, system constraints or ideological differences.

Development involves value judgements. What some consider as 'development' is quickly decried and discarded by others as 'non-development' or 'stagnation'. To some people, the building of a liberal democratic welfare state within the framework of a capitalist economic order is the goal of development. To others, the reordering of society on socialist lines is the road to human progress. The Socialists themselves are divided as to the means and methods of ushering in the socialists society. Some believe in collectivist and guild socialist paths, i.e., in the peaceful democratic, non-violent, constitutional methods while others vote in favour of the syndicalist and communist method, i.e, in the sanguine, revolutionary, totalitarian, methods of liquidation of the propertied class, expropriation of capitalists, landlords and businessmen in order to socialize the means of production and build a socialist society. To some the means have to be as good as ends while others insist that ends justify means.

The affluent West offers the package of industrialization and modernization, involving wide-scale application of science and technology to accelerate production in agriculture and industry as well as for development of infrastructural facilities, as the recipe for economic and social change. Even as the socialist model of development reiterates its faith in industrialization and modernization, the 'monolithic', school of socialists strongly advocate the 'one best' method of ushering in socialist society, whereas the 'milieu' or 'contextual' school of thinking believes in the 'national roads to socialism'. Caught between the horns of these dilemmas, the developing nations who have been reduced to destitution by centuries of colonial rule and who have mounted their challenge against poverty, unemployment, illiteracy, ignorance and illhealth, have become dependent on industrialized nations, and are forced with new threats to their hard won political freedom. Their crippling dependence on the developed countries for foreign capital, technology, know-how and information have brought them face to face with a new type of imperialism in the garb of multi-national companies.

India has embarked upon planned development through democracy ever since the fifties with a view to build up a rapidly expanding and technologically progressive economy and a social order based on justice and offering equal opportunities to every citizen and marked by deconcentration of wealth, income and economic power. India's model of development through democracy manifests the policy of gradualism. incrementalism and constitutionalism. The influence of the Western Model is writ large on the Indian experiment to the extent that it relies heavily on democratic and peaceful methods of bringing about social and economic change. At the same time considering the inherent dangers of the free market economy, the planners and policy makers have created a 'mixed economy' wherein the public and private sectors will coexist and jointly carry out the planned change. The influence of the socialist model on the Indian paradigm can be seen in the faith of the founding fathers of the Constitution to establish a Sovereign, Democratic, Socialist Republic of India.

In the context of India devlopment includes the realization of true democracy, social, politcal and economic as well as the attainment of social justice, economic growth, removal of poverty, unemployment and inequality and national integration. The Community Development Programme launched in India in 1952 and the Democratic Decentralization system of Panchayati Raj introduced in 1958 have been designed to achieve these developmental goals with the active participation and involvement of citizens in the development programmes. Since 1991 India has experienced a paradigm shift in favour of market-led economic liberalization model of development.

At the conceptual level development is planned and directed change in social, economic, political, administrative and cultural fields and is driected towards those objectives which are accepted as desirable and worthy of achievement by the society as a whole. These objectives include increase in production, social, political and economic equality, and freedom, cultural growth and particiapation of citizens in the process of development decision making.

Development is a total concept. It has quantitative and qualitative aspects. The development of some aspects to the neglect of others many lead to social lag and unbalanced growth among people and regions. It produces tangible and intangible results. It involves material and non-material elements. Although the latter enter into the picture, for a sense of well being it is the material aspects that have to be given consideration. The total well being has to be measured in terms of facilities and services that are available and the fulfillment of the basic needs of human beings in terms of food. shelter, clothing, education and health.

Development is thus protean, multi-dimensional. It has national, international, temporal, spatial, social, cultural, economic, political and administrative aspects. Its is not just industrialization or modernization though it involves both. It is not a unilinear but a dialectical process because it releases opposing forces and, it involves ethical and normative considerations.[71]

In empirical terms development is liberation not only from political domination, colonialism and imperialism but also from economic dependence on other nations and freedom from poverty, disease, illiteracy, ignorance, unemployment and malnutrition. In a nutshell, devlopment is human ascent, freedom from all kinds of exploitation and cultural awareness.

(7) Sustainable Development Approach

Since the mid seventics the ***Sustainable Development*** approach has become one of the critical approaches to development analysis, development policy planning and administration. As Noorjahan Bava points out the pursuit of the policies of unbridled *laissez-fairism,* crass commercialism, colonialism, imperialism and modernism resulting in the reckless and mindless exploitation of renewable and non-renewable resources of nature-the natural capital, the destruction of flora and fauna, the pollution of air, water, land and forests, depletion of the stratospheric ozone, build-up of green house gases, rise in the sea level, global warming, destruction of bio-diversity, climate changes-all threaten the very existence of the planet Earth. "The highly intensive per capita consumption to support the unsustainable life styles of the population in the industrialised nations coupled with intensification of the technometabolism of these countries" on the one hand and population explosion, poverty and pursuit of economic development sans environmental concern have also accelerated the environmental degradation in the world-both developed and developing.[72]

Noorjahan Bava emphasizes that development and environment are not antithetical to one another as some conservationists believe, but they are complementary and *synergic* to one another. Protection of Environment is and should be an integral aspect of economic, political and social development. This calls for a holistic, systems approach to sustainable development policy and administration to ensure (1) protection of natural environment and (2) Promotion of human welfare and well-being i.e. initiatives must be built into sustainable development policy to ensure "macro coherency" to prevent environmental degradation and decay and "micro coherency" in order that rights, needs and interest of local people in general and of the marginal groups like tribals and hillarea people in particular are protected.[73]

(8) The Human Rights Approach

Eversince the adoption of the United Nations Declaration of Human Rights, the human rights approach to development has become very important. Human rights-civil, political, economic and cultural constitute the central aspects of development. IN fact development and human rights are synonyms. This approach has been dealt with in detail in the Third Series: Human Rights and Criminal Justimce Administration.[74]

NOTES & REFERENCES

1. Szymon Chodak, *Societal Development: Five Approaches with conclusions from Comparative Analysis* (New York, Oxford University Press, 1973), P. 10
2. John G. Gunnell, "Development, Social change and Time', in Dwight Waldo ed., *Temporal Dimensions of Development Administration* (Durham, North Carolina, Duke University Press, 1970), pp. 74-75

3. Ibid pp. 16-17.

4. T.B. Bottomore, *Sociology* (India, George Allen and Unwin, 1972, p.292.

5. C.P. Bhambhri, "Political Change", S.K. Sharma, ed. *Dynamics of Development-An International Perspective* Delhi, Concept Publishing Company 1979), vol. 1, p.282

6. These approaches were identified by Sorokin. For details see Mohinder Paul Kaushal, A study of Community Development As a Process of Social Change (Unpublished), Ph. D. Thesis, Punjab University, Sept. 1966, pp.94-96.

7. M. Ginsberg, 'Social Change', *British Journal of Sociology,* IX (3), 1958.

8. W.F. Ogburn, *Social Change* (New York Press 1922).

9. Talcott Parsons. The Social System (Glencoe, Illinois, Free Press, 1957); Robert Merton, *Social Theory and Social Structure,* (Glencoe, Free Press, 1951); Marion Levy, *The Structure of Society* (Princeton. N.J.: Princeton University Press, 1952). "Structural-Functional Analysis," *International Encyclopedia of Social Science,* vi, 21-29; David Easton, "An Approach to the Analysis of the Political Systems", *World Politics,* Vol. ix, April, 1957. G Almond and James Coleman, (eds;) *The Politics of Developing Areas* (Princeton, Princeton University Press; 1960) and Almond Gabriel and Bingham Powell, (eds,) *Comparative Politics: A Developmental Approach (Boston, Little Brown, 1966).*

10. *Robert Dahl, "The Science of Public Administration," Public Administration Review,* VII, 1947, pp. 1-11; Roscoe Martin, "Technical Assistance: The Problems, of Implementation, *Public Administration Review;* XII, 1952, p. 266; Fred W. Riggs, *The Ecology of Public Administration.* (New Delhi, Asia Publishing House 1961).

11. Szymon Chodak, op. cit. pp. 55-68.

12. Talcott Parsons and Edward Shils regarded the pattern varibles or dilemmas of orientations as categories for the description of value orientations of inividuals and of cultural and social systems. They used them as alternative modes of action, preference or behaviour. They suggested five pattern variables:
    1. Affecivity-affective neutrality,
    2. Self-orientation-collective orientations.
    3. Universalism-particularism.
    4. ascription-achievement.
    5. diffuseness-specificity.

See Talcotte Parsons and Edward Shils, eds. *Toward A General Theory of Action* (New York, Harper and Row, 1951).

13. Bert Hoselitz, *Sociological Aspects of Economic Development* (Glencoe, Illionois,, The Free Press, 1960; p.60.

14. Fred W. Riggs, *Administration in Developing Countries: The Theory of Prismatic Society* (Boston, Houghton Miffin Co.,) 1964.

15. Ibid, p.31
16. Szymon Chodak, op. cit. p. 150.
17. 'Status Withdrawal' means disregard for one's role in society or one's beliefs and aspirations.
18. Szymon Chodak, op. cit., p.164.
19. Mc Clelland, *The Achieving Society* (Princeton, N.J. Van Nostrand, 1961).
20. "The achievement Syndrome" includes preference for moderate calcultated risks, energetic innovative activity, high sense of responsibility, prospective planning of individual action and probability of success."
21. Szymon Chodak, op.cit., p.167.
22. Szymon Chodak, op.cit.p. 188.
23. Joseph P. Schumpeter, *The Theory of Economic Development:* An Inquiry into Profits, Capital, Credit, Interest and the Business Cycle. Translated from German by Redvers Opie (Cambridge, Mass., Harvard University Press, 1961), p.16 and pp. 63-65.
24. Faisal, S.A., *Al-Salem. The Ecological Dimensions of Development Administration.* (New Delhi, Associated Publishing House, 1977), p.133.
25. Richard T. Gill, *Economic Development: Past and Present* (N.J. Englewood Cliffs,: Prentice Hall, Inc., 1966) pp.4-5.
26. W.W. Rostow, *The Stages of Economic Growth: A Non Communist Manifesto* Cambridge, England, Cambridge University Press (1962), pp.8-10. Rostow says that the 'take-off stage' is one when the rate of effective saving and investment may rise from 5per cen to 10 per cent or more; at 'Maturity' stage some 10 to 20 per cent of the national income is invested and at 'age of mass-consumption', the leading sectors of the economy shift towards durable consumer goods and services.
27. For criticism of Rostow, see Faisel Al Salem, op.cit., pp.135-36 and Simon Kuznets, *Economic Growth and Structure* (New York, Norton and Company, inc. 1965) pp. 232-33).
28. United Nations, *Development Administration: Current Approaches and Trends in Public Administration for National Development.* (New York, U.N. Publication ST/ESA/SER/-E/3, 1975), pp. 32.-34
29. For the classical models of economic development see Gerald Meir and Robert E. Baldwin, *Economic Development: Theory, History, Policy* (New York, Wiley, 1957) p.2; Irma Adelman, *Theories of Economic Growth and Development* (Stanford, Stanford University Press, 1961); Gustar Rains, "Economic Growth Theory, *International Enclopaedia of Social Science;* Ralph Braibanti and Joseph Spengler, (eds), *Tradition, Values and Socio-Economic Development* (Durham N.C. Duke University Press, 1961)p.9.

30. For criticism of national income approach see Kamal Nayan Kabra, "Notes Towards a Theory of Indicators of Development", *Indian Journal of Public Administration*. July-September 1977, Vol. XXIII, No.3 pp. 487-88; Bert F. Hoselitz, "Economic Growth: Non-economic Aspects", International *Encyclopaedia of Social Sciences*, IV, (2968), p.422 and Joseph Spengler, "Bureaucracy and Economic Developent" in *Bureaucracy and Economic Development* pp.204-05.

31. V. Subramaniam, "Ideology and Development : Variations Of an Old Theme," in S.K. Sharma, Ed. *Dynamics of Development: An International Perspective*. (Delhi, Concept Publising Comp, 1977), Vol.II, p.200.

32. U.N. Development Administration, op.cit, p.8; D.V. Mc Granahan, et al eds. *Contents and Measurement of Socio-economic development* (U.N. Research Institute for Social Development) New York, Prager Publishers, Inc. 1972).

33. Malcolm Adiseshiah, "Planning and Development", in S.K. Sharma ed. *Dynamics of Development* Vol. II, p.283.

34. As many as 120 books on political development were published in the United States between 1960-1976 the bulk of which appeared between 1960 to 1972, according to Ralph Braibanti, "Political Development: Contextual Non-Linear Perspectives", in S.K. Sharma ed. *Dynamics of Development*, Vol 1. op.cit.p178.

35. Ferrel Heady, *Public Administration: A Comparative Perpective*, (New York, Marcel Decker, Inc., 1979),, Second Edition, p.85.

36. Ibid, op.cit. p.86.

37. S.P. Verma, "Theories of Political Development: A Critique's Search for an Alternative Approach," in *Dynamics of Development*, opp. 191-208.

38. i) Pye, Lucian W. (ed.), *Communications and Political Development* 1963.

   ii) La Palombara, Joseph (ed). *Bureaucracy and Political Development*, 1963.

   iii) Ward, Robert and Rustow. Drankaart A. (Eds); Political Moderniztion in Japan and Turkey, 1964.

   iv) Coleman, James S. (ed)., *Education and Political Development*, 1965.

   v) Pye, Lucian W. and Verba, Sydney, *Political Culture and Political Development*, 1965.

   vi) La Palombara, Joseph and Weiner Myron (eds.), *(Political Development*, 1966.

   vi) La Palombara, Joseph and Weiner Myron (eds.), *Political Parties and Political Development*, 1966.

   These works have been published by the Princeton University Press.

39. Lucian W. Pye: *Aspects of Political Development* (New Delhi, Amerind Publishing Co., 1966) P.P.33-45.

40. Ibid, P.P.45-47.

41. Gabriel A. Almonó and G. Bingham Powell, Jr. (eds): *Comparative Politics: A Development Approach* (Boston, Little Brown and Company, Inc., 1966,) P.P. 299-300.
42. Sammuel P. Huntington "Political Development and Political Decay, "*World Politics,* XVII, April 1965, p.p. 386-93.
43. Daniel Lerner, *The Passing of the Traditional Society* (New York, Free Press of Glenoce, Inc.,) 1958.
44. Karl Deutsch "Social Mobilization and Political Development", *American Political Science Review* LV, September 1961, pp.493-514. Unlike the systems approach with its behavioural and empirical orientation, the social process approach emphasises the causal relationships between variables and correlates one pattern of action with another.
45. S.P. Verma, Op.cit.p.199.
46. Ibid, p.200.
47. Helio Jauguaribe, *Political Development: A General Theory and Latin America Study* (New Youk, Harper and Row publishers, 1973).
48. Leonar Binder, *Crises and Sequences in Political Development* (Princeton, Princeton University Press, 1974).
49. Some of notable works on modernization are:

    Daniel Lerner, *The Passing of Traditional Society* (New York, Free Press of Glencoe, Inc: 1958) p.401; Alex Inkles and David H. Smith eds. *Becoming Modern* (Cambridge, Harvard University Press, 1974) pp. 15-15; Monte Palmer, *The Dilemmas of Political Development* (Itaska, III: F.L. Peacock Publishers, Inc. 1973) pp.3-4.
50. David E. Apter, *The Politics of Modernization* (Chicago, University of Chieago Press, 1965); Myron Weiner, *Modernization: The Dynamics of Growth* (Forum Lectures, 1966); C.E. Black, *The Dynamics of Modernization* (New York, Harper and Row, 1966): Danakwart Rustow, *A World of Nations, Problems of Political Modernization* (Washington, D.C., The Brookings Institution, 1967); Cloude E Welch, Jr: ed *Political Modernization; A Reader in Comparative Political Change,* Belmont, California, Wordsworth Publishing, Co., inc. 1967): S.N. Eisenstadt, "Modernization and Conditions of Sustained Growth", *World Politics,* XVI, July 1964.
51. Alfred Diamant "Political Development: Approaches to Theory and Strategy", in John D. Montgomery and William J. Siffin, eds;

    Approaches to Development: Politics, Administration and Change (New York, Mc. Gramhell, 1966 p.25.
52. Edward Shils, *Political Development in the New States* (The Hague: Monton and camp. 1962) p.10.
53. Ralph Braibanti, 'Political Development: Contextual Non-linear Perspectives' in *Dynamics of Development,* Vol.I, op.cit; pp.179-181.

54. Satish K. Arora, 'Pre-empted Future? Notes on Political Development, in Rajini Kothari ed., *State and Nation Building* (New Delhi, Allied Publishers, 1976), p.24 (Hereafter the book will be cited State and Nation Building only).

55. Nathan M. Shamuyarira, 'Political Development in New African States', *State and Nation Building.* op.cit.p.237.

56. Inayathullah, "Toward a Non-Western Model of Development" in Daniel Lerner and W. Scvana, eds, *Communication and Change in the Developing Countries* Honolulu, East-West Centre, 1967), P.100-101.

57. Samuel P. Huntington, 'Political Development and Political Decay,' *World Politics.* 17, 1965, pp.386-430.

58. D.L. Sheth, "Comparative Political Analysis and Nation Building," in *State and Nation Building.* op.cit.pp.72-91.

59. N. Shamuyarira. op. cit., pp.235-240. While Ralph Braibanti challenges the linear view of development and the division of societies into 'developed' and 'developing' ones and in its place advocates 'the contexual, non-linear perspective' which will emphasize the "milieu" aspects of a society in the process of social change. Albert Tevoedjre explains how the acceptance by developing nations of the Western model of economic growth measured in quantitative terms had brought about their 'crippling dependence on developed world for imports, capital and aid' and calls for review of the concept of development in terms of different environmental needs. Albert Tevoedjre, Need to Develop Indian Management Models, *The Times of India,* Jan. 18, 1981, p.3.

60. Rajni Kothari, 'State and Nation Building in the Third World,' *in State and Nation Building,* pp.3-20.

61. Jose A. Silva Michelena, 'Comparative Analysis of Development and Underdevelopment' in *State and Nation Building,* op.cit.pp.99-101.

62. C.P. Bhambhri, 'Political Change' *Dynamics of Development* Vol. I op cit. pp.287-89.

63. G. Frank, "Development of Underdevelopment", in G. Frank (ed.) Latin *America: Under Development or Revolution* (Monthly Review Press 1967).

64. Marcos Kaplan, "The Power Structure in International Relations, *"International Social Science Journal.* Vol.XXXVI. No. 1,1974, pp. 95-107.

65. Bernstein ed., *Underdevelopment and Development* (London Penguin, 1973).

66. Shamuyarira, op.cit.pp.241-251.

67. Ibid, op.cit.p.259.

68. Ibid. op.cit, pp.260-62.

69. Ratna Ghosh and George Kurian, 'Some Ambiguities in the Concept of Development', *The Indian Journal of Political Science,* Vol. 40, No. 2, June 1979, pp. 162-63.

70. Ibid, op.cit. p.157.

71. Ibid, op. cit. p.163.

72. Noorjahan Bava, "Environmental Stewardship and Sustainable Development: Policy and Administration in India" in R.B. Jain ed. *Environmental Stewardship and Sustainable Development*, New Delhi, Friendrich Ebert Stiftung, 1997, p.190.

73. Ibid, p.191.

74. For details on human rights approach see Noorjahan Bava, "The Editor's Introduction: Democracy, Development and Human Rights" in Noorjahan Bava ed. *Human Rights and Criminal Justice Administration*, New Delhi, Uppal Publishers, 1999.